The Politics of Public Debt

Studies in Critical Social Sciences Book Series

Haymarket Books is proud to be working with Brill Academic Publishers (www.brill.nl) to republish the *Studies in Critical Social Sciences* book series in paperback editions. This peer-reviewed book series offers insights into our current reality by exploring the content and consequences of power relationships under capitalism, and by considering the spaces of opposition and resistance to these changes that have been defining our new age. Our full catalog of *SCSS* volumes can be viewed at https://www.haymarketbooks.org/series_collections/4-studies-in-critical-social-sciences.

Series Editor
David Fasenfest (Wayne State University)

Editorial Board
Eduardo Bonilla-Silva (Duke University)
Chris Chase-Dunn (University of California–Riverside)
William Carroll (University of Victoria)
Raewyn Connell (University of Sydney)
Kimberlé W. Crenshaw (University of California–LA and Columbia University)
Heidi Gottfried (Wayne State University)
Karin Gottschall (University of Bremen)
Alfredo Saad Filho (King's College London)
Chizuko Ueno (University of Tokyo)
Sylvia Walby (Lancaster University)
Raju Das (York University)

The Politics of Public Debt

Financialization, Class, and Democracy in Neoliberal Brazil

Daniel Bin

Haymarket Books
Chicago, IL

First published in 2019 by Brill Academic Publishers, The Netherlands.
© 2019 Koninklijke Brill NV, Leiden, The Netherlands

Published in paperback in 2020 by
Haymarket Books
P.O. Box 180165
Chicago, IL 60618
773-583-7884
www.haymarketbooks.org

ISBN: 978-1-64259-361-7

Distributed to the trade in the US through Consortium Book Sales and Distribution (www.cbsd.com) and internationally through Ingram Publisher Services International (www.ingramcontent.com).

This book was published with the generous support of Lannan Foundation and Wallace Action Fund.

Special discounts are available for bulk purchases by organizations and institutions. Please call 773-583-7884 or email info@haymarketbooks.org for more information.

Cover design by Jamie Kerry and Ragina Johnson.

Printed in United States.

10 9 8 7 6 5 4 3 2 1

Library of Congress Cataloging-in-Publication Data is available.

To Márcia and Ana Bin

As with the stroke of an enchanter's wand, [the public debt] endows unproductive money with the power of creation and thus turns it into capital, without forcing it to expose itself to the troubles and risks inseparable from its employment in industry or even in usury.

KARL MARX

∴

Well, all hope is not yet lost; as soon as I've saved up enough money to pay back what my parents owe him—another five or six years ought to be enough—I'll most definitely do just that. This will be the great parting of ways. For the time being, though, I've got to get up, my train leaves at five.

FRANZ KAFKA

∴

Contents

Acknowledgements IX
Preface X
List of Figures XII

Introduction 1

1 **The Politics of Financialization** 8
   1   Crisis of Accumulation and Reaction of Finance 10
   2   Financial Expansion of the Brazilian Economy 19
   3   Fictitious Capital as a Concrete Social Relation 31

2 **Capitalist State and Financial Hegemony** 39
   1   Capitalist Economy and Capitalist State 42
   2   Financial Hegemony in the State Apparatus 54
   3   The Class Character of Macroeconomic Policy 62

3 **Fiscal Superstructure, Expropriation, and Exploitation** 83
   1   The Financialization of Class Exploitation 85
   2   Exploitation beyond Labor Exchange 90
   3   Public Debt, Taxation, and Redistribution of Surpluses 94
   4   Public Debt and the Rise in the Rate of Exploitation 103
   5   State Spending and Appropriation of Income 114

4 **Macroeconomic Policy and Economic Democracy** 121
   1   Capitalism *or* Democracy 123
   2   Depoliticization of Economic Policy 130
   3   Selective Bureaucratic Insulation 134
   4   Monetary Expectations and Inducements 146
   5   The Talking Shop of Macroeconomic Policy 154
   6   Economic Democracy *and* Democratic Socialism 167

Conclusion 177
Afterword: The 2016 Coup d'État 185

Bibliography 191
Index 204

Acknowledgements

The first version of this book was published in Portuguese in late 2017 by Alameda Casa Editorial (São Paulo, Brazil) with the title *A superestrutura da dívida: financeirização, classes e democracia no Brasil neoliberal* [The superstructure of debt: financialization, class, and democracy in neoliberal Brazil]. Earlier, portions of the book appeared in (i) "The politics of financialization in Brazil," *World Review of Political Economy*, Spring 2016, pp. 106–126; (ii) "The class character of macroeconomic policies in Brazil of the real," *Critical Sociology*, May 2014, pp. 431–449; (iii) "Fiscal superstructure and the deepening of labour exploitation," *Capital & Class*, June 2015, pp. 221–241; and (iv) "Macroeconomic policies and economic democracy in neoliberal Brazil," *Economia e Sociedade*, December 2015, pp. 513–539.

Many have contributed in various ways to this work, whether directly or at important moments for its results. I would like to thank Alfredo Saad-Filho, David Fasenfest, Ruy Braga, Francisca Coelho, Alexandre Siminski, André Biancarelli, Ângela Rubin, Antônio Brussi, Brasilmar Nunes (in memoriam), César Leite, Cláudia Berenstein, Eduardo Raupp, Eduardo Rosas, Erlando Rêses, Fábio Bueno, Evilásio Salvador, Gustavo Quinteiro, Gustavo Souza, Immanuel Wallerstein (in memoriam), James Rubin, Jeffrey Hoff, João Gabriel Teixeira (in memoriam), João Peschanski, Karine Santos, Laura Dresser, Lourdes Mollo, Luiz Pericás, Mara Loveman, Marcello Barra, Marcelo Dalmagro, Marcelo Medeiros, Marcelo Rosa, Marcia Wright, Marcos Cunha, Maria Fattorelli, Matías Scaglione, Michael Lebowitz, Michael von Schneidemesser, Pablo Mitnik, Paulo Monteiro, Paulo Navarro, Pedro Demo, Radhika Desai, Raphael Seabra, Ricardo Antunes, Roberto Menezes, Rodrigo Ávila, Sadi Dal Rosso, Steve Fleetwood, Teresa Melgar, Tod Van Gunten, Tom Hinds, Zhongbao Wang, Alameda, Brill, Capes, CNPq, FAPDF, the University of Brasilia, the University of Wisconsin-Madison, and the anonymous reviewers and editors at the journals mentioned.

I am most grateful to the late Erik Olin Wright for his support during the year I spent at Wisconsin Sociology Department, where the book's theoretical foundations were developed. I am indebted to him for much of the inspiration and work that led to this book. I certainly was not able to communicate the analytical precision with which Erik responded to the ideas I presented him. Yet his conviction that analytical precision must be our constant pursuit shall last forever.

Preface

This book originated with my doctoral dissertation in sociology that was approved by the University of Brasilia in June 2010. Its theoretical foundations, however, were developed in 2008—during the term I spent as a visiting scholar at the University of Wisconsin-Madison as part of my doctoral studies—when the last large global capitalist crisis exploded nearby, in New York. In addition to the procrastinations typical of someone who had 'just defended' a dissertation, the text was only published as a book in Portuguese much later because of some pragmatism. I wanted to hear from other people—in addition to the members of the dissertation committee—who could contribute to the original arguments before presenting them for the critique I hope this revised version of the text can stimulate.

Following this objective, I began by extracting some articles from the original dissertation, which were then presented at academic meetings and other events dedicated to the issues in question. I was able to discuss them in Brasilia, Buenos Aires, Curitiba, Denver, Geneva, Las Vegas, New York, Pelotas, Recife, Rio de Janeiro, San Francisco, and Sydney. This led to the publication of the four articles I mentioned above, each of them related to a chapter in this book. I have implemented many of the recommendations of the dissertation examiners, considerations presented at meetings, and suggestions by the journals' reviewers and editors. Although I was not able to address others and did not agree with some, they all contributed to the 'final' content of this work. Of course, I alone am responsible for all of its deficiencies.

The more significant differences between this book and the dissertation are mainly due to recommendations from reviewers of the scholarly journals that I accepted and implemented during the revisions. Many of the recommendations required new research in addition to the material that I had already gathered. However, the major emphasis of the study concerned the period that includes the two governments of Fernando Henrique Cardoso (1995–2002) and the two governments of Luiz Inácio Lula da Silva (2003–2010). Nevertheless, I have brought all of the statistical series that are in the version presented here up to date whenever data was available. I have also analyzed the events that I considered most significant for macroeconomic policy that occurred from 2011 to 2015, during the government of President Dilma Rousseff.

When the manuscript for the book in Portuguese was close to conclusion, a coup d'état in mid-2016 overthrew President Rousseff's second government. This forced me to question how I should approach this event, considering I had not analyzed the Dilma governments as much as I had those of the governments of Cardoso and Lula. A prudent option, and perhaps recommendable for historical sociology, would be to 'ignore' the coup. Another option, which was riskier, but possible under the conditions—the coup had just been taken place and the context was still chaotic—would be to present a hypothesis based precisely on the entire study that I had undertaken.

This research focused on the political economy of macroeconomic policies led by Cardoso's and Lula's parties and their associates, who included both politicians as well as members of the capitalist class. I believe that analysis of the path of the Brazilian economy since the mid-1990s helps one to understand how Brazil once again reached this situation: that in which its government was deposed for no longer being able to mediate the struggle between labor and capital in such a way as to guarantee capital the advantages it considers satisfactory. I decided to raise this hypothesis in an afterword to this book.

The thesis fulfilled one role; the articles, another; and this book benefits from all of them to bring its arguments to a public that I would like to see go beyond the academy. In these times when almost everything proposed by the ruling classes and their organic intellectuals is presented as inevitable, especially when the issue is economic policy, I dare to hope that these arguments can have some repercussion on the political realm. And revising the Portuguese version of the book published in late 2017 gave me the opportunity to clarify some aspects about Brazilian politics that might be of interest to a broader public.

If the arguments that I develop in the following pages are capable of provoking uncomfortable doubts about some of the ideologies propagated by the hegemonic thinking about macroeconomic policy—to exclude it from democratic debate and keep it under the control of the ruling classes—I believe that the book will have been of some usefulness.

Daniel Bin
Brasilia, March 2019

Figures

1. Short-term interest rates, selected countries, 1960–2015.
   Source: Calculated by the author based on data from the International Monetary Fund and the Organization for Economic Cooperation and Development   13
2. Public debt and short-term interest rate, United States, 1960–2015.
   Source: Calculated by the author based on data from the Internation Monetary Fund, the Organization for Economic Cooperation and Development, and the U.S. Department of the Treasury   15
3. Short-term interest rates, selected countries, 1980–2015.
   Source: Calculated by the author based on data from the Institute for Applied Economic Research, Brazil, the International Monetary Fund, and the Organization for Economic Cooperation and Development   20
4. Inflow of foreign financial capital, Brazil, 1980–2014.
   Source: Calculated by the author based on data from the Central Bank of Brazil   22
5. Short-term interest rate and inflation, Brazil, 1980–2015.
   Source: Calculated by the author based on data from the Institute for Applied Economic Research, Brazil   23
6. Fictitious capitals and gross fixed capital formation, Brazil, 1988–2014.
   Source: Calculated by the author based on data from the Central Bank of Brazil, the journal *Conjuntura Econômica*, and the Institute for Applied Economic Research, Brazil   25
7. Investment funds and securitized public debt, Brazil, 1990–2015.
   Source: Calculated by the author based on data from the Brazilian Financial and Captial Markets Association (Anbima in its Portuguese acronym) and the Institute for Applied Economic Research, Brazil   27
8. Public debt and implicit interest rates, Brazil, 1991–2015.
   Source: Calculated by the author based on data from the Central Bank of Brazil and the Institute for Applied Economic Research, Brazil   29
9. Public debt and fiscal results, Brazil, 1991–2015.
   Source: Calculated by the author based on data from the Institute for Applied Economic Research, Brazil   30
10. Risk premium on external debt, Brazil, 1995–2005.
    Source: Calculated by the author based on data from the Institute for Applied Economic Research, Brazil   53
11. Delinking of revenues and primary fiscal result, Brazil, 1994–2015.
    Source: Calculated by the author based on data from the Institute for Applied Economic Research, Brazil   67

FIGURES   XIII

12   Inflation in Brazil and unemployment in Metropolitan São Paulo, 1985–2015.
     Source: Calculated by the author based on data from the Institute for Applied
     Economic Research, Brazil   71
13   Central government borrowing requirement, Brazil, 1995–2015.
     Source: Calculated by the author based on data from the Institute for
     Applied Economic Research, Brazil   74
14   Tax collection and primary fiscal result, Brazil, 1990–2015.
     Source: Calculated by the author based on data from the Institute for
     Applied Economic Research, Brazil   81
15   Public debt and tax collection, Brazil, 1991–2015.
     Source: Calculated by the author based on data from the Institute for
     Applied Economic Research, Brazil   97
16   Securitized public debt, interest rate, and investment, Brazil, 1991–2014.
     Source: Calculated by the author based on data from the Institute for
     Applied Economic Research, Brazil   99
17   Indirect and direct taxes, Brazil, 1990–2015.
     Source: Calculated by the author based on data from the Institute for
     Applied Economic Research, Brazil   100
18   Nominal fiscal deficit and change in tax revenue, Brazil, 1995–2015.
     Source: Calculated by the author based on data from the Institute for
     Applied Economic Research, Brazil   106
19   Gross and net taxations, and interest, Brazil, 1995–2015.
     Source: Calculated by the author based on data from the Institute for
     Applied Economic Research, Brazil   109
20   Functional distribution of income, Brazil, 1990–2014.
     Source: Calculated by the author based on data from the Brazilian
     Institute of Geography and Statistics   112
21   Productivity of labor in industry, Brazil, 1992–2015.
     Source: Calculated by the author based on data from the Institute
     for Applied Economic Research, Brazil   113
22   Holders of debt securities, Brazil, 2000–2015.
     Source: Calculated by the author based on data from the
     Central Bank of Brazil and the Institute for Applied Economic
     Research, Brazil   116
23   Selected expenditures by the central government, Brazil, 1995–2015.
     Source: Calculated by the author based on data from the Institute for
     Applied Economic Research and the National Treasury Secretariat,
     Brazil   119
24   Changes in composition of the National Monetary Council, 1964–1994.
     Source: Elaborated by the author based on data from the Central Bank of
     Brazil   137

25 Gross fixed capital formation and interest rate, Brazil, 1970–2014. Source: Calculated by the author based on data from the Institute for Applied Economic Research, Brazil   139
26 Interest, delinking of revenues, and investments, Brazil, 1995–2015. Source: Calculated by the author based on data from the Central Bank of Brazil, the Institute for Applied Economic Research, and the National Treasury Secretariat, Brazil   141
27 Expected and set targets for the Selic interest rate, 2001–2015. Source: Calculated by the author based on data from the Central Bank of Brazil   152
28 Decision makers on securitized public debt interest, Brazil, 2000–2015. Source: Calculated by the author based on data from the Central Bank of Brazil and the Institute for Applied Economic Research, Brazil   159

Introduction

in class struggle/ all weapons are good/ stones/ nights/ poems
PAULO LEMINSKI

∴

The financial crisis that spread from the center of global capitalism to the rest of the planet in late 2008 raised anew for discussion themes that had been treated by most observers as beyond question. One of them refers to the thesis that the economy should be regulated exclusively by markets, with a minimum of state interference. Although this has never been empirically observed and is not theoretically plausible—state and capitalism depend on each other—a crisis of global proportions was necessary to revive the debate. To some degree caused by joint actions of finance and governments of countries at the center of the global economy, the crisis had to be attacked precisely by a state rescue of the largest beneficiaries of those actions. Those who affirmed that the state had decreased its presence in the economy were challenged by even clearer evidence that the state was always ready to come to the rescue of capital. The trillions of U.S. dollars distributed by governments around the world to save large corporations, financial or not, revealed the false neoliberal rhetoric of the minimal state.[1]

Another important debate refers to the belief that the economy could prosper detached from the material base of production, for example, via financial mechanisms. This, as various scholars have shown, proved to be as fictitious as were these mechanisms. Marx's thesis, in his posthumous third volume of

---

1 The term neoliberalism refers to the combination of two sets of ideas that guided the thinking of the group known as the Mont Pelerin Society, which met for the first time in 1947 sharing concerns about the supposed threats to the capitalist social order. Its members included illustrious figures such as Ludvig von Mises, Milton Friedman, Karl Popper—for some time—and the leader of the group, Friedrich von Hayek. They defined themselves as liberals in the traditional European sense due to their fundamental commitment to the ideas of individual freedom. The neoliberal label indicated the adherence of the group to the free market principles of neoclassical economics, which emerged in the second half of the nineteenth century in contrast to the classical theories of Adam Smith—except the idea of the invisible hand—David Ricardo and, of course, Karl Marx. Neoliberal thinking gained academic respect with the awarding of the Nobel Prize for economics to Hayek in 1974 and to Friedman in 1976 (Harvey 2005).

Capital, about how interest-bearing capital reveals itself as such only at the time of the production of material surplus, once again proved to be correct. The same financial expansion that had reinforced the centrality of the United States and the United Kingdom in the world economy—a centrality that was simultaneous to processes of significant deindustrialization—imposed precisely on these two countries deep economic retractions after the eruption of the crisis in 2008. Given these aspects, I understand that the debate that focuses on the question in terms of the intensity of state intervention in the economy is unproductive. This intervention has always existed under capitalism and shall continue to occur in various forms while this is the mode of production.

Thus, one of the critiques of state intervention that I consider relevant concerns, more than its intensity, the direction that it takes. For example, from whom does the state extract and to whom does it allocate the surpluses that it transitorily appropriates? This is as much a political as an economic question and therefore requires a political debate about economic decisions. Contrary to what free market apologists say they believe, a market is a realm where economic forces confront each other with not only economic weapons, but also with political ones. These include ideologies, which can be substituted depending on the class or fraction of class that remains hegemonic at times of crisis, as took place between the last two modes of regulation of capitalism. Between the mid-1930s and the mid-1970s, the dominant economic ideology was that which saw the increase of consumer income as the stimulus for growth; at the conclusion of this period, the ideology that became hegemonic was that which defended that this stimulus would come from the increased income of those who save (Przeworski 1998).

Another ideology forged since then is that the economy would be a domain that exists independently and is distinct from the other spheres, particularly politics. Nevertheless, as we see today with even greater clarity, the economy has at its essence a political dimension, given that social conflict is organic to it. If this is correct, and since the current stage of capitalism is increasingly influenced by phenomena that develop in the realm of financial markets, they deserve a sociological examination. The truism "economic worlds are social worlds" (Fligstein 1996: 657) also applies to the world of finance. The influence of this sphere goes beyond the process of allocation of resources, and has important implications for the social, political, and cultural contexts, as well as connections with institutions such as the state and the legal system (Preda 2007). The issue was already a broad concern in the classic sociological analyses. Both Karl Marx and Max Weber considered markets as more than just allocation systems (Preda 2007). For both, as for Émile Durkheim, a monetary theory would make little sense if it were not part of a broad explanatory theory of society (Deflem 2003).

INTRODUCTION

Upon reviewing the literature dedicated to sociological research about financial markets and banks, Lisa Keister (2002) noticed that the various concepts studied treated financial relations as social relations and the systems of financial relations as social structures. Even financial crises and instabilities had roots of a political and social nature. In this way, the capital that circulates in financial markets is part of, has implications for, and is shaped by, other spheres of social life that are not only economic in a strict sense. This financial capital is currently a condition for the expropriation and accumulation of economic surpluses, and thus has significant implications on the political sphere.[2] Therefore, if finance is so relevant in the social structure, where it interacts with the political, legal, ideological, and state spheres, a sociological analysis of the financial superstructure appears suitable when one observes the Brazilian economy of approximately the past two decennia, from the mid-1990s to the mid-2010s.

A starting point for analytically connecting the political and financial spheres is to study how the latter is related to the state, as well as the implications of this relation for democracy. The transition from a dictatorial regime to a formally democratic regime was one of the most outstanding phenomena in recent Brazilian political history, similar to some of its Latin American neighbors. After more than twenty years of military dictatorship (1964–1985), at the end of the 1980s the democratization process re-established in the country the most important institutions of modern liberal democracy. In addition to formally independent republican branches, Brazilian society came to coexist until recently—at least until the parliamentary coup of 2016 that imposed an unelected president—with universal free and periodic elections, party plurality and formal individual liberties. A new Constitution was also promulgated to substitute the one that had been drafted under the military dictatorship.

---

2 The best known concept of finance capital is possibly that introduced by Rudolf Hilferding (2006 [1910]), for whom the power of banks over industry was growing in his time due to industry's dependence on the banks' money-capital. Hilferding believed that in the most advanced stage of capitalism the concentration of property would lead to finance capital's control over the entire capitalist system. According to Wagner (1996), this terminology was ambiguous because it at times related finance capital to the transformation of money-capital into industrial capital—that is, to the domination of the former over the latter—and at times to the direct domination of banks over industry. My discussion does not take this path, which indicates a sharp distinction between financial, industrial, and commercial capital, and I also do not conceive of an eventual domination of the first kind of capital over the others. This latter aspect would actually not apply to the Brazilian case, in which the oligopolistic character of the banking system, high interest rates, and the facility of association to foreign capital were sufficient to contain the temptation of large banks to seek direct control over industrial activity (Saes 2001).

New political rights were established, including the opening of institutional routes for greater participation of society in the affairs of the state.

The Constitution of 1988 also consecrated social rights that institutionalized policies associated to the welfare state. In terms of effective measures, Brazil remained quite distant from the advances found in countries that were pioneers of these policies in the Global North, but the path had been opened. The universalization of public healthcare and education, the expansion of the number of beneficiaries and of the minimum benefits of social security and social assistance were rights conquered by society at the time of re-democratization. The new Constitution determined that specific portions of revenue would be dedicated to specific budget expenditure items. In this way, some policies would potentially depend less on the particular government in power, signaling a certain distancing of the Brazilian state from its history of clientelism. On the other hand, soon after formal institutions of liberal democracy and social welfare policies began to be structured, in the mid-1990s this trend suffered an inflection. This involved the arrival in Brazil of the neoliberal wave that had been irradiating from the Global North during the two previous decades.

The adhesion to neoliberal theses imposed a new political-economic reality on Brazilian society, which meant a reversal in the recently inaugurated democratizing trend, especially in relation to the economy. With the implementation of the Real Plan in 1994, which was a mark of this neoliberal shift, a process began that deepened the distance between what one may call economic democracy and the liberal democracy that had been rehearsing its return since the mid-1980s. The Real Plan, by stopping hyperinflation, which had been inculcated in social representations as the greatest of all socioeconomic evils, was crowned as one of the greatest conquests of Brazilian society in the 1990s. In this context, inflation control came to have priority and thus any economic policy, as well as its decision-making mode, was justifiable as long as it sought currency stability.

The democratic implications—here I consider, in addition to procedural questions, economic inequality and the class relations that reproduce such inequality—of economic policy can be noticed in a phenomenon quite familiar to economics, but whose social implications are more important than that discipline usually considers. This is the public debt, which synthesizes practices developed in the realm of the capitalist state that tend to reproduce economic inequality and thus erode the democratic politics. In sociological terms, public debt engenders a special class relation between debtors and creditors. This relation tends to deepen the transfer of surpluses from the productive classes, that is from workers, and other materially disadvantaged segments—such as those dependent on social welfare policies—to a reduced segment of appropriators, in this case, finance.

The fact that public debt does not engender direct exploitation, as it takes place in economic operations sensu stricto—those that occur in the capitalist infrastructure—makes the public debt a special relation between classes, which is established by means of the state. The debt synthesizes a series of policies developed to assure its sustainability, and which in turn denote the anti-democratic inflection mentioned previously. The context delineated until here about what the public debt has represented in the past nearly twenty years in Brazilian society in terms of appropriation of surpluses and democratic evolution point to the following hypothesis: *by potentially raising future rates of exploitation of the labor of others and serving the expropriation of the fruits of this labor by the part of finance, and by being administered without substantive participation of the ruled classes in the political decisions related to it, the public debt, as well as the macroeconomic policies that sustain it, reproduce the class and anti-democratic characters of the Brazilian state.*

This hypothesis encompasses two main abstract questions that I raise to develop my argument, which I will support with historical evidence. First, there is a gap between liberal democracy and economic democracy, the latter form being a requirement for substantive democracy. Second, but as a complement, I understand that this gap is also generated by the economic inequality that the public debt contributes to reproduce and by the way that it is administered. Thus, this kind of debt is a social relation from which results a deepening of the anti-democratic character of the capitalist state, which has taken different forms in different societies over history. This can be seen in variations in the handling of public debt, with varying gradations of democratic practices. There were moments in which the debt, even if addressed in an insulated manner, was not as important and its effects were not so broad that they gained greater public attention than other issues. Thus, the hypothesis I have just raised refers specifically to a given spatial and historical context, that of neoliberal Brazil that ranges from the mid-1990s to the mid-2010s.

This book is organized in four chapters, a conclusion and an afterword, which was included because of the coup within the Brazilian capitalist state that took place in mid-2016. Chapter 1 addresses the social context in which state and social classes articulated with each other with financial logic as an important guide for action. To do so, I review some preceding aspects and other more recent ones that have respectively steered and maintained the Brazilian state using this financial logic. This logic, we shall see, has important connections with a specific social relationship with which the study is concerned, the public debt, and with its implications for class exploitation and democratic politics. I first develop a theoretical discussion to situate the public debt within the problematic of the fictitious economy, which nevertheless has a concrete dimension in terms of material consequences for broad social segments, with special impacts in moments of crisis. I also describe in the first chapter aspects of the international context from which certain conditions were established for the development of the financial expansion of the economy.

In Chapter 2, the analysis focuses on the specific way that the Brazilian state reproduced and revealed its class character in the context of a new mode of regulation. In this sense, a contribution to the understanding of the role of the state in social relations is made by qualifying its interventions in the economy. This involves recognizing and differentiating activities that it performed and that, depending on the context, were more or less intense. Firstly, I develop theoretical questions about how the state in general acts to maintain capitalist relations. I then develop an analysis of more specific aspects, in which the Brazilian case is treated with greater emphasis, to explain how structural policies—especially fiscal and monetary ones—have served this objective. An important theoretical aspect present in the second chapter is the distinction between forms of state intervention, which allows examining the common neoliberal claim that the state should retreat from economic action.

The objective of Chapter 3 is to study how the public debt served the expropriation of surpluses and its potential to raise rates of exploitation of the labor of others. In this way, I call attention to the need for mediations by the state for this process to take place. The amounts and other quantitative dimensions involved, and the institutional apparatus—legal devices, sovereign risk, state technocracy—of the public debt assure to finance capital profits, liquidity, and risks not always available in the sphere of material production. Special attention is given to the issue of interest, more than to the debt itself, because I understand that interest indicates a potential rise in the rate of exploitation of the productive classes—the workers—by the appropriating ones. The public debt, as a stock of fictitious capital, is not accumulated labor—"the capital does not exist twice over" (Marx 1991 [1894]: 597)—however, interest on the debt can raise the rate of exploitation of labor to attain satisfactory rates of return on the various types of capital.

In Chapter 4, I analyze decisions about some of Brazil's main macroeconomic policies and the country's public debt vis-à-vis a certain concept of democracy. I focus the discussion on two issues: economic inequality and some of its implications for democratic policy; and the question of people's participation—either direct or through representatives—in economic decisions that affect the material well-being of all society. In this chapter, the central themes of the research are treated in such a way that public debt, expropriation of surpluses, class exploitation, and economic democracy appear in an articulated manner: by mediating relations of expropriation or exploitation, and by being conducted at the margin of any substantive political debate, public debt has made Brazilian capitalist democracy even less democratic.

CHAPTER 1

The Politics of Financialization

> [There is] a structure of successive humiliations that begins in the international markets and financial centers and ends in the home of each citizen.
>
> EDUARDO GALEANO

∴

We are in a moment of history in which financial logic imposes itself not only on the economy, but also on social life in general. Behavioral standards once relatively restricted to private capitalist domains have expanded to various social spheres, such as education, culture, public safety, healthcare, social security, etc. Nearly anything that can be considered a commodity—even if this requires some effort of persuasion—has been led towards the formation of new markets. Services once considered strictly public are widely provided commercially by private companies. Means of subsistence that once had communal characteristics have become the object of contemporary forms of what Karl Marx once called enclosure in his concept of primitive accumulation. Large conglomerates, some of them led by finance, make their not always invisible hands increasingly present in various social realms, expanding the phenomenon that Ellen Meiksins Wood has called "commodification of life" (Wood 2005: 11). In sum, capital ceaselessly advances over new social domains seeking to accumulate surpluses or resolve its crises.

In terms of social relations that have still not been commodified, many have come to have the capitalist market as a reference. In the case of state government, the option for monetarism, for example, raised financial logic to a first level concern in the formulation of policies, not only economic, but also those regarding social welfare.[1] These became subordinated to the imperatives of

---

1 Monetarism is an economic theory that arose in the early 1970s that challenged the then dominant Keynesian theory and became part of the recommendations of international organizations, like the International Monetary Fund. Its main principles were: (i) inflationary control even at the cost of unemployment; (ii) the implementation of rigid fiscal policy based on the rule of steady growth of the money stock; (iii) the option for fixed policy rules

inflationary control and a supposedly greater concern for fiscal equilibrium. This is because, to the degree that nation states were placed at the mercy of fiscal discipline, whether because of the potential effects of capital flight or because of direct institutional pressure (Arrighi 1994), the context of financialization also created constraints for respective societies. Thus, if in the longer history of the modern state this state is capitalist, in a more recent history it is the financial-capitalist character of it that has been highlighted.

For the social relations that were already guided by capitalist logic, the increased influence of finance provoked important changes in the social process of accumulation. The appeal to consumption became increasingly accompanied by the offer of financing, in a relation of mutual incentives. The old formula of finance to activate production gave room to the logic of produce to generate financing. More options for savings were created, ranging from the traditional savings account to modern investment funds. The latter are actually described by the ideologues of finance as mechanisms capable of benefiting not only those who invest in them, but society in general by supposedly expanding the sources of financing for economic activity. Investment funds are also said to discipline companies' managers to seek the most profitable investment, which would in turn lead to more efficient resource allocations. In this way, financial mechanisms would rationalize production under new forms of domination of labor, as is the case of the ideology of corporate governance, which made viable new forms of sharing productivity gains, now between productive capital, labor, and finance (Salama 1998).

In a broader sense, the neoliberal wave, which began to expand globally in the 1970s, resulted in the restoration of the class power of finance, which until then was constrained by the Keynesian consensus. Neoliberalism did this by reaffirming money as a commodity, as capital, placing the currency in an even more important position for social relations. This conferred finance economic and political powers significantly higher than those that it enjoyed in the Keynesian-Fordist period. As Gil Eyal (2000) affirmed, monetarism is a technology not only of government of economic life, but of social life in general, with the imposition of its representations over a broad spectrum of problems that then came to be steered and stabilized by organized financial markets. For Gérard Duménil and Dominique Lévy (2004a), the neoliberal era is the era of finance and, in the words of Roberto Grün, Brazil was facing the cultural dominance of finance, which imposes the preeminence of its ways of seeing reality and framing the country's problems (Grün 2007a).

---

over discretionary powers of policy makers; and (iv) flexible exchange rates and commercial opening to international competition (Eyal 2000).

e analyses may be exaggerated, it is a fact that financial ex- ...ped only by economic phenomena, but also involves politi- ...s (Bourdieu, Heilbron, and Reynaud 2003). The role of financial ...rkets as fundamental institutions of advanced societies was already visible in the 1980s (Preda 2007). With the rise of neoliberalism as a dominant ideology and practice, market logic triumphed over public goods, making the state subservient to economic imperatives (Kellner 2002). Even if this subservience had always existed in the history of capitalism, the greater global integration of markets and the unprecedented expansion of the fictitious economy made finance deeply and broadly influential in various spheres of social life. In this way, to summarize, the years after the 1970s witnessed the coexistence of fictitious accumulation, coercion over labor, debt servitude and deregulation of conditions that had been keeping within private spheres the risks that have now been increasingly socialized (Bonefeld 2010).

The central thesis of this chapter is that the most recent financial expansion of the economy took place within a context of structural reorganization of economic and political relations. The role of the state was fundamental in this process, even if the neoliberal prescriptions called for its reduction, which, however, took place selectively. The ruling classes throughout the world felt threatened when, in the 1970s, economic growth began to collapse, real interest rates became negative and lower dividends and profits became the rule (Harvey 2005). Under the pretext that state intervention distorted the 'normal' functioning of the economy, and for this reason the latter was not working appropriately, neoliberalism took the planet by storm, advocating that economic activity should be regulated exclusively by free markets. Underlying that discourse was the real intention of re-establishing the economic power of the ruling classes whose profits had been reduced by the redistributive policies of the welfare state. Expanding profits of the financial type has been one of the results of neoliberalism and the financialization it engendered.

1   Crisis of Accumulation and Reaction of Finance

Without disagreeing with the ideas that affirm that the liberalization of the economy made crises more frequent, deepened them or created new ones (Duménil and Lévy 2001; Evans 2008), I follow the hypothesis that the neoliberal shift was a response to a crisis of broader structural dimensions. Crises are a constitutive element of capitalism (Hilferding 2006 [1910]), which, by means of them, regenerates itself and modifies the conditions of exploitation (Salama

1978). This means that crises are not exclusive to neoliberalism, whose structural dimensions to which I refer go beyond the sphere of production. The latter is necessary but not sufficient for understanding the socioeconomic order whose foundations were propagated first in the central countries in the 1970s, and then reached the periphery of the world economic system with greatest impetus in the mid-1990s. In the same way that economic crises cannot be explained only by phenomena restricted to the sphere of production—it is also necessary to consider the contradictions present in the political system (Offe 1984a)—part of the explanation about the reaction to such crises is also in the political system.

Upon taking this route to study the reactions to the crisis that I understand inaugurated the conditions that led to the centrality of finance in contemporary capitalism, class relations are fundamental. The opening of global markets that began in the mid-1970s was one of the responses of the ruling classes to the crisis that led to the end of the Keynesian consensus. Another was the rise in interest rates promoted in the U.S. economy, at the end of that decade, whose effects were experienced in most of the world economy. The class character of these movements is revealed, for example, in the increase of financial profits at the expense of lower returns on productive investment, which in turn led to increases in unemployment, public indebtedness, and social violence (Duménil and Lévy 2001; Salama 1998). In political terms, both measures took place within an institutional framework marked by fundamental participation of the state, which stepped away from some activities to strengthen others, in contradiction to neoliberal rhetoric.

The history of capitalism has been a succession not only of crises, as classic Marxism suggested about the inescapable downfall of this mode of production. As early as the beginning of the past century, Rudolf Hilferding assumed that capitalism could stabilize itself against economic crises and potentially continue to exist forever (Wagner 1996). Nevertheless, what can be said with certainty is that crises are a constitutive part of this mode of production. For Duménil and Lévy (2004a), it is not an accident that the current transformations of capitalism have followed structural crises. If on one hand they point to the self-destruction of the system, on the other, they can open up new possibilities for the deepening of labor exploitation. From the eruption of financial disasters, for example, dominant elites can emerge even more powerful (Harvey 2005). This was the case of the Brazilian crises of the late 1990s. Upon comparing the periods of 1990–1997 and 1998–2004, the average return on direct foreign investment rose from 0.36% to 0.85% and that of portfolio investments from 1.65% to 2.58% in relation to GDP (gross domestic product) (Dufour and Orhangazi 2007).

As can be seen, crises do not necessarily threaten capitalism. As Giovanni Arrighi portrayed, the history of this mode of production has been characterized by "long periods of crisis, restructuring and reorganization" (Arrighi 1994: 1). According to him, after three long cycles of accumulation, each one composed of a phase of material expansion followed by a phase of financial expansion, capitalism has now attained its fourth cycle, which is precisely that of financial expansion.[2] Arrighi affirms that a new cycle of accumulation overlapped the then existing one to thus recover the capacity for accumulation threatened by crises generated within the structure to be substituted. In each one of these cycles, the financial expansion results from the fact that production and trade are not capable of guaranteeing cash flow as well as pure financial deals (Arrighi 1994). According to Arrighi,

> the recurrence of systemic cycles of accumulation can thus be described as a series of phases of stable expansion of the capitalist world-economy alternating with phases of turbulence in the course of which the conditions of stable expansion along an established developmental path are destroyed and those of expansion along a new path are created.
> ARRIGHI 1994: 235

But we can also think of these phases of turbulence also within Arrighi's broad cycles. One of these phases of turbulence, which generated deep consequences for the world accumulation process, was that which erupted in the final decade of the Keynesian consensus, more precisely in the late 1970s. That regime had been a response to the accumulation crisis sparked by the reduction of consumption after World War II. Under the Keynesian model, at the same time that it left the private sector free to decide about investment and administration at private companies, the state was involved more in the control of the level of economic activity, regulating interest rates, credit, currency, and supervising financial institutions (Duménil and Lévy 2001, 2004a). The state also became more active in fields like education, research, and industrial policy, as it was in the creation of social protection systems in healthcare, retirement, and unemployment.

---

2 Arrighi identifies four systemic cycles of accumulation, each of them characterized by the fundamental unity between a main agent and the structure of the global process of accumulation: (i) the Genovese, which lasted from the fifteenth to the early seventeenth century; (ii) the Dutch, which extended from the late sixteenth through most of the eighteenth century; (iii) the British, which lasted from the second half of the eighteenth to the beginning of the twentieth century; and (iv) the American, which has extended from the late nineteenth century until the present.

One of the results of this configuration, shaped by controls over finance and by the compromise synthesized in the objectives of full employment and social protection, was to limit the levels of profitability of the financial classes, which was revealed, for example, by the behavior of interest rates. Figure 1 shows that, in some of the main economies of the center of world capitalist system, the context was of relatively low interest rates until the late 1970s. During the period from 1960 to 1979, annual ex post real interbank interest rates averaged 1.1% in Germany, 0.5% in Japan, and 0.9% in the United States. When real rates in general reached negative levels, particularly in the second half of the 1970s, the liberalism of the Keynesian type began to make room for a kind of new liberalism. In this way, in the period from 1980 to 1999, average real interbank rates in those countries rose to 3.2%, 2.6%, and 3.1%, respectively. In the following decade, these rates fell again, but by then the financial mechanisms had already reached the extraordinary dimensions revealed in the crisis of 2008.

The Keynesian model was not sustained and signs of crisis multiplied during the 1970s, the majority of which restricted capital accumulation. Steep rises in oil prices, low rates of economic growth and technological evolution, unemployment, wage stagnation, labor militancy, fiscal crisis, collapse of fixed exchange rates, increased global competitiveness, falling profits and dividends, depressed stock markets, and nominal interest rates unlikely to be higher than inflation were the main elements of the crisis. It was precisely the decline of

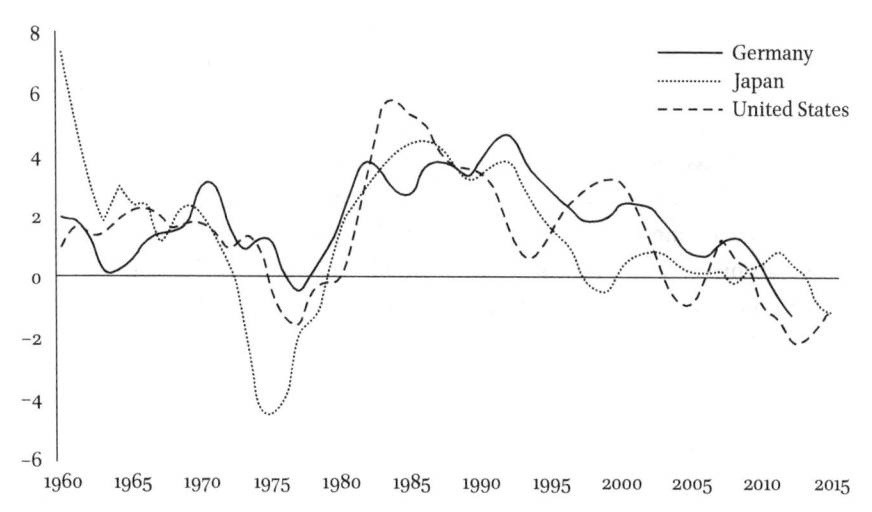

FIGURE 1 Short-term interest rates, selected countries, 1960–2015
Notes: (i) percentage scale; (ii) ex post real interbank interest rates; (iii) three-year moving averages.

profits in the central countries and their consequences for the income of the ruling classes that delineated the transformations that followed (Duménil and Lévy 2001, 2004a). Along with the deregulation of markets, a new monetary ideology promoted by the United States changed the economic environment from low to high real interest rates, which discouraged productive investment and steered economic activity towards finance (Foster and Magdoff 2009; Krippner 2005). A similar movement would also be observed in other economies worldwide.

One of the main events that marked the switch in direction to financial hegemony was the change in U.S. monetary policy sparked by what Duménil and Lévy (2001: 587) called "the 1979 coup." At a time when inflation began to soar, priority was given to its eradication, and the method chosen was to raise interest rates claiming that this would encourage individual savings (Duménil and Lévy 2004a). The ex ante real interest rate rose from an annual average of 0.8% during the 1973–1979 period to an average of 4.8% in 1979–1989 (Bowles, Gordon, and Weisskopf 1990). But the discourse did not pronounce that inflation was also corroding the real return on financial investments and that, therefore, it was necessary to staunch these loses (Duménil and Lévy 2004a). The change in monetary policy was the preamble to a series of measures that sought to restore confidence in the U.S. dollar and once again centralize private financial capital in the United States (Arrighi 1994).[3]

This gave shape to the transformations that, according to Duménil and Lévy (2004a), would lead to the restoration of the domination of finance, revealing a movement of a political nature and of a clear expression of class struggle. The evolution of the ratio between real interest rate and the growth rate of GDP in the seven main capitalist economies corroborates and synthesizes part of this hypothesis. According to data compiled by Minqi Li (2004), the average of this ratio, which was 2.4 in the 1919–1939 period and that fell to 0.3 in 1946–1958, returned to the original level in the 1985–1997 period, when it reached 2.3. This shows that financial assets were more profitable and attractive than investments in production in the first and third of these periods. They respectively correspond approximately to the periods that Duménil and Lévy (2011: 15) refer to as "a 'first' and a 'second financial hegemony.'"

---

3 These measures, in addition to rising real interest rates, were (i) deregulation that virtually gave total freedom of action to corporations and domestic and foreign financial organizations within the United States; (ii) public indebtedness, which transformed the country from the world's largest creditor into the world's largest debtor; (iii) military expansion in the context of the Cold War; and (iv) demonstrations of force against unfriendly regimes in the so-called Third World (Arrighi 1994).

THE POLITICS OF FINANCIALIZATION 15

In sociological terms, 'the 1979 coup'—the rise in U.S. interest rates—signified the change of direction given to economic surpluses transferred between classes and their fractions in financial operations, for example, lending. This is because an inflation rate higher than the nominal interest rate causes the interest paid by the debtor to be more than offset by the depreciation of the debt, with this difference being a transfer of surpluses, in real terms, from the creditor to the debtor. In sum, "inflation hurts creditors and benefits debtors" (Carruthers 2005: 368). When nominal interest rates exceed inflation, the phenomenon takes place in the reverse direction, that is, the creditors receive a portion of the surpluses that are redistributed through financial transactions. Evidence of this can be found in figure 2, which shows that the public debt and real interest rates in the United States followed similar trends, at least until the eve of the financial crisis that erupted in 2007–2008.

From the 1960s until the mid-1970s, declining real interest rates drove the tendency for the debt level to also decline. From the mid-1970s until the early 1980s, when these rates became negative, the level of public debt remained stable. After 'the 1979 coup,' when the U.S. government started to pay higher interest rates, the public debt began to increase. From an average of 41% of GDP during the 1960–1979 period, it rose to an average of 51% in 1980–1999. The annual ex post real interbank interest rate, which had averaged 1% in 1960–1979, rose to 3% in the 1980–1999 period. This rate fell to an average closer to zero in the 2000–2015 period, but then the level of debt was already nearly

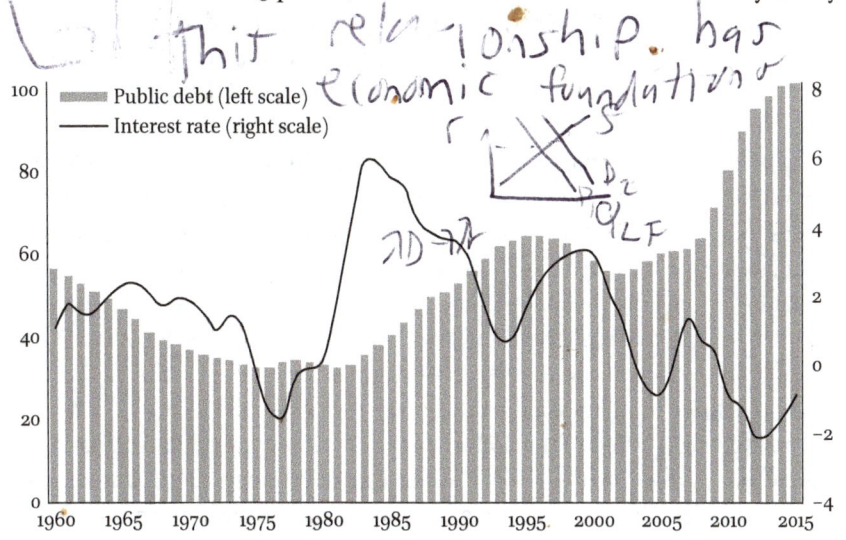

FIGURE 2   Public debt and short-term interest rate, United States, 1960–2015
Notes: (i) public debt as a percentage of GDP; (ii) ex post real interbank interest rate in percent; (iii) three-year moving averages.

80% higher than that in the 1960–1979 period. It averaged 73% of GDP in 2000–2015 and 91% if one considers only the 2009–2015 period, after the financial crisis of 2008 erupted. These figures show that since the early 1980s the financial classes expanded their share in the appropriation of economic surpluses. This was the great feat of neoliberalism as a class project that sought to strengthen finance as a privileged fraction of capital (Harvey 2010).

That accelerated debt expansion cannot be substantially explained by the accrued interest on outstanding debt, as took place in Brazil. It is explained—and this applies to the United States as well as to Brazil—mainly by the fact that higher real interest rates had created a favorable scenario to increased indebtedness, contradicting the wisdom of classical economics. This very scenario was marked by the greater facility for the state to finance fiscal deficits, which in turn nourished its propensity to incur new deficits, and by capital's intensified search for more profitable financial outlets. When interest rates on the public debt are higher than the returns on investment in production, the bonds issued by the state become more attractive. At the same time, governments see indebtedness as a source of anticipation of future taxes. This was the equation that allowed, for example, the United States to finance the recurring fiscal deficits significantly driven by military spending in the Reagan era.

The other phenomenon that I highlight as being determinant for the current configuration of capitalism was the opening of international financial markets, which actually began before and influenced the change in U.S. monetary policy previously mentioned. This opening allowed finance to move money-capital throughout the world economic system when and where a more profitable option appeared, and was key to re-establishing the political power and profitability of finance capital. Antecedents to this opening had already been seen since the early 1970s, when the U.S. pressure for free circulation of financial capital became concretized with the collapse of the Bretton Woods system (Carcanholo and Nakatani 2001; Vernengo 2006). The fundamentals of that system were fixed exchange rates, limits on capital flows and international financial institutions capable of guaranteeing credit to countries with this need. The Bretton Woods system had also established the U.S. dollar—which at the time was convertible into gold—as the global currency to be used in international trade.

The exclusivity given to the dollar provoked tremendous global demand for the currency, to which the United States responded with direct investment, imports, foreign aid, and military assistance. This led the country to successive deficits in external accounts in the 1950s and 1960s, which in turn generated crises of confidence that led other countries to try to convert the dollars that they held into gold. With this, between 1971 and 1973, the United States abandoned the convertibility of the dollar into gold, leading to the extinction of the fixed exchange rate system. The new development ended the requirement imposed by the Bretton Woods system that the United States should maintain equilibrium in its balance of payments. Thus, dollars could continue to inundate global markets, but since then without a clear control over the value of the U.S. currency. During the 1970s, the average annual growth of the volume of Eurodollars was 25% compared to a 10% growth in the supply of dollars in the United States and to a 4% increase in the volume of international trade (Harvey 1990).

Between 1970 and 1973, the money supply grew 40% in the United States and between 1972 and 1973 70% in Great Britain, thus initiating an inflationary process (Frieden 2006). The latter was attacked with the rise in interest rates that we saw earlier in the phenomenon described as 'the 1979 coup.' While inflation was a threat to finance, because it reduces the real values of assets, the new increased money supply created new opportunities for the financial class to profit. The fact is that the path was open for the United States to print more dollars to the degree that other countries were prepared to absorb them, which, in the periphery of the world economy, took place largely by means of external indebtedness (Corbridge 1993).

The collapse of the Bretton Woods system and the subsequent elimination of capital controls promoted by the United States and its agents—namely the IMF and the World Bank—allowed central banks to compete worldwide for speculative capital flows, thus provoking the rise of real interest rates (Vernengo 2006). Seeing its domination threatened, the United States changed its opinion in relation to the controls that had been imposed by the Bretton Woods agreement. The Economic Report of the President of 1973, supposedly drafted by Milton Friedman, affirmed that free international mobility of capital should be treated equally to free trade in goods and services, and controls should be suppressed (Duménil and Lévy 2004a). Limits on the circulation of capitals were eventually revoked in the United States in 1974, in the United Kingdom in 1979, in continental Europe between 1986 and 1988, and in all of the OECD countries in 1989 (Duménil and Lévy 2004a).

The rise in interest rates and the opening of financial markets thus established important bases for the current configuration of global capitalism. Conditions were thus established for capitalist *accumulation*—that is, the production of surplus-value—to cede space to the *expropriation* of surpluses by financial means. The logic of monopoly rents, which since then has focused on financial assets and politically protected intangible assets, in some form overcame the logic of revolutionizing the means of production (Evans 2008). This delineated what we now call financialization, which some commentators define as the phase of capitalist development characterized by an economic pattern in which profits would mainly come from financial channels instead of productive activities (Krippner 2005, 2011). These channels, Greta Krippner adds, have made the provision or transfer of net capital viable, with the aim of obtaining interest, dividends, or future capital gains.

The reactions of finance—the rise in interest rates and the liberalization of markets—to the crisis of accumulation and the essential role of the state to do so show that in the actually existing neoliberalism the state retreat was a fallacy. Neoliberalism is a pastiche of political prescriptions inspired by an economic-political theory that maintains that human well-being would advance more by means of individual liberties and one's entrepreneurial capacities, within an institutional framework characterized by guaranteed private property rights and by markets and trade free from state interference (Babb 2007; Crouch 2011; Harvey 2005). The neoliberal doctrine also affirms that the state's only role should be to create and maintain institutional conditions that assure these practices, by guaranteeing, for example, the soundness and integrity of the currency. It would also be a role of the state to maintain the military, police, and legal functions needed to assure property rights and the correct functioning of markets. In sum, state intervention in the economy should be held to a minimum. One alleged reason is because asymmetries of information and influences created by state intervention could favor certain social groups.

Yet, as David Harvey (2005), highlighted, in addition to incoherencies internal to the theory, such as the concomitance of disbelieving in state power and demanding strong action to defend the right to private property and individual and corporate liberties, neoliberal practice presents other contradictions: (i) the state is expected to provide accessory actions, limited to establishing conditions for market operations, but it is simultaneously expected to promote an environment favorable to business and act as a competitive entity in global politics; (ii) the more neoliberalism advances in an authoritarian manner to promote the market economy, the more difficult it becomes to maintain its legitimacy in terms of individual liberties, thus revealing its anti-democratic character; (iii) at the same time that it is crucial to maintaining the integrity of the financial system, the irresponsible individualism of its agents produces speculative volatility, financial scandals, and chronic instability; (iv) while the virtues of competition are promoted, the reality shows the consolidation of multinational oligopolies and monopolies; and (v) the option for market freedoms and the commodification of everything possible tends to erode forms of social solidarity, compromising the very social order. For this reason, Eric Hobsbawm correctly concluded that "the theories on which neo-liberal theology was based, while elegant, had little relation to reality" (Hobsbawm 1995: 564).

Upon concluding this section, a warning is in order about the argument that capitalist crises point to solutions by means of reorganizations within the system itself. Based on what was said until now, it cannot be concluded that capitalism is safe from itself. For Göran Therborn (2007), there is a possibility that the current phase of capitalism represents a threat to the system itself, given that financial expansion is an expression of, and a vehicle for, a deep crisis of the existing global hegemony. Even if finance capital is hegemonic, it should remain at levels compatible with the actual valorization of productive capital. If it does not, the results will be the decline in the volume of surplus-value to be distributed among the various forms of capital—industrial, commercial, and financial—as well as a general crisis of accumulation and or the decline of capital (Jessop 1990, 2010). Therefore, as powerful as it may appear, the current order is unsustainable, because it is incapable of protecting society and the environment, as well as capital itself from the chaos of its own markets (Evans 2008).

2 Financial Expansion of the Brazilian Economy

Similar to what had taken place in the Global North, the main result of Brazil's liberalizing policies was to place finance capital at the top of the list of beneficiaries of these policies. Measures that irradiated from the multilateral financial agencies—for instance, the International Monetary Fund and the World Bank—and governments of the countries of the center of the global economy, some of them implemented in the latter, quickly reach the periphery. Movements in this direction were already seen in Brazil in the first civil government after the military dictatorship—that of President José Sarney (1985–1990)—when various anti-inflation plans were launched and failed. In the government of President Fernando Collor (1990–1992), in addition to new attempts at inflation control, which also failed, the economy began to be opened to international capital and privatizations of state companies initiated. In the government of President Itamar Franco (1992–1994), which was installed when Collor was ousted from office due an impeachment process, Brazil lifted controls on financial capital outflows, which inserted the country in the international circuit of financial 'valorization' (Paulani 2008).

According to Jorge Garagorry (2007), it was precisely after Collor's impeachment that international finance attained effective hegemony in Brazilian society. Garagorry affirms that between the governments of Sarney (1985–1990) and the first Lula government (2003–2006), it was during the Collor government (1990–1992) that Brazil paid less interest on public debt. That was a result of the reduction in the federal debt caused by the sequestering of bank savings and deposits decreed under the anti-inflation plan known as the Collor Plan, in 1990. The fall of President Collor, Garagorry concluded, came to be a correction in direction by the part of the ruling class by "defenestrating its creature," who would have not been up to the task of implementing the policies that were priorities for finance (Garagorry 2007: 254). This recalls Karl Marx's comparison of the democratic model of the Paris Commune to the limited idea of democracy materialized in representative democracy. He affirmed that "companies, like individuals, in matters of real business generally know how to put the right man in the right place, and, if they for once make a mistake, to redress it promptly" (Marx 2010 [1871]: 333).

In July 1994, the Real Plan was launched and one of its foundations was a restrictive monetary policy, with the main objective of containing inflation. Like the U.S. Federal Reserve (Desai 2013: 195), the Central Bank of Brazil became "almost hysterically intolerant of inflation." This could be considered 'the 1994 coup,' which in some measure reproduced the monetarist turn marked by the rise in U.S. interest rates set by 'the 1979 coup.' One difference was that in Brazil, a succession of 'coups' of this kind followed as responses to returns of high inflation or to financial crises. Since then, the Brazilian state has been paying the world's highest interest rates, as shown in figure 3 (see also figure 1). During the period the Real Plan was in effect (1994–1998), the annual ex post real interbank interest rate averaged 22% in Brazil, compared, for instance, with 7.2% in Korea, 7.6% in Mexico, and 5.8% in South Africa. After the collapse

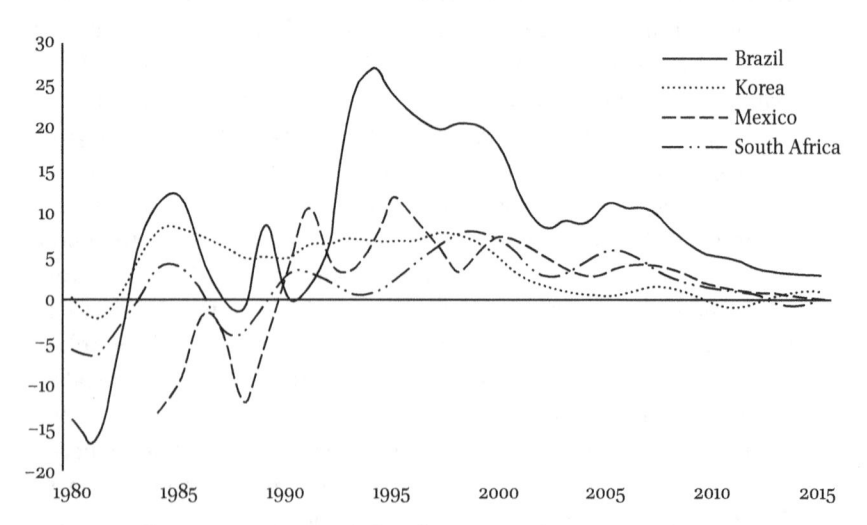

FIGURE 3   Short-term interest rates, selected countries, 1980–2015
Notes: (i) percentage scale; (ii) ex post real interbank interest rates; (iii) three-year moving averages.

of the Real Plan, in 1999, when inflation targeting was adopted, Brazil continued to pay the highest interest rates. During the 1999–2015 period, the ex post real interbank rate averaged 7.3% in Brazil, 0.9% in Korea, 2.7% in Mexico, and 2.5% in South Africa.

The main objective of the Real Plan was monetary stabilization. However, it had broader ambitions. Its premise was that only a drastic reduction of inflation could create an environment attractive to foreign investments, and that only the massive inflow of these investments would provide the bases for long-term economic growth (Rocha 2002). Relying on this strategy to restore foreign confidence and thus attract capital, the Brazilian government encouraged the inflow of short-term speculative funds in an attempt to accumulate foreign currency reserves. For this reason, in addition to the world's highest interest rates, the government granted investors permission to remit financial capital out of Brazil at any moment (Rocha 2002). The model also included the deepening of concessions to the private sector of various activities that until then were operated directly by the state, which took place by means of breaking up monopolies and privatizations.

As can be seen in figure 4, one of the results of this new political orientation was an expansion of the inflow of financial capital into the country, in both direct investment and portfolio investments, loans and others. The annual average of financial inflow of foreign capital rose from 7 billion U.S. dollars during the 1980–1994 period to 36 billion dollars during the 1995–1998 period. The situation changed in early 1999, when the Real Plan collapsed—the pegged exchange rate regime was substituted by inflation targeting—after a succession of global financial crises, in particular in Southeast Asia in 1997 and Russia in 1998. However, in the long-term, Brazil remained an important destination of global financial flows. The inflow of this type of capital, which had fallen to an annual average of 15 billion dollars in 1999–2005, resumed its increasing trend in 2006, reaching an annual average of 105 billion dollars during the 2006–2014 period.

This route taken by the Brazilian state expanded an uncomplicated but efficient system to transfer surplus-value to finance. The intuitive simplicity of both monetarism and deregulation facilitated the acceptance of the model by society at the same time that it masked the sale of profitable assets, both direct and portfolio (Potter 2007). Of the annual average of 36 billion U.S. dollars that entered Brazil in 1995–1998, 15 billion were in direct investment and 21 billion in portfolio investments, loans and others. Liberalization, deregulation, privatization, and other policies said to be modernizing, which had been implemented since the early 1990s, sought to attract foreign capital as the most recent neoclassical formula for diffusion of the development of capitalism

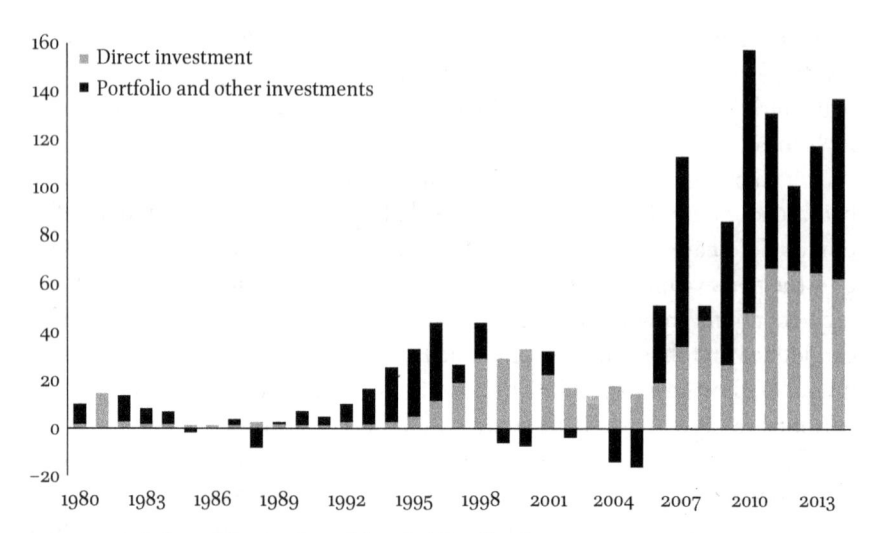

FIGURE 4   Inflow of foreign financial capital, Brazil, 1980–2014
Notes: (i) nominal values in U.S. dollars billion; (ii) balance of payments statistics from the 5th edition of the International Monetary Fund Balance of Payments and International Investment Position Manual; (iii) series discontinued by the Central Bank of Brazil in February 2015.

from the center to the periphery (Rocha 1994). In synthesis, Brazil was doing its part to construct "the emerging financial regime … designed to facilitate global capital mobility in search of profits via cheap labor[-power]" (Asimakopoulus 2009: 179).

The idea to take advantage of abundant liquidity in international markets and attract foreign investments to develop the economy thus helped justify the policy of consistently high interest rates. According to João Sicsú (2006) this was the only formula envisioned to do so. In addition, the understanding that inflation must be reduced to attract those investments also warranted the high interest rates. The dominant premise that any intervention was justifiable to keep inflation low (Wilson 2002) gained support in Brazil. The fight against hyperinflation counted on immense popularity among those who had been suffering from increasing prices because they could not protect their income, at the same time that it aligned financial interests to the neoliberal agenda (Potter 2007). This conjugation thus served to sustain the financial hegemony by coordinating the interests of finance with those over whom the hegemony was exercised, namely the working class and ordinary people and consumers in general. As Adam Przeworski recalled (1985), economic hegemony is only maintained if that coordination takes place, which occurs when the interests of the subordinated social fractions are served to some degree. Thus, if

THE POLITICS OF FINANCIALIZATION 23

society sought low inflation to protect itself from the inflation tax, it would be willing—or it was convinced—to support higher interest rates to control inflation.

Hyperinflation was truly contained, as can be seen in figure 5. Despite some instabilities along the path inaugurated in 1994, it was maintained at levels and for a time that led it to be celebrated as the great conquest of Brazilian society, in particular for the poorest stratum. The annual average consumer price index fell from an astounding 728% in 1980–1994 to 7.4% in 1995–2015. Nevertheless, the discourse told only part of the story, failing to disclose that part of what the new order gave with one hand it took away with the other. Eliminating the inflation tax, as well as attracting foreign capital, had a price, which was mainly paid by the classes that would allegedly be the main beneficiaries of the development promised by neoliberalism. It is synthesized by the rise in short-term real interest rates, whose annual average rose from 6.5% in 1980–1994 to 10% in 1995–2015 (16% in 1995–2002 and 6.4% in 2003–2015). This was eventually reflected in increases in the public debt and in the level of taxation, as well as in restrictions on non-financial state spending (see figures 13, 15, and 23).

The increased domestic public debt since the mid-1990s and interest rates among the world's highest provided finance significantly profitable and liquid investment alternatives. Thus, the Brazilian state contributed to the financial expansion of the economy through domestic indebtedness, which, by judging mainly by the attractiveness that it represented for finance, became one of the

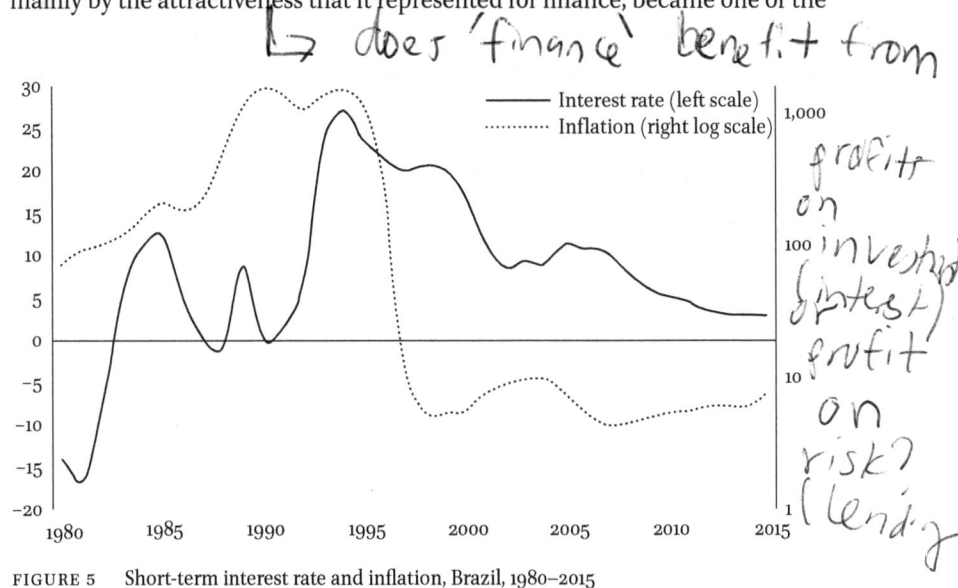

FIGURE 5 Short-term interest rate and inflation, Brazil, 1980–2015
Notes: (i) percentage scales; (ii) ex post real interbank interest rate; (iii) three-year moving averages.

most significant elements of the financialization movement. The stock market also considerably expanded. I emphasize that government bonds and corporate stocks are precisely the items highlighted by Karl Marx in his definition of fictitious capital, whose evolution I use as evidence of the financialization of the Brazilian economy. As Pierre Salama (1998) teaches, the degree of financialization of a country can be measured by the relation of financial assets to total assets.

With the liberalization of international capital flows, some of the fictitious type quickly multiplied in Brazil, as can be seen in figure 6. At the same time, there was a decline in investments in production represented by gross fixed capital formation. The portion of GDP invested in fixed assets for productive activity fell from an average of 21% in the 1988–1994 period to 17% in the 1995–2014 period.[4] Meanwhile, fictitious capital, formed here by the domestic federal debt securities and shares of companies negotiated on the São Paulo stock exchange—known as the BM&FBovespa—rose from an average of 62% to 86% of GDP between these same periods. It must be highlighted that this percentage reached 139% in the year prior to the financial crisis of 2008, and even with the trend to decline that it then began, remained on average close to 100% of GDP from 2008 to 2014.

The items that form fictitious capital in figure 6 are capital because they represent to their owners a potential for valorization; they are fictitious because the eventual realization of this expectation for price appreciation does not create any additional value for the economy. This realization, however, assumes its concrete social character when these capitals serve the expropriation of the productive classes by the appropriating classes. In the case of the fictitious capital represented by corporate stocks this means of expropriation can take place through a novelty that came in the wake of neoliberalism. This is the ideology of corporate governance, which, roughly speaking, prescribes that corporate management should give priority to the appreciation of the money-capital of shareholders. This logic is different from that of the previous period when the valorization of individual capitals was fundamentally sought through material production.

This does not mean that the relevance of material production has weakened, because capitalism depends on this production. Nonetheless, for many individual capitalists production became a secondary objective. Their fundamental

---

4   When there is no indication, the GDP and the other data from the national accounts used throughout this book are those found in the Brazilian System of National Accounts reference 2010. When necessary, in particular for the older series, data from the System of National Accounts reference 2000 were used, which will be mentioned when pertinent.

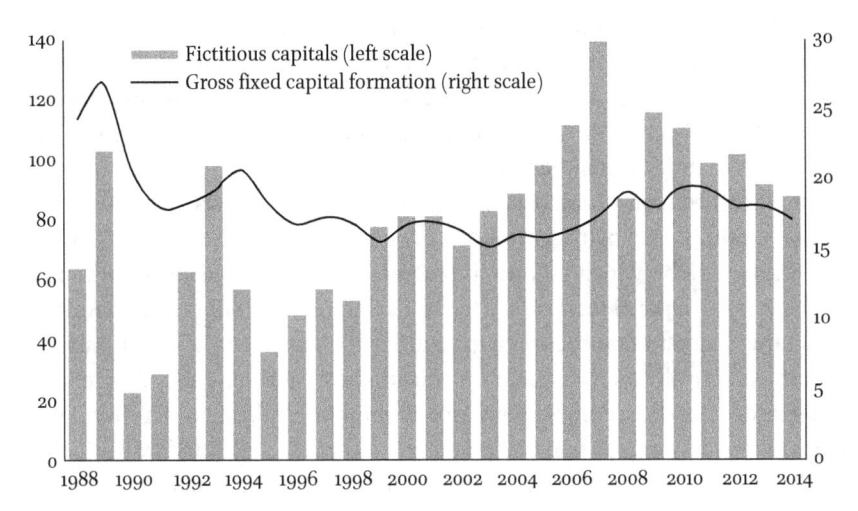

FIGURE 6 Fictitious capitals and gross fixed capital formation, Brazil, 1988–2014
Notes: (i) percentages in relation to GDP; (ii) fictitious capitals composed by the year-end positions of the outstanding domestic federal securitized debt and the market price of the shares of the companies traded on the São Paulo stock exchange BM&FBovespa; (iii) gross fixed capital formation and GDP retrieved from the System of National Accounts reference 2000, where 2014 is the last year in the series.

objective is now financial appreciation, so that increased material wealth is one means among others to accumulate capital. According to François Chesnais (2005b), since the 1980s, shareholders have been employing considerable energy and legal or quasi-legal means to subordinate industrial executives, transforming them into people who interiorize the attributes and codes of conduct born from the power of the stock market. Their priorities, Chesnais adds, are very different from those of the industrial managers who they succeeded. Now, large corporate groups are directed by executives who, above all other concerns, guide their work by watching the share prices of the company that hires them.

Many of the administrative ideologies that have been promoted since then, such as corporate governance, brought with them rising rates of exploitation of labor by the part of the appropriating classes in the guise of shareholders. Unlike the industrial or commercial capitalists, finance capitalists—who may be shareholders—are driven by the opportunities for valorization of the fictitious capital that they hold or can come to hold. In this sense, finance did come to control industry and trade as indicated by Rudolf Hilferding (2006 [1910]), although in a different way. It is not only banks that exercise strong influence on industry and commerce. It is finance in general that exercises this influence via globally connected stock and capital markets. It is finance capital that exercises influence on nation states, especially by means of the public debt.

The Brazilian public debt is now one of the destinations of money-capital not productively invested that, nevertheless, appears to become valorized—in a fictitious manner, given that it does not engender exploitation of productive labor—in the circuit of finance. Banks and investment funds—the latter are mostly administered by the former—concentrate in their hands nearly all of the Brazilian debt, which, in turn, has come to account for a large portion of the country's financial market (see figure 7). Complementarily, the public debt made this market an appropriate ground for the expansion of fiscal sources, because practically any person or organization can now lend to the state. Another aspect of this complementarity is mentioned by Jennifer Hermann (2002) who emphasizes that the tendency towards global standardization of public debt under the form of securities tradable on secondary markets is explained by the need that governments came to have to sell bonds with conditions—interest rates, maturity, etc.—that could also meet their economic policy objectives. From this arose a mutuality of reproduction between public debt and financial markets, corroborating Robert Boyer (1999) when he affirms that the state is not only responsible for correcting market deficiencies, but also for creating new markets.

In relation to this point I call attention to a relatively new mechanism in the Brazilian financial market. Its evolution can be seen to parallel the very process of domestic public indebtedness. It is the investment fund, the amounts of which rose at a pace similar to that of the domestic federal securitized debt, as shown in figure 7. This is even clearer in the portion of federal debt securities in the composition of the portfolios of these funds, which averaged 65% during the 2000–2015 period (see bars in figure 7). Even if this period is relatively brief, the behavior of the other two indicators leads us to believe that federal bonds had been similarly representative in the period beginning with the Real Plan, in the mid-1990s (see lines in figure 7). In a word, it was the securitization—the transformation of contractual debt into marketable securities—of the Brazilian public debt and the growth of this debt that were the main movements that made viable the development of the investment fund market in Brazil.

An important aspect of the investment fund is its meaning for finance in terms of the risk associated to sovereign debt. This kind of fund pools money-capital from savers and investors who want their financial resources to be professionally managed. The money is then employed to purchase assets, which may include public debt bonds. This apparently involves a relationship

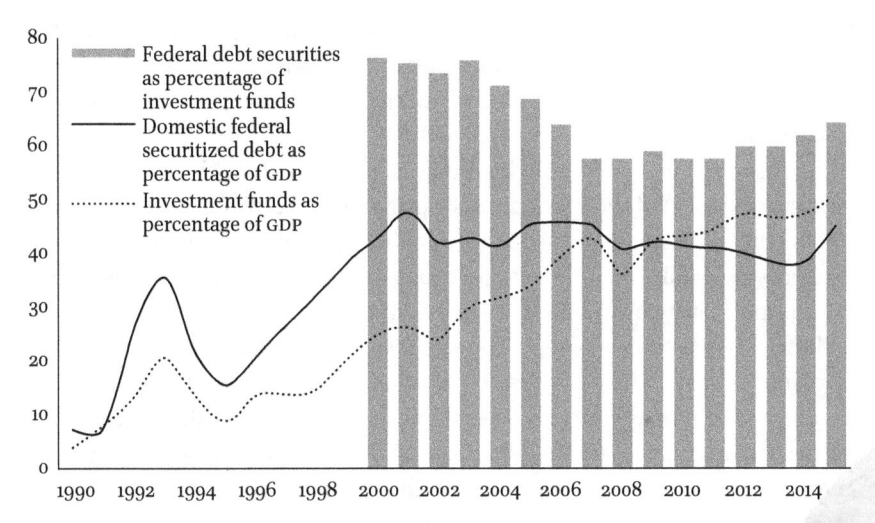

FIGURE 7 Investment funds and securitized public debt, Brazil, 1990–2015
Notes: (i) outstanding debt securities and total net asset value of investment funds at the end of each year; (ii) federal debt securities as percentage of investment funds is available only from the year 2000.

similar to the operation of collecting, now through an investment fund, resources of savers and lending them to borrowers through the purchase of securities issued by the latter. However, the intermediary that manages the investment fund does not necessarily hold the creditor's rights, as would a traditional financial agent acting as a lender. Most of these rights are held by those who purchase shares in the investment fund, and they consequently run the credit risk. For funds that purchase public debt bonds, if the state does not make the payment due upon maturity, the corresponding bonds lose value, leading to the depreciation of the shares of the fund, thus imposing losses on its shareholders. Even if this occurs, the mangers will already have appropriated the fees charged from the shareholders as remuneration for managing the fund.

The expansion of the market for investment funds supported by domestic public debt involves another relevant aspect. As I have said, the growth in this market in Brazil also signified expanding the sources of financing for government fiscal deficits, which until the 1980s were concentrated in contractual debt with foreign banks. This movement of mutual reproduction between financial expansion of the economy and public debt was also coherent with the removal of barriers to the worldwide flows of capital. This structure created alternative financing sources for the state at the same time that it provided profitable alternatives to finance capital. It also expanded the options available to domestic finance, including retail investors, to lend to the Brazilian state and thus earn part of the income previously steered largely towards international finance.

On this point my analysis differs from many that commonly criticize the financial expansion of the economy as favoring *foreign* capital. Even if this were totally true—it is not, because in the Brazilian case native capitalists were also favored—it would have little relevance for an analysis from a class perspective. Furthermore, it involves an incorrect critique from a theoretical perspective and a useless one from a practical perspective, because it is based on a distinction, in this case between foreigners and non-foreigners, that adds virtually nothing to the fundamental issue of capitalist exploitation. This approach was quite striking in the external debt crisis of the 1980s, when the rhetoric of a certain portion of the left wing made tough references to international finance capital. In times of privatizations and financial expansion, this approach remains present. Nonetheless, more than politically useless, it can be a risky approach to the degree that the attack of the left wing on *international* capital also involves establishing an opposition between foreigners and natives even within the ruled classes. And this division, it is known, is always welcome by the ruling classes. It is important to remember that "the national governments are *one* as against the proletariate!" (Marx 2010 [1871]: 354; emphasis in original). Capitals, apparently national or international, also compose *one*, when they face the proletariat.

The critique that I consider relevant concerns the hypothesis that attracting capital from one or another location of the world-system can lead to changes in the rate of exploitation. This is different from analyses with an, at times, nationalist coloration that I just mentioned. They unconsciously wind up taking the perspective of the exploiter by accepting the simplification that distinguishes national and foreign, insinuating that the latter would be *the* adversary in relation to the one who makes such distinction. But if we take the perspective of the exploited we must ask if the qualitative change—substituting one exploiter for another, in this case, from different places in the world economy—is not in reality translated into a quantitative change. I am referring to the conclusions of Nakatani and Herrera (2007) that the conversion of external into domestic debt that took place in peripheral countries has meant an increased rate of exploitation because domestic lenders have levied higher interest rates than foreign lenders. This is the apparent case in figure 8, which shows the changes in the domestic and external debts in Brazil and their respective implicit nominal interest rates.

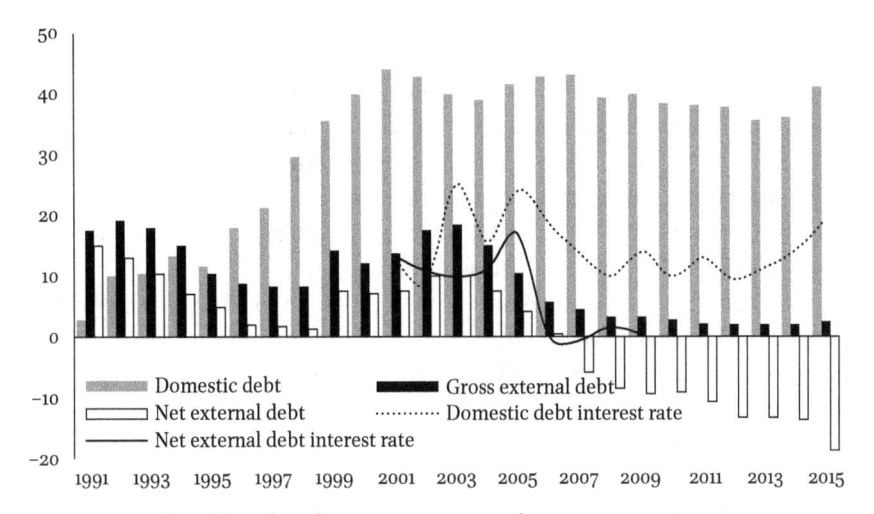

FIGURE 8   Public debt and implicit interest rates, Brazil, 1991–2015
Notes: (i) percentage scale; (ii) debts of the central government as percentages of GDP; (iii) implicit nominal interest rates.

Figure 8 shows a deepening movement of the transfer to finance of surpluses collected by the Brazilian state. While the average domestic debt increased from 14% of GDP in 1991–1998 to 40% in 1999–2015, that of the gross external debt fell from 13% to 7.6% of GDP between these same periods. The annual average of the implicit nominal interest rate on the domestic debt was 14% in 2001–2015 vis-à-vis the 4.6% rate on external debt. This more expensive domestic debt also financed the formation of foreign exchange reserves, whose returns were similar to the interest rates on external debt. In sum, the decline of the external debt, which since 2006 has been more than offset by foreign exchange reserves, was financed by another more expensive debt, the domestic one. Thus, one notices that finance, whether domestic or foreign, can impose rates of expropriation according to the economic and political conditions framed by this specific form of class relation. In Brazil the difference between external and domestic rates made the tax system a mechanism for the transfer of surpluses to those with access not only to international financial markets, as Morais, Saad-Filho and Coelho (1999) argue, but with access to financial markets in general, including the domestic ones.

This made Brazil a relatively safe harbor for finance. As I have shown, this was made viable by attractions such as low inflation and high real interest rates (see figures 3 and 5). But these were not sufficient, because high interest rates are only converted into significant profits when the debt is also significant.

Thus, the other factors that guaranteed advantages to finance were what I call sustainable public debt and equally sustainable nominal fiscal deficits. In the few years before the launching of the Real Plan for which relevant data are available, the Brazilian outstanding public debt changed approximately according to the nominal fiscal results of the central government. Since then, due to a monetary policy marked by high real interest rates, the public debt also rose, as seen in figure 9. Its annual average rose from 28% of GDP in the 1991–1998 period to 47% in the 1999–2015 period.

Evidence that interest rates were the main cause for the growing debt is seen in the fact that the nominal fiscal deficits were, in most of the series analyzed, accompanied by primary fiscal surpluses. While the average of the latter was 1.4% of GDP in 1991–2015, that of the nominal fiscal deficits reached 4.1% of GDP in the same period. One point to highlight is the stability that these items came to have—as did the outstanding public debt—especially since the adoption of inflation targeting, in 1999. After rising significantly until the early years of the decade of 2000, when this trend reversed, the debt remained at a level much higher than observed in the 1990s. This is what I just referred to when I mentioned sustainable debt and sustainable fiscal deficits. In this case, however, the term sustainable does not have the ideological connotation that bourgeois economists give to it, which is that the debt and fiscal results will be 'sustainable' as long as they can be supported by the public budget. From the

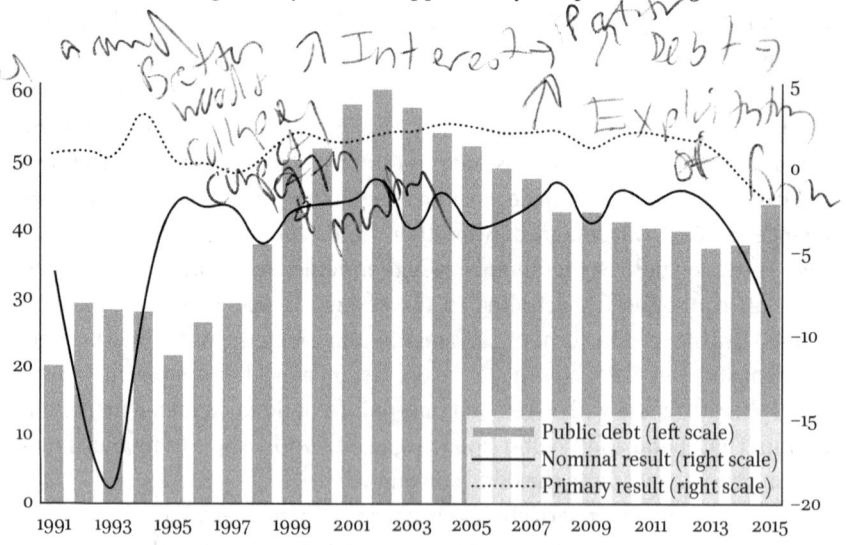

FIGURE 9   Public debt and fiscal results, Brazil, 1991–2015
Notes: (i) percentages in relation to GDP; (ii) monthly averages in each year of the domestic federal debt securities held by the public plus gross external debt of the central government.

class perspective of finance, the term sustainable means that both debt and nominal deficits, in addition to being supportable in fiscal terms, should continue to exist and thus make viable the expropriation of surpluses through financial mechanisms.

3 Fictitious Capital as a Concrete Social Relation

What we have seen in the two preceding sections suggests that one of the consequences of financialization was to grant money-capital an apparent self-reproducing capacity. It expanded socioeconomic relations beyond their connections with the material economy present in the financings of production and the circulation of commodities. Karl Marx had perceived, for example, that

> the credit system ... in its first stages ... furtively creeps in as the humble assistant of accumulation, ... but it soon becomes a new and terrible weapon in the battle of competition and is finally transformed into an enormous social mechanism for the centralization of capitals.
> MARX 1990 [1890]: 777–778

One result was that the beginning of the past century "mark[ed] the turning point from ... the domination of capital in general to the domination of finance capital" (Lenin 1975 [1917]: 52). Nonetheless, this type of centralization and domination takes places in spheres that can be quite distant from the point of production of commodities. While the financial crises observed in the past two decades served to centralize capitals, they have also shown the relevance of the fictitious economy for this process and for capitalism itself in its current stage.

In this phase, financial contracts spread across markets at an unprecedented velocity, moving amounts whose growth was not nearly accompanied by material production. The expansion of the distance between these two spheres crystalized what today is usually understood as the distinction between the fictitious and the real economy. The latter is composed of production, commerce, and services, which are articulated in a globally integrated system of accumulation. The fictitious economy is associated to legal contracts that are materially independent of production, which do nothing to change the volume of socially produced wealth. They only represent expectations for a transfer of economic surpluses between agents and eventually turn these expectations into actual redistribution. An extreme example of fictitious capital is the derivative, which can allow investors to make types of bets based on opposing expectations among agents about the price that a given object—for example, a foreign currency, to use only one possible reference—might have on the maturity or expiration date of the contract.

Another example of fictitious capital are bonds issued by the state to borrow money for a given period and interest rate. From the perspective of the creditor, it is capital because it will return in a higher sum after the maturity of the bond; it is fictitious because it does not represent any existing productive capital, but rather a part of tax collection to come from future material production (Hilferding 2006 [1910]; Marx 1991 [1894]). Its fictitious character is more clearly revealed when we analyze it in an aggregated mode. If at the level of the individual capitalist it represents real capital to its owner, at the level of society it is nothing more than illusory capital (Carcanholo and Nakatani 2001). This aggregated view, however, brings about a sociological problem, for it ignores the concrete character of this special type of social relation that is subjacent to fictitious capital. Members of societies do not live—eat, reside, pay taxes, earn interest—in an aggregated manner.

Indications of the process of financial expansion can be found in Karl Marx's work about the fictitious character of interest-bearing capital, which, even in a process detached from production, seems to carry with it a certain self-reproducing capacity. For Marx, this type of capital "appears as money breeding money" and its "return does not appear as a consequence and result of a definite series of *economic* processes, but rather as a consequence of a special *legal* contract" (Marx 1991 [1894]: 466, 470; emphases added). In this same fashion, Giovanni Arrighi (1994) teaches that the general formula of capital M–C–M'—where M means money-capital, C commodity-capital and M' money-capital increased at the end of the accumulation cycle—represents not only the logic of individual capitalist investment, but a recurring pattern in the history of capitalism. This history, Arrighi adds, has alternated between epochs of material expansion—the M–C phase of accumulation—and epochs of financial rebirth and expansion—the C–M' phase. Within the first, money-capital sets in motion a growing mass of commodities; in the second phase, through financial contracts, money-capital prescinds with production and trade. Here, the process of 'accumulation' can thus take place by the means represented by the abbreviated Marxian formula M–M', which indicates money-capital increased in value without any intermediary productive stage.

This variation from M to M' without the intermediation of C involves the transfer of surpluses from one class to another without any material good being produced or traded between them. Moreover, it can signify a transfer of surplus-value without any of these social classes being directly involved in the production process. This can be brought about through a social relation based on the need or intention of one agent to borrow money for which another does not find a more profitable alternative. It can also be based on opposite expectations between these agents, as in the case of the derivative. They are relations that can function with their own dynamics, at times without any connection with the real economy. In this way, capitalists have found something that they deeply value: freedom of choice. Money-capital also attains this prerogative when it is apparently freed from the form of a commodity (Arrighi 1994) without, however, failing to be itself a commodity (Deutschmann 1996).

Complementing the somewhat exaggerated reasoning of David Harvey (2005: 33) that "neoliberalization has meant ... the financialization of everything," the latter has led to the liberalization of even money in terms of its reproductive capacity. For Geoffrey Ingham, this would be characteristic of capitalism itself, because it "is constituted not only by formally free capital and labour[-power], but also by 'free' credit creating banks," which are capable of creating money (Ingham 1998: 13–14). This provides an indispensable capacity to the appropriating classes, which is the flexibility to quickly reconvert investments into money in order to give them a more profitable destination as soon as one is presented. Unlike fixed investment, it is financial capital that is extremely mobile across national borders (Frieden 1991). For this reason capitalists prefer liquidity, and what makes them capitalists is their interminable search to reach the end of a process with more money-capital than they had at the beginning, regardless of the means employed, either production, trade, or finance (Arrighi 1994).

It was precisely this reduced rigidity that expanded the options for confronting the crisis of accumulation observed during the Keynesian-Fordist period. It did so by giving capitalists the capacity to make high sums of money-capital travel throughout the world at unprecedented speed in search of more profitable outlets. Once again capitalism offered proofs that it is a robust and flexible social order, capable of rapid institutional reorganizations (Wright 1999). These included state deregulation and the development of new financial instruments and channels for transactions, the latter facilitated by technological resources that are able to instantaneously connect different world markets. But this is a process that cannot occur without troubles. After all, no value can be distributed, from a macroeconomic perspective, without first having been produced (Fine 2001; Mandel 1990).

From time to time, the distance between real values and fictitious prices reaches proportions that cannot be sustained. One of the reasons can be the lack of trust among the various agents in the capacities of their counterparts to honor the respective obligations. Prices of financial assets depend on the probability of these assets being liquidated, among other factors (Nesvetailova 2006). In addition, they cannot remain detached from material production for too long. Thus, when there is a reduced probability of the liquidation of fictitious assets, the distance between their prices and the values of the capital accumulated is shortened by the decrease in prices. And it is precisely the frequency and intensity of the distancing between prices and fundamental values that characterizes the instability intrinsic to markets for financial assets (Carneiro 1996). In addition, the situation can delineate the contours of a self-fulfilling prophecy, because agents who believe that their assets will depreciate shall seek to realize them, thus provoking new drops in prices. In any case, crises of this nature act as mechanisms of moderation between speculative capital and the productive base of the economy through destruction of part of that capital (Carcanholo and Nakatani 2001).

But these crises can assume much more dramatic contours in terms of social impact. Were they restricted to the supposedly closed circuit of finance, their consequences would also be restricted to this realm, with no great traumas for society as a whole. Events like the external debt crisis that struck the periphery of global capitalism in the 1980s would have been only crises for creditors and not deep social crises if the actual debtors were not the working classes and the vast subaltern social layers. In the real world, the consequences of financial relations impact all of society, but with different effects for each one of the classes or class factions that compose it. For example, in emerging markets that are widely open, expectations of reduction of liquidity can lead foreign creditors to withdraw their investments, which can lead to results such as deflation, recession, or economic depression (Nesvetailova 2006).

In situations like this, of potential capital flight, the adoption of exorbitant interest rates becomes the remedy for keeping capitals within the country (Camara and Salama 2005; Vernengo 2006). This is what took place in Brazil in mid-1998, with the crisis caused by the Russian debt default. In September of that year, in "a day of generalized capital flight, which signified a speculative attack against Brazil," the Monetary Policy Committee (Copom in its Portuguese acronym) of the Central Bank raised the nominal interest rate for financial liquidity assistance (TBan in its Portuguese acronym) from approximately 30% to nearly 50% per annum.[5] The new level of interest rates caused the Selic rate, to which 64% of the domestic federal securitized debt were pegged, to

---

5 Banco Central do Brasil. Comitê de Política Monetária. "Atas do Copom: 28a reunião (extraordinária)." 10 de setembro de 1998. If a source was not available in English, its respective reference was used in its original language, namley Portuguese. Any reference that may not provide enough information to locate the source will be provided in detail upon request.

reach an average of 36% per annum in real terms in the four final months of 1998.[6] As a comparison, in the same year, the average of the ex post real interbank interest rate in Russia was some 25% per annum.

This is an example of a measure by the Brazilian state that signified responding to the threat of the propertied classes to remove their investments, offering them an even greater portion of the surpluses to be raised through taxes. Rises in interest rates have impact on the public debt, implying an increase in income for its creditors. The consequences are increased taxes, reduced spending, generally those for welfare or investments, the issuance of more debt or a combination of them, all with their respective material impacts supported by the producing classes. For this reason, economic crises unaccompanied by political transformations invariably fall on the shoulders of workers (Przeworski 1985). Either during or after crises, raising the rate of surplus-value is one of the main objectives of capital (Mandel 1991). Ernest Mandel also affirms that the large-scale reconstitution of the reserve army of labor during crises and depressions allows this rise in the rate of surplus-value, not only by means of increased productivity, but also by reducing real wages.

Another point to highlight is that if the state could never be considered autonomous in relation to capital, in times of financial expansion the control of finance over the state appears to be even greater. Globalization compromised state sovereignty in both spatial terms, due to the distance between globally integrated markets and nationally referenced state apparatuses, and temporal terms, because capital mobility restricted the normal cycles of state policy and also limited its agents (Jessop 2010). Nevertheless, as Bob Jessop also warns, this does not mean that the role of the state has declined because of global integration of markets. The process of financial expansion, as we have seen, was largely sustained by the state. Although the latter is responsible for the general conditions of accumulation (Offe 1984a; Wright 1999), the state also serves as the harbor of last resort when financial crises become too severe.

The financialization of the economy expanded this need for state protection in light of financial crises, which in recent decades became increasingly frequent. Mexico in 1994, Southeast Asia in 1997, Brazil and Russia in 1998 and Argentina in 2001 were some with large global repercussions. The most serious was that revealed with the fiasco in the U.S. mortgage system. It erupted in late 2008, but years earlier some observers had already noticed that "a housing market bubble [was] ... approaching its peak" (Li 2004: 25) and that the U.S.

---

6 The Selic rate is the benchmark interest rate of the Brazilian economy. Selic is the Portuguese acronym for the Special System of Settlement and Custody (Sistema Especial de Liquidação e de Custódia), which is managed by the Central Bank of Brazil.

centrality in globalization, as well as its total adoption of the financial regime of accumulation, could make it the epicenter of the financial and economic crises in the future (Chesnais 2002). All of those crises developed in a context marked by deep liberalization of markets, which eroded the stability supposedly favorable to economic development. But this situation also revealed the neoliberal contradiction of demanding reduced state intervention in the economy at the same time that it was up to the state itself to play the role of stabilizer.

These and the other contradictions of neoliberalism discussed indicate that if it did not attain the *alleged* objectives, such as expansion of economic growth and social welfare, it did help attain its *undeclared* goal of reestablishing the economic power of the ruling classes, in particular its financial fraction. The course of the neoliberal disaster revealed the increase of the inequalities between poor and rich and the brutality of those who are dominant (Therborn 2007). Its model, fixed in monetary stabilization, fiscal equilibrium, financial and commercial liberalizations, deregulations of labor relations, and privatizations did not consider the social and ecological costs stemming from the neoliberal reforms (De la Barra 2006; Li 2004). In economic terms, what was seen was a rise in interest rates, thus, of the cost of money-capital, a drop in both savings and investment, and consequently the deceleration of growth in output (Carneiro 1996).

These economic implications of neoliberalism and of the financialization that it made viable call attention to one of the points very often treated inadequately when considering the distinction between the fictitious economy and the real economy. The process of financialization appears to suggest that financial activity takes place independently from material production. However, this autonomy is at most relative, never absolute (Foster and Magdoff 2009). A first reason is logic and recalls the Marxian theory that "interest ... originally appears, originally is, and remains in reality nothing but a part of the profit, i.e. the surplus-value" (Marx 1991 [1894]: 493). In broader terms, this is to say that finance cannot exist independently of production, because the money-capital of a lender cannot valorize without first being converted into money-capital in the hands of those who use it in production (Hilferding 2006 [1910]).

A second dimension that reveals the inseparability between finance and production is historical, and moreover, helps us to understand the neoliberal era. As we saw previously, neoliberalism in general and financialization in particular were class reactions that sought to restore the level of profitability of capital. One of its targets was the cost of variable capital, which rose during the Keynesian consensus in the various forms of the social wage. Despite the rhetoric about state intervention being a threat to the values disseminated by neoliberal propaganda, the actually existing neoliberalism was much more pragmatic. This is because capitalism is a mode of production characterized by the persistent search for the endless accumulation of capital with the goal of accumulating more capital (Wallerstein 1979, 2013). In this sense, the promotion of the neoliberal creed and the corresponding discourse was at most an ideological recourse. On the other hand, its practice, in which financialization was one of the most evident manifestations, sought to restore profit levels.

Considering the old Marxian formula for the rate of profit 's ÷ [c + v],' financialization was an attempt to confront the decline in this rate by attacking its denominator, that is, the costs of constant (c) and variable (v) capital.[7] An example of the reduction of constant capital (c) was the privatization of productive structures already in operation, thus providing investment alternatives for over-accumulated private capitals so that their owners would not have to wait for constructions of new productive structures. In Brazil, privatizations represented 29 billion of the 120 billion U.S. dollars of financial capital that entered the country under the form of direct investment during the 1996–2000 period, when most of them took place (see figure 4). But it is in the second factor of the denominator of the Marxian formula of the profit rate—variable capital (v)—that finance operated more significantly in order to raise this rate.

Finance was the practical arm in neoliberalism's efforts to reduce the costs of variable capital by cutting welfare policies—which, after all, determine the social wage—that had once been implemented to attenuate the distributive conflicts between capital and labor. This was true in the first movements of the neoliberal advance and also in more recent ones. Probably, what is most significant about this "strange non-death of neoliberalism," of which "virtually everything" remains even after the crises of 2008 (Crouch 2011: viii, 179), is that the crisis itself, accelerated by the neoliberal model, continued to serve as a justification for so-called austerity measures. And the latter invariably affected the working class via reduced labor costs. We shall see this in detail in coming chapters, thus, I only mention social security as an object of regressive reforms implemented by all Brazilian governments since the mid-1990s. Other items of the social wage, such as healthcare, sanitation, education, culture, housing, urbanization, and unemployment benefits, combined, had their federal government spending reduced from an annual average of 3.9% of GDP in 1990–1998 to 3.4% in 1999–2015.

The connection between production and financialization is also perceptible in a geopolitical characteristic typical of peripheral countries, which is dependence in relation to the U.S. dollar in international transactions. During the

---

7   s means surplus-value.

Cardoso governments (1995–2002), the current account—balance of trade, services and income, and unilateral transfers—accumulated a deficit of 186 billion dollars, which was financed by a total inflow of financial capital of approximately 188 billion dollars. During the Workers Party (PT in its Portuguese initials) governments the situation became quite distinct. After a period of surpluses in the current account, which totaled 45 billion dollars in 2003–2007, Brazil returned to run deficits in these transactions, which reached 379 billion dollars in 2008–2014. Nevertheless, considering the entire 2003–2014 period, the deficit in the current account (334 billion dollars) was more than offset by the inflow of financial capital, which totaled 642 billion dollars, yielding a surplus of 314 billion dollars in the balance of payments. During this period, international currency reserves grew continuously, increasing from 38 billion dollars in 2002 to 374 billion in 2014.

In sum, a global financial structure pressured Brazil to generate the surpluses demanded by the connection between finance and material production, and this pressure has intensified worldwide with the commercial and financial liberalization of recent decades. This, combined with the logic that values redistributed by financial means must first be generated in material production, and combined with the historical reality that the neoliberal measures sought to restore profit rates through the reduction of the costs of both constant and variable capital, helps us to understand the financialization process. It also helps to grasp that it was not a self-referenced process, disconnected from the production of surplus-value. I am not denying that finance has assumed an outstanding position, both for the economy and for politics or policy-making. We will see later that the capitalist class rules by means of the alliance among all its fractions, but the functioning of this alliance depends on the hegemony of one of them, which unifies the class power (Poulantzas 1973, 1978b). And in the past two decades in Brazil—or four on the global scale—finance has been this fraction and the state its political arm, as it was for industry and had been for export-oriented agriculture at previous moments.

CHAPTER 2

Capitalist State and Financial Hegemony

> Whenever a Coketowner felt he was ill-used—that is to say, whenever he was not left entirely alone, and it was proposed to hold him accountable for the consequences of any of his acts—he was sure to come out with the awful menace, that he would "sooner pitch his property into the Atlantic." This had terrified the Home Secretary within an inch of his life, on several occasions.
> CHARLES DICKENS

∴

One of the issues anticipated in the previous chapter concerned the supposed distinction between politics and the economy alleged by the neoliberal discourse that claims the state should not interfere in the market for the sake of a rationality supposedly attainable only through the freedom of individual action. Nevertheless, if instead of analyzing neoliberal discourse, the internal contradictions of neoliberal prescriptions and the practices that result from them are examined, it becomes clear that the supposed opposition between state and economy is false. Capitalism and state mutually imply each other and far from a retraction of the latter, what has occurred since the 1980s at the center of the world economy—and a bit later at its periphery—was a repositioning of the state in relation to the modified social context that it contributed to establishing. The fact is that the economy is embedded in a civil society that is both structured by the state and helps to structure the state (Block and Evans 2005). As Bob Jessop teaches,

> states do not exist in majestic isolation overseeing the rest of their respective societies but are embedded in a wider political system (or systems), articulated with other institutional orders, and linked to different forms of civil society. A key aspect of their transformation is the redrawing of the multiple 'lines of difference' between the state and its environment(s) as states (and the social forces they represent) redefine their priorities, expand or reduce their activities, recalibrate or rescale them in the light of new challenges, seek greater autonomy or promote

> power-sharing, and disembed or re-embed specific state institutions and
> practices within the social order.
>
> JESSOP 2007: 6

The recent transformations in the forms of economic action of the state also denote Colin Hay's affirmation that it "is a dynamic and constantly unfolding system" (Hay 1999: 170). This complicates any effort to conceptualize the state, even when one restricts the definition to its capitalist character. Since there is no abstract theoretical solution to the problem about how capital assures its political rule, the key to understanding the capitalist character of the state can be found in specific conjunctures of interactions between the circuit of capital, strategies or regimes of accumulation, forms of state, and the balance of political forces (Jessop 1990). The modern form of capitalism, for example, is marked by financial expansion of the economy—also called financialization—that is expressed in the shift of the center of gravity from production to finance (Foster and Magdoff 2009). The financial systems that developed since the 1970s changed the correlation of forces in global capitalism by gaining much more autonomy in relation to other types of companies and the state (Harvey 1990).

These introductory words, as well as those in Chapter 1, indicate the importance of understanding the concept of state by analyzing its connection with capitalism in the phase of neoliberal financialization and also through the continual and mutual dependence between state and capital. Therefore, even if classic Marxism does not have a systematic and coherent or specific theory of state (Harvey 2006a; Jessop 1990, 2007), this tradition allows finding some consistent explanations for the relation between capital and the state. The objective of this chapter is not to present an inventory of these theories, but to identify the role of the state in the concrete social phenomena that this study addresses. For this reason, I will try to respond to the following question: what was the politico-economic character of the Brazilian state and how did it operate within the social relations found in the general context of the financialization of the economy and the more specific context of the expansion of the country's public debt as a relevant class expression of this process?

To begin, I adopt Ellen Wood's definition that the state is "a means of appropriating surplus-product—perhaps even as a means of intensifying production to increase surplus—and as a mode of distributing that surplus in one way or another" (Wood 1981: 83). To this concept should be aggregated the consideration of the prominence that finance has acquired in the neoliberal phase of capitalism. The term finance in this study refers to "the upper fractions of the capitalist classes and to financial institutions in any social arrangement in which these fractions of capitalist classes control financial institutions"

(Duménil and Lévy 2011: 13). We therefore face what David Harvey calls the "state-finance nexus," which "describes a confluence of state and financial power ... where the state management of capital creation and monetary flows becomes integral to ... the circulation of capital" (Harvey 2010: 48). In times of financialization, the state remains indispensable to capital *accumulation*, but playing a prominent role in the *redistribution* of economic surpluses.

Regardless of what commentators say about the decline of the state, there is no evidence that global capitalism has found a more effective instrument for maintaining order and guaranteeing the conditions for accumulation (Wood 2003). More specifically, there is no evidence that the state's role in establishing stable legal and institutional conditions for agents in the markets has been reduced (Fligstein 2001b). Markets, even in their neoliberal version, cannot work without this state function (Harvey 2005). The Brazilian situation is similar, since its semi-peripheral economy developed closely accompanied by the state, which has continued under the advanced form of financialization (Oliveira 2006). According to Francisco de Oliveira, some examples of this proximity are: (i) the massive pension funds of workers at state-owned companies that grew under the military dictatorship (1964–1985); (ii) the Worker's Support Fund (Fundo de Amparo ao Trabalhador in Portuguese), which was created by the Constitution of 1988 and is now the biggest source of resources for the public Brazilian Development Bank (BNDES in its Portuguese initials); and (iii) the search for foreign investment through pension funds and the banking system that are largely dependent on public debt securities.

This introduction indicates some fundamental concepts and their mutual dependencies that will be developed throughout this chapter and the book as a whole. State, class, expropriation, and exploitation are part of a totality that is also revealed in the realm of fiscal policy, which synthesizes results of the class struggle. As James O'Connor indicated, "the volume and composition of government expenditures and the distribution of the tax burden ... are structurally determined by social and economic conflicts between classes and groups" (O'Connor 2002: 2). Furthermore, "tax finance is (and always has been) a form of economic exploitation and thus a problem for class analysis" (O'Connor 2002: 203).[1] Therefore, in the fiscal superstructure, classes are seen struggling for monies levied by the state, which can then be redistributed as

---

1 O'Connor is not precise when he refers to taxation as economic exploitation. In strict Marxian terms, taxation is a relation that occurs not in the economic infrastructure, but in the superstructure, because it is conducted by legal means. It is beyond the scope of this section to deepen this discussion; it suffices to keep in mind that taxation and state expenditure comprise a system that can influence the processes of class exploitation and expropriation (I shall discuss this in the next chapter).

interest payments to finance capital, subsidies to productive capital, welfare benefits for workers, and in other forms.

1   Capitalist Economy and Capitalist State

The definition of state, which also considers the definition of capital, involves concepts that are located between extremes. One of these, close to the Marxist tradition, considers the state as an instrument in the hands of capitalists, which would be dedicated to creating and maintaining their class advantages. The other is the neoliberal conception, which considers the state as an impediment to the full potential of capital accumulation to the degree that its intervention in the economy would impede what is considered the 'natural' functioning of free markets. If the first extreme involves a simplified view of a mechanical use of the state by capitalists, the neoliberal conception neglects the fact that accumulation is dependent on the state's institutional and bureaucratic apparatuses. Recognizing these weaknesses and seeking to avoid them, my analysis begins by considering the state not as independent of capital—which in some way is present in both the extremes mentioned—but as organic to it.

In the neoliberal conception, the distinction between state and capital appears with greater clarity because it advocates the minimum possible state intervention in the economy to provide more rationality. Conceptualizations that tend toward this extreme have gained prominence and illuminated discourses and practices in the past nearly four decades. This rhetoric, bolstered by academic legitimacy and the social reach of the corporate media, has competently served the ideology that preached the reduction of the role of the state in the economy. At the same time, capitalists contradictorily turned to the state to sustain conditions of accumulation that until then were considered to be threatened. Thus, neoliberalism empirically signified a repositioning of the state in relation to the politico-economic situation reached in the 1970s. What took place was not a reduction of its role but a reconfiguration, a change in the pattern of intervention of the capitalist state in the economy (Filgueiras and Gonçalves 2007; Saes 2001). The "free market," for example, was "endorsed as a stateless sphere under state protection" (Bonefeld 2010: 19).

At the same time that this situation revealed the falsity of the neoliberal claim that the state is a threat to the economy, it reinforced the actuality of the core elements of the Marxist theories that address the mutual implication between these spheres. Despite the differences between the current phase of capitalism and previous ones, theories of state remain necessary, as do those with Marxist approaches (Hay 1999). These theories, Colin Hay adds, are justified by the importance of the state to the dynamics of accumulation, and the Marxist approach is useful because of the contradictions that these dynamics continue to reveal. One example of this is the environmental crisis that is aggravated by capitalism's need for constant growth with sponsorship from the state. In this same line, the justification of the pertinence of these Marxist approaches can be found in the economic crises generated by the strengthening of finance, which is also sponsored by the state.

Nevertheless, as I have mentioned, the concept of the state that appears to prevail among Marxist thinkers also distinguishes it from capital by considering it "a neutral instrument to be manipulated and steered in the interests of the dominant class or ruling 'elite'" (Hay 1999: 165). However, were this the case, the ruled classes should be able to resolve this problem by capturing the state, which according to this thinking, would be a possibility for all political forces (Jessop 1990; Salama 1978). This could lead to a change in direction of the class favoring operated by the state apparatus. But an eventual capturing of the state does not change its capitalist character, even if certain changes may occur, for example, in the controlled redistribution of economic surpluses. Moreover, it is logically impossible for the ruled classes to capture the capitalist state without the fractions that lead this movement coming to defend interests of capital that they originally challenged. For Claus Offe,

> the capitalist state can no longer be characterized as an *instrument* of 'the' interest of capital (an interest which is neither homogeneous nor 'generally understood'); rather, this state is characterized by constitutional and organizational structures whose specific selectivity is designed to reconcile and harmonize the 'privately regulated' capitalist economy with the processes of socialization this economy triggers.
> OFFE 1984a: 51; emphasis in original

That is, if state's objective is to harmonize an economy that is capitalist, state and capital remain mutually dependent on each other.

In the concept delineated elsewhere by Offe (1975) the state's relation with the process of accumulation encompasses four elements: (i) exclusion, which means that the state is not capitalist per se, because production does not occur within it and is not controlled by it, but takes place in private units of accumulation; (ii) maintenance, which indicates that the state has, in addition to authority, a mandate to create and maintain conditions necessary to accumulation, which means controlling potentially anti-capitalist threats, such as working class militancy or those stemming from behavior that is incompatible with the production of surplus-value, for example, those considered deviant or criminal; (iii) dependence, which indicates that the state, its decision-making power, the personnel in its apparatuses, its agencies and entities, all depend on the continuity of the accumulation process, because only in this way are the resources created that make taxation possible; and (iv) legitimation, which indicates the need for the coincidence and harmonious coexistence of the three previous elements.

The imperative that the state not subvert its capitalist character requires from it an image of organization of power that considers the common interests of society, allows equal access to power, and is receptive to the justified demands. In sum, "the existence of a capitalist state presupposes the systematic denial of its nature as a capitalist state" (Offe 1975: 127). Thus, state intervention in the economy assumes a class character that is not always perceivable due to the formal universalism inscribed, for example, in the conception of the state as a promoter of social welfare. This character refers not to state arbitration or neutrality, but to the exercise of the class power by means of the state, which "*mediates* social relations between ruler and ruled" (Therborn 2008 [1978]: 169; emphasis in original). It also does not signify, Göran Therborn adds, that the state places itself between the classes to terminate their struggles, but to the contrary, that it connects them in an asymmetrical relation of domination and exploitation.

This asymmetrical class relation, however, is not unilateral, because the ruled will always raise demands and protests towards the rulers. For this reason, the state cannot be defined as an instrument at the service of a class or fraction of class. Were it a univocal tool in a system of domination, the state would become impoverished (Ianni 2004 [1989]) and would not serve the proposal of reproduction of capitalist relations, which it thus fulfills by opposing itself to both the workers and individual capitalists (Jessop 1990; Salama 1978). The capitalist state is also not an instrument in the hands of the ruling classes, because it remains relatively autonomous from each of its fractions in their contradictory relations (Poulantzas 1976, 2000 [1978]). This autonomy that maintains its legitimacy (Offe 1975) is sustained by the distinct resources and powers of the state, which, however, also has distinct vulnerabilities and depends on capital accumulation (Jessop 1990, 2007).

Norbert Elias (1993 [1939]) rightly observed that the state's monopoly of violence could only be consolidated by means of the state's monopoly of taxation and by the reciprocity between these monopolies. It follows that as a tax state it depends completely on capital accumulation (Bonefeld 2010). Therefore, the state is by no means autonomous in relation to the general interests of capital.

According to Nicos Poulantzas (2000 [1978]), the state represents the long-term political interests of the bourgeoisie as a whole.[2] To do so, it participates in processes that are essential to capital accumulation. These include spending on research, training, infrastructure, fiscal incentives, and state acquisitions, for example. All are actions aimed at creating and maintaining conditions necessary to economic relations and to increasing the productivity of capital (Fligstein 2001a; Offe and Ronge 1975, 1984). They thus involve the state's role to socialize the private costs needed for capitalist production (Offe 1984a).

This indicates that if the purpose of capital is to accumulate surplus-value, the state is the political means for doing so (Bonefeld 2010). This was the role of the Brazilian state during the efforts towards industrialization, when it invested in capital intensive sectors that were not attractive to private capitalists since they required a relatively long time to become profitable. That was carried out, inter alia, by creating state-owned companies such as the Companhia Siderúrgica Nacional in 1941, Vale do Rio Doce in 1942, the Brazilian Development Bank (BNDES in its Portuguese initials) in 1952, Petrobrás in 1954, and Eletrobrás in 1962. Even at the center of global capitalism, the economic bases were launched with strong support from the state. In the United States, the pioneer actions of the federal and state governments in the construction of economic infrastructure and in the direct support for basic activities were fundamental to attracting capital and, therefore, to the development of that country in the first half of the nineteenth century (Furtado 2007 [1959]).

In addition, the apparent reduction of state intervention should be considered as a way to support accumulation. In England, industrial capitalism was only able to develop after the abolition of the social protections that impeded the formation of a competitive labor market precisely in the most active phase of the Industrial Revolution (Polanyi 2000 [1944]).[3] More recently, using as an

---

2   Diverging from Poulantzas, whose analysis he considers functionalist, Jon Elster (1982) affirmed that, because the capitalist class is not a formal organization, with a singular decision-making center, the state is a means by which that class can promote its collective interests. Elster is not receptive to the idea of the capitalist character of the state, and affirms that Marx also recognized this when he said "that the noncapitalist state was beneficial for capitalism" (Elster 1982: 458). Upon reviewing some recent approaches to the concept of state, Bob Jessop (2007) concluded that they converge in not understanding the state as a collective capitalist to the degree that it is not an institution above society, but rather one among a number of institutions. Nevertheless, Jessop adds, this is a problem not resolved by theory of state, and he sees as paradoxical the idea of the state as simply another institution within the social formation at the same time that this state holds the greatest responsibility for maintaining the social cohesion of the social formation of which it is a part.
3   The main protective mechanism was the Speenhamland system (1795–1834), which guaranteed a minimum income to the most poor, regardless of their original income. According to

example the experience of the Soviet economy, theoreticians—even liberal ones—and international financial institutions have recognized that the state had essential responsibility in the construction of the institutions needed for the flourishing of markets (Boyer 1999). The ulterior trajectory of the Russian economy, Robert Boyer adds, has taught that it was not sufficient to banish the monopoly of political power and centralized planning for a market economy to prosper. The recurrent difficulties in the Russian economy that followed the dissolution of the Soviet Union are just one example that indicates that markets cannot establish themselves on their own.

But it is in the institutional apparatus that state support to capital is revealed most clearly, as in the mechanisms that guarantee property rights, contract enforcement, and other rules for sharing surplus-value. For example, segments like the so-called informational economy, or that of entertainment, whose assets take the form of ideas, images or cultural representations—such as the formula for Coca-Cola, Windows, Mickey Mouse—instead of tangible goods, do not require a weak state; to the contrary, they require a sophisticated and active state able to repress acts contrary to property rights (Block and Evans 2005; Evans 1997). In relation to the rules for sharing surplus-value, the need for an institutional apparatus is especially visible in the financial realm. When one recalls that the return on that which Karl Marx (1991 [1894]: 470) characterized as "interest-bearing" capital is "a consequence of a special legal contract," the state reveals that it is indispensable to the process of financial expropriation.

Equally, when impediments to accumulation arise, a combination of strategies are established between state and capital to overcome them (Wright 1979). This was the case in the implementation of Keynesian policies after World War II. It also took place with economic changes that marked the end of the Keynesian consensus, which was especially noticed in the change towards policies for high interest rates and the deregulation of global financial markets, thus contributing to the financial expansion of the economy. The role of the state at the time of the neoliberal shift was to support the re-establishment of the economic advantages of the classes that saw themselves threatened by social welfare policies and by high inflation that had been imposing significant losses on finance. For this reason, the state allied itself to capital in its attacks on the working classes, seeking to restore the levels of profitability that had been limited by the Keynesian consensus. As John O'Connor (2010) observed,

---

Karl Polanyi, the system was assailed by the middle class using the maxim that, under the regime of the economic-rational individual, no one would submit oneself to wage labor if he or she could survive while doing nothing.

the new form of neoliberal competition, within nation-states or between them as well, produced significant gains for capital at the expense of labor. But since this new form of competition depended on the mobility of capitals, it required that the state establish and maintain the conditions necessary for this mobility.

These aspects support the idea that capitalism and state are historically interlinked. The state is necessary to the fortune of capital, which can only maintain large-scale profits, and for an undefined period, through restrictive practices supported by state power (Arrighi 1994). For this reason the success of capitalists depends less on their business competence—the courage to assume risks, inventiveness and ability to predict changes in demand—than on the results of state policies that restrict the freedom of the market by fixing prices and establishing protectionist measures (Bonefeld 2010; Offe and Ronge 1975, 1984). Examples of this are the ongoing disputes within the World Trade Organization concerning subsidies granted by central countries to sectors of their economies that, without these subsidies, could not compete with corresponding productive sectors in peripheral countries.

Even in times of globalization, states remain crucial to the shaping of the global economy (Block and Evans 2005; Evans 2008; Wood 2005). One of the reasons for this is that national elites depend on them to preserve their power and enter global markets (Fligstein 1996). It is the state that is responsible for implementing policies, given that it detains the legitimate—in the Weberian sense—monopoly to do so. It was to the state and quasi-state organizations, like the International Monetary Fund and the World Bank, that finance turned to replace priorities such as full employment, national integration, and economic development with the neoliberal policy focused on monetary stability (Duménil and Lévy 2001, 2004b; Potter 2007). In the case of Latin America, the influence from the United States, which in the past was wielded through the State Department and the Pentagon, came to be wielded by the departments of the Treasury and Commerce, both working along with the International Monetary Fund and the World Bank (Marini 2011 [1991]).

State action is also needed to respond to capitalist crises in financial markets, or those of a broader social scope, which can threaten the stability of the system and harm capitalist reproduction. Despite the neoliberal discourse about the need for the state to remain distant from economic relations in favor of the free market, were the state not present to resolve crises, the threats to capital would be even greater. It is important to recognize how significant were the trillions dollars in bailouts granted by the governments of various countries to rescue finance and the rest of the capitalist economy from themselves when the U.S. subprime mortgage fiasco erupted in 2007–2008. Actually, this was not a new role for the state. In 1984, the Continental Illinois National Bank and Trust Company—at the time the seventh largest U.S. bank, with relations with more than 2,200 banks—became insolvent and, instead of being liquidated, received funds from the state-run Federal Deposit Insurance Corporation, under whose control the bank remained until it was reprivatized in 1991 (Kaufman 2002). By the end of the process, the U.S. Federal Deposit Insurance Corporation had taken on a loss of about 1.1 billion dollars.[4]

State officials are constantly responding to some form of crisis (Fligstein 1996); if they do not adopt certain fiscal and monetary policies, chaos would ensue in international financial systems (Evans 1997). The state is thus the institution turned to when threats appear to stability. It must sustain the continuity of exploitative relations and intervene in a crisis to limit disruptive effects to certain fractions of capital (Salama 1978). In fact, at a certain point, a reduction in the state's power to intervene in the economy increases the collective exposure to risk more than it increases the possibility for individual gains (Evans 1997). For this reason, amid the financial crisis that erupted in 2007–2008, even George Soros, one of the world's most celebrated and wealthy speculators, appeared to call for a certain level of state regulation. This was after, in the previous year, he had reaped 2.9 billion dollars through the administration of his speculative funds.[5] In late 2008, Soros declared before the U.S. House of Representatives that

> the globalization of financial markets allowed financial capital to move around freely and made it difficult for individual states to tax it or regulate it. Deregulation of financial transactions also served the interests of the managers of financial capital; and the freedom to innovate enhanced the profitability of financial enterprises. ...
>
> The new paradigm has far-reaching implications for the regulation of financial markets. Since they are prone to create asset bubbles, regulators such as the Fed[eral Reserve], the [Department of] Treasury, and the [Securities and Exchange Commission] must accept responsibility for preventing bubbles from growing too big. Until now financial authorities have explicitly rejected that responsibility.[6]

Soros's words reveal the prudence of finance in the face of the large bubble threatening the system that, however, should be allowed to continue to

---

4 U.S. Federal Deposit Insurance Corporation. "Managing the crisis: the FDIC and RTC experience 1980–1994 (Vol. 1)." 1998: 558.
5 Jenny Anderson. "Wall Street winners hit a new jackpot: billion-dollar paydays." *The New York Times*. April 16, 2008: A1.
6 U.S. House of Representatives. "Statement of George Soros before the U.S. House of Representatives Committee on Oversight and Government Reform." November 13, 2008: 6–9.

generate bubbles as long as they do not reach levels that are extremely risky to the system. Finance—as the words of George Soros expressed at that time—was also being prudent by requiring that regulation not be excessive, but only that necessary and sufficient to maintain markets functioning in a minimally secure manner. At the end of his testimony, Soros expressed the concern that,

> in view of the tremendous losses suffered by the general public, there is a real danger that excessive deregulation will be succeeded by punitive re-regulation. That would be unfortunate because *regulations are liable to be even more deficient than the market mechanism*. As I have suggested, regulators are not only human but also bureaucratic and susceptible to lobbying and corruption. It is to be hoped that the reforms outlined here will preempt a regulatory overkill.[7]

These words are an example of what Marxist theory teaches about the capitalist state being responsible for protecting capital from itself and from the interests of particular capitalists. The apparent contradiction raised in the demand of this speculator who had profited with crises, but who was also concerned about the need for some control over them, is coherent with his class situation as a leading rentier. Despite liberal discourse, class interests must prevail over the interests of individual capitalists, and the role of the state is to sustain this prevalence. Thus, if the capitalist state has to act against Soros's personal interest to preserve the interests of the class to which he belongs, it will. No capitalist would publicly defend the contrary. When the speculator spoke of regulation, he did not do so to request limits on financial profitability, but to call on the state to fulfill its structural responsibility to protect capital and its conjunctural responsibility to stabilize financial markets.

What we have seen until now does not deny that the state did reduce its presence in certain activities in which it had traditionally performed. However, the process was not uniform in the economy as a whole. Upon analyzing results of the adjustment programs prescribed by the International Monetary Fund and the World Bank, Thomas Biersteker (1990) observed that this did not take place in all activities or with the same intensity in each one of them: (i) actions on the exchange rate, money supply, fiscal adjustments, and even trade and financial liberalizations tended to increase or at least maintain the state's macroeconomic influence; (ii) in the same manner, a state active in the mediation of conflicts between labor and capital was maintained;

---

7   U.S. House of Representatives. "Statement of George Soros before the U.S. House of Representatives Committee on Oversight and Government Reform." November 13, 2008: 11; emphasis added.

(iii) functions such as state production and planning were reduced, and the regulation that had been taking place through these means was converted into support for private investment, as took place by means of privatizations; and (iv) the function of redistribution of surpluses was reduced by ending subsidies, price controls, and wage indexation.

In general, that which Biersteker found in various other countries came to occur in a similar way in Brazil. State action continued to have important macroeconomic effects, especially in terms of monetary policy, particularly by maintaining interest rates higher than those observed in similar economies worldwide. Its mediating role in the relations between capital and labor also remained important despite threats to weaken labor laws, like those proposed by Michel Temer's government after 'the 2016 coup.' State involvement in production and planning were reduced by privatizations carried out mostly in the late 1990s. Regulatory action gained some distance from government influence through the increased operational autonomy of regulatory agencies. In terms of the state's redistributive functions, while indirect measures such as wage indexation and price controls were terminated, direct measures such as income transfer programs were created or expanded, especially during the Lula governments (2003–2010).

Another way that the state redistributes economic surpluses has gained importance and signified an expansion of state participation in the Brazilian economy. It was carried out through a complex composed of taxation and public debt, which operates in such a way that a significant portion of economic surpluses coming from tax revenues are transferred to pay off this debt. This process is not always perceived as redistribution, because the term is generally applied to processes through which the state transfers surpluses from the rich to the poor. Nevertheless, there are situations in which the state does exactly the opposite. There are peculiar forms of expropriation of the productive classes by the appropriating ones that are processed precisely with state mediation. Actually, some of them would not even be possible without this kind of mediation.

The redistributive function of the state involves a dialectic in which the resources obtained by one social segment necessarily come from an other. Its economic result sensu stricto is that of a zero-sum movement, but in sociological terms it involves a redistribution of surpluses between classes and thus engenders conflict between them.[8] The legitimacy the state has to mediate

---

8 The affirmation that this is a zero-sum movement can be questioned by affirming that the redistributive action of the state can result in steering money-capital to activities that generate an increase in output. However, this is not correct because the act of simply reallocating

these conflicts thus serves redistribution. By placing itself between classes, it assumes the dual role of mediating conflict and redistributing surpluses, roles that may be reciprocal in such a degree that it is not possible to establish a clear distinction between them. To consider the public debt as an example of this double role of class mediation and redistribution can help cast light on this issue.

The public debt is one of the empiric expressions that illustrates the mistakenness of the instrumental idea that the state is a tool in the hands of creditors or capitalists of the financial type. I understand that it is more reasonable to consider the state and its own creditors to be financial and political allies. In financial terms, it is in the interest of creditors that the state has the capacity to pay off its financial obligations; politically, they are interested in the maintenance of the regime through which the loans were taken, because this raises the chance that they will be paid back (Carruthers 1996). In this sense, the public debt reinforces the idea referred to previously of the state as a relatively autonomous institution in relation to classes and their fractions. Unlike the perspectives that see finance subordinating the state when the latter reports to the former and, moreover, when the state makes an effort to show that it deserves trust by the part of finance, it is precisely the need to do so that indicates the inexistence of direct subordination.

Were the state subordinated to, or an instrument in the hands of, finance, the relation itself would guarantee finance what it expects of the state. In the same manner, governments would not have to make an effort to convince investors that they deserve to be trusted.[9] An example of this was the Letter to the Brazilian People (Carta ao Povo Brasileiro in Portuguese), which, despite the title, the then candidate and later president of Brazil from 2003 to 2010, Luiz Inácio Lula da Silva, also addressed to finance during the electoral campaign of 2002. His objective was to stall the crisis of confidence generated by the fear that the Brazilian state may not honor its financial obligations under a government led by the Workers Party, which was expected to win the

---

money-capital does nothing to change the aggregated output. It can change the share of each agent in the appropriation of surpluses, which are nevertheless results of production, of labor. Production, of course, can be activated by credit, for example, but this does not mean that credit creates surpluses. A loan, after all, is a legal transaction that has no relation with the actual process of capital reproduction (Marx 1991 [1894]).

9 "Remember this saying, *The good paymaster is lord of another man's purse*. He that is known to pay punctually and exactly to the time he promises, may at any time, and on any occasion, raise all the money his friends can spare." This is an aphorism preached by Benjamin Franklin (1706–1790), quoted by Max Weber in his book on 'the spirit of capitalism' (Weber 2001 [1904–1905]: 15; emphasis in original).

presidential election according to polls at the time. In that letter, Lula defended the need for a transition that would abandon the neoliberal model under the premise, however, that if he were elected his government would maintain "respect for the country's contracts and obligations." He also affirmed that it would "preserve the primary fiscal surplus as much as necessary to prevent the domestic debt from increasing and destroying trust in the government's capacity to honor its commitments."[10]

As a candidate, Lula made the promises that finance wanted to see fulfilled, and the fact that they were is revealed in figure 10, which displays the changes in the risk premium on the main Brazilian external debt security at the time, the C-Bond. Expressed in basis points, which indicate a surcharge in relation to interest rates on the U.S. debt, this premium is an expression of the level of confidence that finance had in Brazil's capacity to honor its external debt payments. After having maintained an average of 810 basis points throughout nearly all of the Cardoso governments, namely from January 1995 to June 2002, the index skyrocketed to an average of 1,770 points in the second semester of 2002. That was the period of the presidential campaign in which Lula was eventually elected. The index reached its peak of about 2,050 basis points in October 2002, the month of the election of the candidate whose party had in the past defended positions in conflict with the interests of finance. With those positions withdrawn—the promises of the Letter to the Brazilian People were being fulfilled—in the first year of the first Lula government (2003) the risk premium dropped to less than one quarter of the level it had reached in the month of the election.

As I have discussed in this section of the book, the normative debate about the alternatives between the state distancing itself from the economy in favor of the 'free' market or intervening to deal with the imperfections of this market is not fruitful. This debate does not go beyond considering the structural limits of capitalism, and merely discusses variations within it. The consequence is the mistaken nature of perspectives that see the state as an antonym of market (Preda 2007) or even the state's role as being a drag on capitalist accumulation (Wright 1999) whose neoliberal remedy would be less state and more market. It is also true that there are no guarantees that more state means less centralization of wealth and thus greater material equality. Government regulations and interventions seek to influence the terms under which capitalists exercise

---

10 Fundação Perseu Abramo. "Carta ao povo brasileiro, por Luiz Inácio Lula da Silva." 22 de junho de 2002. If a source was not available in English, its respective reference was used in its original language, namely Portuguese. Any reference that may not provide enough information to locate the source will be provided in detail upon request.

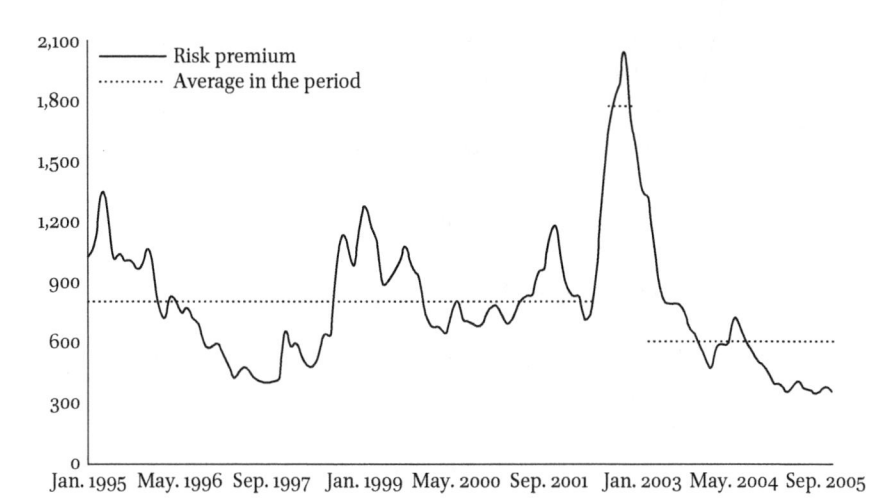

FIGURE 10 Risk premium on external debt, Brazil, 1995–2005
Notes: (i) scale in basis points; (ii) spread of the Brazilian C-Bond over the U.S. treasury securities; (iii) the series covers the period from January 1995 to October 2005, when it was discontinued.

their power to shape markets (Elson 1988). Karl Polanyi (2000 [1944]) had previously affirmed that state intervention and market system were not mutually exclusive terms. Liberals would appeal to state intervention, Polanyi added, until markets systems were attained and then for their maintenance.

To conclude this section, it is reasonable to claim that, in conjunction with the weakening of the productive, providing, and regulating functions of the state, its role as mediator of class relations continues to be strong and articulated with other dominant forces. To consider governments as irrelevant would lead to the conclusion that national economic elites would have been crushed or absorbed by global capitalist expansion, which is not correct; governments themselves are the main agents in negotiations to open markets of interest to these elites (Fligstein 2001b). Who sits at the round-tables at Mercosur, the BRICS, the International Monetary Fund or the World Bank are not members of the Federation of Industries of the State of São Paulo (FIESP in its Portuguese acronym) or the Brazilian Federation of Banks (Febraban in its Portuguese acronym).[11] Who does so are officials of the Brazilian Ministry of Foreign

---

11 Mercosur is the Spanish acronym for the trade bloc comprised of Argentina, Bolivia, Brazil, Paraguay, Uruguay, and Venezuela. BRICS refers to the association of the national economies composed of Brazil, Russia, India, China, and South Africa.

Affairs, Ministry of Finance or Central Bank, even if they act to support capitalist class interests. In the same manner that fractions of class exercise hegemony in processes of interest to the capitalist class as a whole, this same kind of hegemony is reproduced within the state. This is the subject of the next section.

2   Financial Hegemony in the State Apparatus

The presence of the state as an articulator of economic relations is a trait common to various phases and processes of capitalism. Although it acts according to the interests of the capitalist class in general, it does so under the hegemony of one of its fractions. Evidence of this can be found in the structure of the distribution of power within the state, in which the dominant apparatus is that in which the hegemonic class or fraction retains powers (Poulantzas 1973). We also perceive this in the historical evolution of the Brazilian economy. Until the 1930s, the most important activity was agriculture for export, and thus representatives of that economic sector were the closest to state power at the time. From then until the 1980s, during the efforts at substitution of imports, the industrial elites occupied the positions of influence in the state economic apparatus. After a hiatus that some commentators have called a crisis of hegemony, the 1990s marked the beginning of a trend towards a financial expansion of the economy. The neoliberal shift established monetary and fiscal imperatives that placed finance, its logic, and its representatives in privileged positions to influence economic policies.

After the failure of the Collor Plan (1990), which had not been able to neutralize rampant inflation, a general change in the presidential cabinet, especially in the economic team, led a new political coalition to power during the government of President Itamar Franco (1992–1994) that had begun to be formed under the Cruzado Plan, which was launched in 1986, during the Sarney government (Bresser-Pereira 2007). The intellectuals linked to Sarney's party who composed the nucleus that conducted the theoretical formulation of the Cruzado Plan were followed by economists associated to the Pontific Catholic University of Rio de Janeiro who later regrouped under the leadership of then Minister of Finance Fernando Henrique Cardoso and whose theories became the foundation for the Real Plan, launched in 1994 (Abu-El-Haj 2007; Silva 2003). This established what Bresser-Pereira called the liberal-dependent pact, which involved an exclusionary political arrangement whose principal agents were the large rentiers, the financial agents who received commissions from rentiers, multinational companies, and foreign interests attracted by the overvalued new domestic currency, the *real*.

As had taken place during the Cruzado and Collor plans, the Real Plan placed the agencies responsible for macroeconomic policy at the center of state power. Changes of this type, according to Poulantzas (1969), do not take place from the immediate exterior role of the agency that becomes predominant; they rather occur from the reorganization of the entire state apparatus in response to changes in relations of production and also due to developments in the class struggles. This idea finds support in the Brazilian context of the mid-1980s and which deepened in the 1990s with the beginning of the movements of economic liberalization. Since then, the monetary and fiscal concerns, which had been of paramount importance to the neoliberal logic, came to occupy the center of government attention, making all the other state areas subordinated to financial logic.

Since the launching of the Real Plan (1994), despite the changes in internal divisions of the different governments that followed the plan, the agencies responsible for the fiscal and monetary policies remained hegemonic. During the two Cardoso governments (1995–2002), the cleavage between finance capital and industrial capital reverberated within the government, and was manifest in the division between an extreme neoliberal faction, which dominated the administration under the leadership of the Ministry of Finance and the Central Bank, and a minority moderate neoliberal faction, which controlled less influential areas and gave voice to the clamors of the industrial bourgeoisie (Boito 2007; Loureiro 1998). The Central Bank was the leading protagonist, and attained considerable autonomy, particularly after 1999, when the implementation of inflation targeting gave the Central Bank even more power to use monetary policy to interfere in the economy as a whole and in state administration as well. This situation remained practically unchanged during the Workers Party-led governments, particularly during Lula's two terms (2003–2010).

During the entire period from the Real Plan until today, the Central Bank of Brazil has apparently been above the political debate, which would be justifiable by its responsibility to defend the purchasing power of the currency. The Bank was not concerned if many people, such as the unemployed, had less money, while a few, namely the rentiers, could increase their share in the surpluses appropriated through financial investments. The policy whose core was high real interest rates did keep inflation within the planned levels, but also engendered the redistribution of surplus-value in benefit of those who held public debt securities. It was in this sense that Ary Minella (2007) highlighted the centrality of Central Bank decisions to economic policy, which made it a strategic organization in the maintenance of financial hegemony. This confirmed Poulantzas's (1973) affirmation that it is the hegemonic fraction of the bourgeoisie that guarantees the general interests of the alliance among the ruling fractions, while the specific interests of this hegemonic fraction are guaranteed by the state apparatus.

In a context of growing importance of finance for capitalism, it is not only finance capitalists, but also those from industry or commerce who tend to direct money-capital to financial assets whenever these are more profitable than investments in the material activities of real economy. Nevertheless, the hegemonic fraction is that whose interests are given priority by the state's economic and social policies (Saes 2001). And it was finance, after all, which had its interests mainly served when the economic policies called for high interest rates and deregulation of capital movements. This hegemonic fraction—a hegemony brought about by the state's dependence on finance to fund fiscal deficits—had the opportunity to exercise influence on government based on a logic that made the agencies responsible for fiscal and monetary policies central within the state apparatus.

A fundamental issue is that the influence on the state tends to only be successful to the degree that the channels for interlocution are minimally crystalized. It is essential that only a limited number of specific agencies elaborate the relevant policies, and not deliberative bodies, whether they are the parliament or those with direct participation. Actually, this latter form has been highly scorned by theories of elitist political preferences, such as those of Max Weber and his followers. The centralization-unity of the state is thus established in such a way that some dominant state apparatuses can only be influenced by monopolistic interests by becoming centers of consolidation of state policy and of impediments to measures taken by other state apparatuses that may favor other fractions of capital (Poulantzas, 2000 [1978]). This unity, Poulantzas continues, is established by a chain of subordination of certain apparatuses to others, and by the domination of the state apparatus that crystallizes the interests of the hegemonic class fraction over other apparatuses that may serve other fractions of the power bloc.

This entire movement signifies the bureaucratization of politics, because the executive bureaucracy becomes not only the center of power but also the arena where all power conflicts are resolved under the terms it sets (Mills 2000 [1956]). A situation then arises in which the traditional political leader, prepared only for formal-legal activities, becomes anachronistic, posing a danger to state activity if he or she is not capable of at least evaluating the solutions designed by specialists (Gramsci 2004 [1932]). In this spirit, political forays by finance into the Brazilian state apparatus were not seen as such, but as a search to overcome the barriers that politics imposed on society (Grün 2007b). An emblematic example is given by the representatives of finance—whether inside or outside the state apparatus—who defend the independence of central banks from elected government officials so that the monetary policy decisions are not constrained by political determinations, which, according to neoliberals, would work against the 'natural' and thus 'more efficient' functioning of the economy.

Market rules have a political nature and are the results of power relations delineated from the interaction between market agents and political institutions (Preda 2007). If this is true, the independence of a central bank poses even greater restrictions on democratic controls that are already limited by capitalist democracy. To grant independence to the monetary authority reduces even more the number of agents who can influence decisions that affect society in general, going beyond the already limited popular power that exists in the representative system. This is not merely a quantitative reduction, but an important qualitative change, because it involves concentrating power in the hands of the few and the similar. Actually, the very notion of independence is ambiguous, because one can always ask: independent from whom?

Another important effect occurs in the material results of the disputes between classes or their fractions carried out through the state mediation. The interests of groups with privileged access to information and political influence generally prevail when state institutions impede that same access to others who need it to maintain control over government decisions that also affect them (Bowles, Gordon, and Weisskopf 1990). According to Samuel Bowles, David Gordon, and Thomas Weisskopf, this results in policies favorable to the income of those closest to legislators and bureaucrats, in detriment to the efficiency of the economy as a whole. As an example, they mention the members of the Board of Governors of the U.S. Federal Reserve—the seven members of which serve staggered fourteen-year terms—who generally assure a disproportionate influence of finance on the Bank's decisions. Referring to a not very distant past, William Greider reported that at the same time that citizens in general had no space in the rare political discussions about monetary issues,

> the bondholders, the commercial bankers, the 400,000 financial professionals of Wall Street and their customers, the investors ... were like an ever-present chorus, scolding the Fed[eral Reserve] or applauding it, demanding that their interests be served by the government before all others.
>
> GREIDER 1989: 702

This situation has expanded the power of macroeconomic policy-makers and has had important consequences for democratic politics. It has meant the installation of a type of financial capitalist state within the capitalist state.

The agencies responsible for these policies were allowed to determine levels of state spending in practically all fields of action, even those where political choices could have followed a more democratic procedure, such as parliamentary debate. Budgetary systems like the Brazilian one, that simply authorize the executive branch to spend the amounts allocated without making it mandatory to do so, granted significant discretionary power to state economic technocracy. Similarly, one of the most significant state redistributions occurred because interest rates on public debt were highly influenced by Central Bank decisions taken without any substantive parliamentary debate.

As will be illustrated later on, in the case of economic policy 'socialism' was not necessary to establish a 'dictatorship' of the bureaucracy, as Max Weber once feared. In this realm one observes precisely what Weber deplored, that is, a bureaucracy beyond parliamentary control. This phenomenon is not surprising since bureaucracy has always been the state institution most rebellious to representative democracy (Poulantzas 2000 [1978]), welcoming a poorly informed and thus weak parliament (Weber 1964 [1922]). To redistribute surpluses via financial paths it is essential to control institutions, more than controlling people as takes place in material production. To the degree to which an economic field with its own laws is established and installs its mechanisms for reproduction—whose consistency is guaranteed by the state—direct and personal power over people tends to give space to power over the mechanisms that assure economic capital (Bourdieu 1994). In sum, wealth and power are results that depend on access to the central institutions (Mills 2000 [1956]).

If the state is one of the institutions essential to capitalist reproduction, access to state apparatuses is essential so that its powers or capacities serve that purpose. Yet the state is not an actual agent, which acts and exercises power by its own; it is always groups of politicians and bureaucrats, located in certain parts of the state system, who activate specific powers and capacities inscribed in particular institutions and agencies (Jessop 1990). For this reason, the access by capitalists to the state is not immediate. It requires mediations by the part of a category which, even without detaining capital, acts according to the interests of capital. As Poulantzas (1969) affirms, the capitalist state better serves the interests of the capitalist class when its members do not directly participate in the state apparatus. At this point, inspired by Antonio Gramsci, I insert the category that I call the 'organic intellectual of finance,' who is responsible for the articulation of the state with the financial fraction of capital.

Gramsci (2004 [1932]) noticed that each social group that forms around an essential function of economic production organically creates for itself one or more layers of intellectuals who give it homogeneity and consciousness of its own function in the economic, social, and political fields. According to

Gramsci, in addition to creating themselves, capitalists create technicians of industry, scientists of political economy, the organizers of a new culture, of a new law. These intellectuals are prepared by the ruling classes to preserve the conditions for exploitation and the main material fruit of this exploitation, which is surplus-value. Gramsci also affirms that capitalists, or at least the business elite, seeking their expansion as a class, must have the capacity to organize the entire complex organism of services in society, including the state, or to choose agents—the specialized employees—whom they can trust to organize the general relations outside their companies.

It is for this reason that the superstructures, of which the intellectuals are precisely the employees (Gramsci 2004 [1932]), become relevant. Gramsci locates superstructures on two planes, that of civil society—entities vulgarly designated as private—and that of political society or state. These planes correspond, respectively, to the exercise of hegemony over all of society by the ruling group, and to the direct rule expressed in the state and in legal government. In this relation, the intellectuals are the agents of the ruling group for the exercise of the subaltern functions of social hegemony and of political government (Gramsci 2004 [1932]). The subordinated function exercised by this organic intellectual is to develop the spontaneous consensus given by the large masses of the population to the guidance imposed by the ruling group that is essential to social life. This consensus is historically born from the prestige, and therefore from trust, obtained by the ruling group because of its position and its function in the world of production (Gramsci 2004 [1932]).

Nevertheless, it is within the state that the organic relationship between intellectual work and political domination takes place in a more complete form. As Pierre Bourdieu (2011 [1996]) teaches, the monopolization of universal values and ideas results from a work of universalization that takes place mainly within the bureaucratic field. Specialists external to the bureaucracy called to assist in the reform of institutions do so within a limited repertoire of ideas, often appealing to the best international practices as standards for judging these institutions and the models to be followed (Carruthers and Halliday 2000). Due to the crystallization of intellectual work and to its consequent distancing from the process of material production, the operation of state apparatuses requires command of a given knowledge and discourse that are shaped by the ruling ideology and exclude the popular masses (Poulantzas 2000 [1978]).

Since the time of Brazilian industrialization intellectuals have been occupying prominent positions in the state apparatuses. In the 1930–1945 period, they assumed political and ideological tasks that were required by the growing state intervention in various domains; in the 1945–1960 period, the careers reserved to them were expanded, while recruitment of new specialists also intensified, such as economists, sociologists, and planning and administrative technicians (Miceli 2001). The economists, upon becoming the notable players in the structural changes that took place in Brazil during its industrialization, and by being responsible for analyzing economic facts and proposing guidelines for action, exercised the role of organic intellectuals of the ruling class, giving a technocratic form to the bourgeois revolution in Brazil (Ianni 2004 [1989]). More recently, economists acting as organic intellectuals of finance and installed in the state economic apparatus became essential to the reproduction of the universal policy guidelines of this period, such as monetary stability and so-called fiscal responsibility. At the same time that they denounced the calamity of hyperinflation and drafted plans to contain it, they promoted a true culture of monetary instability, which granted them the legitimacy and authority to, as pedagogues of this instability, diagnose and remedy the country's ills (Neiburg 2005, 2006).

But just as it is logically impossible for the capitalist state to represent the general will, the state bureaucracy cannot be considered neutral in its social relations. This is because, even if they compose a social category with a particular unity, state personnel have class positions, which, in the case of the highest ranks, are among the bourgeois or petit-bourgeois classes (Poulantzas 1973, 1976, 2000 [1978]). Their unity, according to Poulantzas (1969), is established by the objective role of the state, whose totality coincides with the interests of the ruling class. This unity is also established by the social localization of the bureaucrat. For Erik Wright (1998, 2000), despite a lack of definition of class location of the intermediary fractions, those with higher positions in the bureaucratic hierarchies are more aligned to capitalist interests.

In Brazil, the closed and exclusionary style of administration of the economy made the state technocracy an elite above questioning from society or the political class (Diniz 2004). Joined in restricted committees, this elite had the legitimacy to allocate parcels of tax revenues without having to submit these decisions to the debate that would supposedly exist in a genuinely democratic environment. This technocracy thus steered a process that levied surpluses produced by the working classes which, despite their role, were rarely called on to give an opinion about this redistribution.

An analysis of the personal attributes of, and relationships between, organic intellectuals of finance reveals important similarities among them. These are highlighted by their social origins, educational paths, and professional destinations in various moments before or after their passage through the state bureaucracy. Many of them had studied at specific elite schools, had worked in specific economic segments, and returned to these institutions after passage through high government positions. As an 'ideal type' one can consider the image of an economist who switches between professional activities in economics departments at prestigious universities, government economic staffs, private financial institutions, and multilateral financial agencies. The importance of this is that the proximity in social space predisposes them to approximation in terms of the beliefs that they share (Bourdieu 2011 [1996]).

A less abstract finding in this regard is made by Joseph Stiglitz (2002), for whom ministers of finance and governors of central banks are normally very close to the financial community, which is where they come from and where they go to after passing through government. According to Stiglitz—who served as vice-president and chief economist at the World Bank after having led the U.S. Council of Economic Advisers in the Clinton government—it is 'natural' that these individuals see the world through the eyes of financial community. Something similar also took place in Brazil, where "these technicians can be easily captured," in the words of Luiz Carlos Bresser-Pereira, a former minister during the Cardoso administrations who had also chaired the Ministry of Finance in the Sarney government.[12] The educational connections of the economic technocracy are also found in Brazil. Some of its most important members were educated in universities, especially those in the United States, that appear to have homogenized the theoretical schemes and the political and ideological orientations that governed their actions and decisions under the neoliberal creed and prescriptions (Chesnais 1998, 2005a; Loureiro 1998).

The professional connections appear to have followed a similar pattern. Of the nearly forty individuals who have served as governors of the Central Bank of Brazil since 1996, when the Bank's Monetary Policy Committee was created, more than half came from, or went to, private banks, investment management firms or international financial institutions prior to reaching the Central Bank or upon leaving it.[13] Thus, the economic policies of the various governments since the implementation of the Real Plan (1994) had a certain continuity of formulators, ideas and ideologies, all with important connections to finance. One peculiarity of Brazil, according to Lecio Morais and Alfredo Saad-Filho (2003), was that financial organizations had influenced economic activity not predominantly by financing industry or through operations in the stock market, but through ownership of public debt securities. Moreover, Morais and

---

12   Brasil. Câmara dos Deputados. CPI—Dívida Pública. "Transcrição ipsis verbis: reunião ordinária n. 2400/09." 16 de dezembro de 2009: 6.
13   The Monetary Policy Committee is composed of the members of the board of governors of the Central Bank of Brazil. It is responsible for establishing monetary policy and the nominal targets for the benchmark interest rate of the Brazilian economy, known as the Selic rate.

Saad-Filho add, the representatives of finance dislodged old social fractions from the bureaucracy and guaranteed finance's control over the state through the growing power of the Ministry of Finance and the Central Bank.

3   The Class Character of Macroeconomic Policy

The year 1994 marked the beginning of an uncommon period of relative political stability in Brazilian history. In that year, for the first time in nearly forty years, a president of the republic was elected who would complete the full term granted by the popular vote. It was also the year in which the country changed its currency to the *real*. This change was part of an economic stabilization plan considered by its enthusiasts to be quite successful after frustrated attempts in previous years. In the discourse of the ruling classes, Brazil had entered the group of countries on a development path that was monetarily and fiscally sustainable. This new stage peaked in April 2008, when the risk classification agency Standard & Poor's declared a portion of the Brazilian debt to be investment grade. Then President Lula boasted that "Brazil had been declared a responsible country, which has responsible policies, which responsibly cares for its finances ... And what we have now received," Lula added, "is simply the recognition that we have come to be masters of our own destiny by determining the policies that we deem to be suitable for Brazil."[14]

These words reveal the basic contradiction in linking sovereignty to set policy to the certification of good behavior from a third party. It is also important to remember that, a few months later, the large global risk classification agencies—whose certifications of compliance with given economic imperatives had been so highly sought by countries seeking money-capital—were confronted with serious challenges to their credibility shaken by the U.S. subprime mortgage crisis. This highlights what is coherent and truthful in the evaluations of the Brazilian economy in the era of the new currency—the *real*—made by organic intellectuals of finance, by the mainstream economic press, and by members of various governments that followed. To better qualify what they all affirmed, Brazil became a serious and responsible country in the eyes of finance. This qualification is necessary because, in a society of classes, state action is based primarily on capitalist logic, but particularly on the logic of capital's hegemonic class fraction.

---

14 Brasil. Presidência da República. "Discurso do presidente da República, Luiz Inácio Lula da Silva, na cerimônia de instalação e posse do Conselho Deliberativo da Superintendência do Desenvolvimento do Nordeste—Sudene." Maceió, AL. 30 de abril de 2008.

In Brazil of the last two decennia, we saw the formation of a situation in which finance was assured it would have precedence over other classes or fractions in the sharing of economic surpluses transitorily appropriated by the state. Following this hypothesis, the objective of this section is to shed light on how some of the main foundations of macroeconomic policy reaffirmed the class character of the Brazilian state in general, and its financial-class character in particular. To do so, I will analyze three mechanisms of economic policy that in articulation established an institutional apparatus that has consistently favored finance. These are the delinking of federal revenues from constitutionally mandated spending, inflation targeting, and so-called fiscal responsibility.

3.1   Delinking of Federal Revenues

Different redistributive configurations can result from the disputes between classes for the economic surpluses transitorily appropriated by the state. This leads to advantages for some and disadvantages for other classes or fractions of classes that struggle for the appropriation of these surpluses. The simultaneous favoring of all is a logical impossibility. One of the means by which redistributive configurations are shaped is the type of spending made by the state, which can determine that one or more social fractions is favored in detriment to others. There are also methods to establish greater stability in state redistribution in terms of the destinations of the previously appropriated surpluses. Legal mechanisms can prescribe in what way this sharing takes place, for example, by earmarking portions of tax revenues for certain types of budgetary expenditure, making them mandatory. The Brazilian Constitution of 1988 did this, when it was promulgated just three years after the end of the military dictatorship that originated with the coup of April 1, 1964.

Because of the pent-up demand for democratic participation that had been repressed by the dictatorship, the new Constitution was also the result of social forces that had had sufficient legitimacy to make demands and see some of them fulfilled. This participation led to conquests that in principle would not depend on the discretion of an incumbent government to be converted into universal public policies. For example, the Constitution of 1988 determined that the federal government should spend no less than 18% of its tax revenues—excluding social security contributions—on the maintenance and development of education. For states and municipalities, the Constitution mandated that no less than 25% of their respective tax revenues must be spent on public education. It also determined that social contributions destined to form the subsidized savings programs for workers and civil servants (respectively known as PIS and Pasep in Portuguese) must finance unemployment benefits and an annual bonus of a minimum wage for workers with monthly income up to two minimum wages. Furthermore, the revenues from all other social contributions must be spent on social security, namely on healthcare, retirement and other pensions, and social assistance.

This framework granted a significant portion of the Brazilian population the opportunity to count on the basic services of education, healthcare, retirement benefits, and social assistance that the state was required to provide. If on one hand the constitutional entitlements were not a guarantee that the respective services would be executed, on the other, they made the struggle for state outlays more complex than it would have been if the incumbent government had full discretion over these expenditures. But this did not avoid a reduction of the space conquered by the ruled classes. With the financial expansion of the economy and strengthening of the neoliberal logic, the Brazilian capitalist state adapted itself to this new order. As early as the preliminary phase of the launching of the Real Plan, the government partially rolled back some achievements of the Constitution of 1988. As a first step, the government instituted a mechanism that freed up a significant portion of tax revenues that the Constitution determined would be guaranteed to education and welfare programs.

In March 1994, the federal Constitution was amended to create the Emergency Social Fund (Fundo Social de Emergência in Portuguese), which had the declared "objective of financial cleansing of the federal public treasury and economic stabilization."[15] Its main source of funding was 20% of the federal tax revenue that had originally been set aside by the Constitution to fund education, healthcare, and other social welfare programs. Monies that had been dedicated to retirement and other pensions were not affected by this delinking of revenues from constitutional obligations. Originally created for the fiscal years of 1994 and 1995, the Emergency Social Fund was extended, first until June 1997 and then until December 1999, although after 1996 it was renamed the Fiscal Stabilization Fund (Fundo de Estabilização Fiscal in Portuguese).[16] The same 20% that had been delinked from the original constitutional obligations by the first fund continued to compose the new one.

It should be noted that when the original fund was created, it foresaw that the monies freed from the mandatory spending would be "allocated to expenses in actions for healthcare and in educational systems, retirement and other

---

15   Brasil. "Emenda constitucional de revisão n. 1, de 1 de março de 1994." Art. 1º.
16   Brasil. "Emenda constitucional n. 10, de 4 de março de 1996"; "emenda constitucional n. 17, de 22 de novembro de 1997."

pensions and social assistance programs."[17] When it was extended under the name of the Fiscal Stabilization Fund, the constitutional amendment that did so established that the delinked monies would be "applied with *priority* to the expenses" for these policies.[18] That is, the government made the effort to reduce mandatory social spending even more clear, curiously through the ambiguous use of the term 'priority,' which created the loophole that eventually reinforced the release.

The process was consolidated with that which became known as the Delinking of Federal Revenues (Desvinculação de Receitas da União in Portuguese). In March 2000, the federal Constitution was once again amended and, at this time, no fund was established. The same 20% of release first established in 1994 was renewed a few times, first until 2003, then until 2007, 2011, and 2015.[19] Since 1994 the delinking was also affecting the federal tax revenues that the Constitution of 1988 required to be spent on education, but this latter delinking came to be reduced from the original 20% to 12.5% in 2009, 5% in 2010, and zero in 2011, thus re-establishing the original constitutional provision for education.[20] In 2016, in a new extension, now until the year 2023, the delinking was broadened from 20% to 30%—not including the re-established provision for education—of the revenues coming basically from social contributions, excluding those for retirement and other pensions.[21]

What must be highlighted is that the release from the initial constitutionally mandatory spending was one more expression of the class character of the state, now in its financial version. This is because finance was precisely the leading beneficiary of that mechanism. In fact, while capitalists in general prefer liquidity (Arrighi 1994), finance capitalists particularly fear any type of impediment that can represent a threat to this liquidity, for example, when state revenues are mandatorily earmarked for social welfare programs. There is a parallel between money and credit that can cast some more light on the phenomenon of the delinking of federal revenues mechanism.[22] The parallel involves fungibility, that is, the homogeneity of money and its capacity for exchange.

---

17   Brasil. "Emenda constitucional de revisão n. 1, de 1 de março de 1994." Art. 1º.
18   Brasil. "Emenda constitucional n. 10, de 4 de março de 1996." Art. 1º.
19   Brasil. "Emenda constitucional n. 27, de 21 de março de 2000"; "emenda constitucional n. 42, de 19 de dezembro de 2003"; "emenda constitucional n. 56, de 20 de dezembro de 2007"; "emenda constitucional n. 68, de 21 de dezembro de 2011."
20   Brasil. "Emenda constitucional n. 59, de 11 de novembro de 2009." Art. 5º.
21   Brasil. "Emenda constitucional n. 93, de 8 de setembro de 2016."
22   Henceforth, the term delinking of federal revenues will also refer to the other release made since 1994 through the Emergency Social Fund, and the Fiscal Stabilization Fund.

According to Bruce Carruthers (2005), fungibility, which makes money so useful by granting it the power to purchase anything, also carries a problem, which he exemplifies as follows: fungibility means that the money that a parent gives to a child to pay for a haircut can be surreptitiously deviated to purchase candy. Although it may seem a bit odd, this example helps reveal that the delinking of federal revenues gave the Brazilian government greater discretion over a significant portion of the budgetary expenditure. In this case, neoliberals did not find a big problem in contradicting one of their dearest axioms, which calls for fixed rules to limit the discretionary power of policy makers. What the delinking of revenues did was to precisely substitute clear rules on how to spend some tax revenues with increased discretionary government power over the expenditure of the monies released from mandatory social spending.

For finance, however, the problem prior to the delinking of revenues was not in the existence of clear rules, but to *whom* those rules catered. Since they were not in the interest of finance—its members did not need public education or healthcare; they wanted interest on public debt—the constitutional earmarking did not fit the axiom 'rules instead of discretion.' Recalling the story about the candy, Carruthers (2005) emphasizes that lenders, like parents, do not want to see fungible money deviated from its original purpose and, for this reason, they want the loans they make to be less fungible. One way to do this is to convert general money, which can be used for anything, into special money, which should have a predefined destination. This takes place, for example, by means of budget classifications that create restrictions so that a certain type of resource be employed in certain activities. The logic is that these restrictions increase the probability that debt will be paid back (Carruthers 2005). This same logic helps to understand in what way the delinking of federal revenues served the objective of sustaining the Brazilian public debt.

Although it did so in a form that was not formally explicit, the delinking of revenues effectively reserved resources for the payment of public debt services. I propose another abstraction to bring the concept of fungibility closer to this argument, but now through an inversion of the reasoning. In Carruthers's description, the lender imposes on the debtor the condition that the money loaned must be applied in a certain economic activity that is expected will be capable of generating surpluses to pay back the loan. The inversion of the reasoning that I mentioned is in the idea that the increased fungibility of money—namely the delinking of federal revenues—favored creditors to the degree that it avoided that resources that *potentially* could be allocated to debt service be *compulsorily* used for other purposes, like social welfare policies. Thus, if revenue linked to a social policy was less fungible because it was aimed at objects other than servicing the public debt—education, social security, etc.—making it fungible, that is, delinking it, would increase the probability that it would be used to service the debt.

What the delinking of federal revenues did—and not very subtlety—was to inform creditors that the released monies would not automatically be allocated to servicing the public debt, but that, with a similar practical effect, nor would they be allocated for any competing destination, such as the state provision of healthcare or educational services. The released monies then remained free from constitutional restriction to then be disputed and redistributed according to the correlation of forces between classes and other social fractions vying for the budgetary resources in question.

In the first years of the Real Plan, the amounts released allowed the government to face the immediate fiscal restrictions caused by the reduction of the inflation tax that accompanied the lower inflation. Figure 11 shows how it was difficult to stabilize the primary fiscal result in the first period of the new currency, the *real*, from 1994 through 1998. In any case, the reduction of mandatory social spending signified an increase in the amount of non-earmarked monies equivalent to an average of 10% of federal tax revenue in the 1994–2015 period.

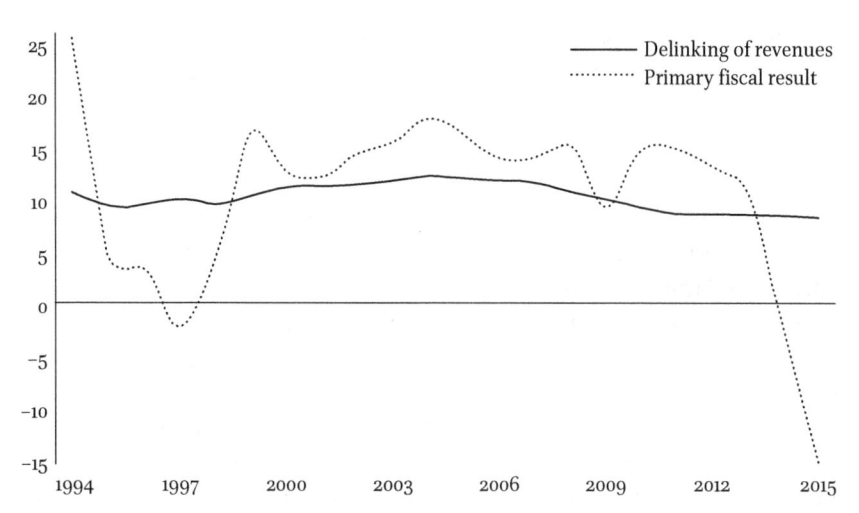

FIGURE 11   Delinking of revenues and primary fiscal result, Brazil, 1994–2015
Notes: (i) percentages in relation to total revenue from federal taxes and social contributions, not including those for retirement and other pensions; (ii) delinking of federal revenues estimated according to the constitutional amendments that created it, the Emergency Social Fund, and the Fiscal Stabilization Fund.

The main point of this configuration is that the Brazilian government understood that it should have mechanisms to service the public debt, and the delinking of federal revenues fulfilled this role. A comparison can be made here between the Cardoso and Lula governments that shows not just a continuity of the policy, but its deepening. Distancing itself from the traditional anti-creditor rhetoric of the Workers Party, the Lula governments clearly indicated their commitment to payment of interest on the public debt. During Cardoso's second term (1999–2002), the portion of the primary fiscal results that exceeded the delinked revenues averaged 2.8% of federal tax revenue; during Lula's two terms (2003–2010), this average rose to 3.5%. It is not surprising that the risk on Brazil's external debt in the first years of the Lula government fell below the level observed in the Cardoso years (see figure 10). Nor is it surprising that a few years later, Brazilian debt was considered to have attained investment grade. The fact that reductions in the primary fiscal results in the first government of President Rousseff (2011–2014) were combined with the loss of that investment grade is also compatible with this reasoning.

The increased freedom of spending that came from the delinking of federal revenues should be relativized by considering what began to take place in 1999. That was the year of the crisis that led the government to allow the exchange rate to float and to adopt inflation targeting as a substitute for exchange rate pegging to control inflation. Since then, with the exception of the years 2009, 2014, and 2015, the amounts released from mandatory social spending came to integrally serve the formation of the primary fiscal surpluses. Primary surpluses were also not attained in most of the pre-1999 phase of the *real* (see figure 11). I will discuss the primary fiscal surplus later, but it is necessary to mention it briefly to clarify the point at hand. The primary result is equal to the difference between non-financial revenues and non-financial expenditures. Thus, the very existence of a primary surplus means that total revenues exceeded total expenditures excluding the interest on the public debt. In practical terms, the goal for primary fiscal surplus acts as a provision to pay interest.

From the data shown in figure 11, it can be concluded that primary fiscal surpluses greater than the increase in the released monies represented an additional effort to contain non-financial spending. It was additional because it impacted also the portion of revenues that had never been constitutionally linked to any spending. Thus, if to form primary surpluses the government also claimed portions of tax revenues that were not constitutionally dedicated, the new tranches that came from the delinking of federal revenues were fully steered to pay interest on public debt, which took place in 1999–2008 and 2010–2013. In 1995–1998, 2009, and 2014–2015, this steering was partial, as is also seen in figure 11. Considering that the first objective of the delinking of federal revenues was the formation of primary fiscal surpluses, in practice it released revenues that had previously been linked for social welfare policies to virtually link them for interest payments.

In a similar way as education and healthcare, which had mandatory portions of tax revenue linked to them since the 1988 Constitution, since 1994 financial classes could obtain their own share of virtually linked revenues. While this was not guaranteed by the constitutional amendments mentioned, no limits were placed on the ruling classes' access to the released monies. In this way, the delinking of revenues made available to finance the same portion that was grabbed from the ruled classes. This increase in the fungibility of resources previously dedicated to specific spending obligations was one of the first steps to granting an advantage to finance in the struggle for the surpluses collected by the state. Nevertheless, since this had not been accompanied by an explicit linking to interest payments, other institutional mechanisms were joined to the delinking of federal revenues to also contribute to the class advantage of finance. I will analyze these additional mechanisms in the next two subsections.

3.2 Inflation Targeting

In the nearly three decennia following World War II, the great socioeconomic concern was for full employment, around which the Keynesian consensus was erected, approximating the interest of capitalists, state, and workers. With the end of the so-called glorious years of capitalism in the late 1970s inflation control gained increased attention and began to guide the concerns of both the state and capitalists. This concern had already been revealed in the first years after World War II, for example in the well-known anti-inflationary measures that the International Monetary Fund imposed on the countries that turned to it for help (Babb 2007). But it was when monetarism became hegemonic in mainstream economics that inflation became the primary concern that guided the main economic policies of most national governments.

The vehement aversion of monetarists to inflation was based on the belief that, in addition to distorting prices and making rational decisions impossible at the company level, it impeded rational steering of the economy as a whole (Eyal 2000). This would thus require actions to make markets the only sources able to provide agents the needed and precise information about economic activity. To do so, inflationary control was the first requirement. This priority was due to the fact that inflation erodes the integrity of the price system, which would be the key supplier of information in a market economy (Babb 2007). However, this understanding is open to debate, given that market mechanisms do not transmit direct information about intentions, desires, and values, but information about the results of decisions already made (Elson 1988). In any case, if monetarist theory is not a sufficient explanation for the change of political priorities, it served well to give theoretical legitimacy to a series of economic policies.

As in so many other movements that irradiated from the center of the world-system, the concern for inflation reached Latin America, where various countries took considerable efforts to contain it. This movement became politically legitimated to the degree that inflation was inculcated in social representations as a type of public enemy. In February 1986, when the Brazilian government launched the Cruzado Plan—one of the many aimed at containing the rising consumer price indices—the then president of the republic said that he was launching "a life or death war against inflation."[23] Runaway prices were considered a social emergency and came to be treated as such at important events in national life, nearly always with strong popular support. This was due in large part to the rhetoric that affirmed that the worst effects of inflation most intensely affected the poor. Since they did not have the ability to protect themselves from the loss of purchasing power of money as did those with access to the financial market, the poor and working classes aligned themselves to the clamors of finance against inflation.

Nevertheless, while inflation was violently affecting the classes with lower purchasing power, it was also reducing the real income, and even the wealth, of those who held financial assets. This second element, however, was not mentioned in the discourses used to justify the stabilization plans, which were presented as routes for 'national salvation.' The process that had begun in 1986 with the quixotic figure of Sarney's inspector (Fiscal do Sarney in Portuguese) peaked with the election of Fernando Henrique Cardoso to the presidency of the republic, in 1994.[24] Cardoso was portrayed as the figure most responsible for the success of Real Plan, which had been implemented while he was minister of finance in the government of President Itamar Franco (1992–1994). The Real Plan finally defeated hyperinflation after the various failed plans of the Sarney and Collor governments. But as Marx once said about the France of Louis Bonaparte, a "society is saved just as often as the circle of its rulers contracts, as a more exclusive interest is maintained against a wider one" (Marx 2010 [1852]: 111–112).

---

23   "O primeiro dia de guerra à inflação." *O Estado de S. Paulo*. 1 de março de 1986: 1.
24   The expression "Sarney's inspector" became popular when in his announcement of the Cruzado Plan, the president of Brazil at the time, José Sarney, said: "each Brazilian will and must be a price inspector" ("O primeiro dia de guerra à inflação." *O Estado de S. Paulo*. 1 de março de 1986: 1).

CAPITALIST STATE AND FINANCIAL HEGEMONY 71

The end to Brazil's suffering from hyperinflation took place concomitantly to the increased favoring of the financial fraction of capital, which was attained through a deepening of the exploitation of the labor of others and a reduction in financing for social welfare policies (I shall discuss this issue in more details in the next chapter). Another effect was the increase in unemployment, as shown in figure 12. In the São Paulo metropolitan region, Brazil's largest economic and populational center, the average unemployment rate rose from 11% in the 1985–1994 period to 17% in 1995–2003, lowering to 14% during the 2003–2015 period.

It is well known that the attempts at inflation control implemented since the so-called re-democratization of Brazil in 1985 failed until the Real Plan was launched, in 1994. Nearly all were followed by periods whose inflation levels became even higher than those that they sought to reduce. In this aspect, the Real Plan had important success, maintaining consumer price indexes under control until today. The issue came to be treated in such a way that any economic policy decision was justifiable in the name of inflation control, which seemed to be supported by most of Brazilian society. One point that at times is not clear is that while society as a whole apparently benefited from lower consumer prices indexes, a minority, specifically the financial classes, benefitted directly, and this was not just apparent, but real. After all, in a class society it

FIGURE 12 Inflation in Brazil and unemployment in Metropolitan São Paulo, 1985–2015
Notes: (i) percentage scales; (ii) the unemployment rate includes hidden unemployment, which is precarious work and unemployment because of discouragement.

cannot be said that economic phenomena have uniform effects on society as a whole. Inflation is one such phenomena.

The benefits to finance came from the fact that the mechanism used to counter the price rises were systematically high real interest rates. Even if this occurred during the entire period in question, it is divided in two subperiods that are distinguishable by the means of inflation control. In the first, when the Real Plan was in force, from 1994 to 1998, the leading mechanism was the exchange rate policy for maintaining the national currency overvalued. The exchange rate pegging, which kept the *real* close to parity with the U.S. dollar, stabilized the prices of tradable goods in the international market, which was reflected in the prices of products traded in the domestic market. One of the reflexes was to encourage imports and discourage exports, with a negative impact on the balance of payments. During the 1994–1998 period, Brazil accumulated a deficit that totaled more than 107 billion U.S. dollars in current transactions, which was financed with the inflow of foreign financial capital (see figure 4).

The second subperiod that is distinguished according to the means of inflation control began after a succession of crises—in Mexico, Southeast Asia and Russia—that, between 1995 and 1998, led to speculative attacks on the Brazilian new currency. By January 1999, the exchange rate pegging policy could no longer be sustained and the Brazilian government abandoned parity with the U.S. dollar. Soon after, the Central Bank indicated that the floating exchange rate did not mean there would be no nominal anchor, but that this anchor would be the benchmark interest rate of the economy. In March 1999, the Central Bank declared that it was

> essential to transmit to society that the economy [would] not operate without a nominal anchor and that the Central Bank ha[d] the capacity to act. In this sense, the performance of monetary authority [would] come to be guided by the commitment to controlling the inflation rate. Given the current situation, one notices that fiscal policy austerity and foreign credit are determinant factors.[25]

On the same occasion, the Central Bank's Monetary Policy Committee sharply raised the goal for the nominal benchmark interest rate from 25% to 45% per annum, which led to a rise in the real ex post rate from 17% to 30% per annum

---

25   Banco Central do Brasil. Comitê de Política Monetária. "Atas do Copom: 33ª reunião." 4 de março de 1999.

between February and March 1999.[26] This level was reduced in the following month, when the Committee admitted "that the nominal interest rate of 39.5% per annum represented a very high real return."[27]

Soon after, in June 1999, fearing that the float of the exchange rate would lead to hyperinflation, the government eventually adopted the inflation targeting regime (Arestis, de Paula, and Ferrari-Filho 2009). Since then, Brazilian interest rates have remained at the highest levels among the world's major economies (see figures 1 and 3). These rates were quite attractive to finance, which was consistent with the Central Bank's understanding of foreign credit being determinant for controlling inflation. In just one month, in March 1999, when the Central Bank's Monetary Policy Committee raised the Selic rate, the share of the securities whose yield was pegged to Selic increased from 57% to 68% of the outstanding domestic federal securitized debt. Comparing the 1995–1998 and 1999–2015 periods, the average portion of securities whose yield was pegged to the Selic rate increased from 28% to 42% of the domestic debt, while the portion whose yield was prefixed dropped from 42% to 26%. This change confirmed that the Lula governments continued, and in some aspects even deepened, the macroeconomic policy begun in Cardoso's second term (Mollo and Saad-Filho 2006; Prates and Paulani 2007).

Upon inaugurating the second subperiod of the *real*, the Central Bank's Monetary Policy Committee declared that "price stability in a floating exchange rate regime [would be] guaranteed by the fiscal austerity sustained and by a monetary austerity system compatible with fiscal policy." It also affirmed that, "since in the short-term fiscal policy [was already] set, the effective instrument for controlling the inflationary pressures [would be] of a monetary nature, that is, interest rate."[28] In this way, the Central Bank used the instrument

---

26   Until the 32nd meeting of the Central Bank's Monetary Policy Committee, when it decided to allow the exchange rate to float, the benchmark interest rate set by the Committee was known as the Central Bank rate (TBC in its Portuguese initials). When this rate was terminated, after the 33rd meeting the Committee began to set goals for the Selic rate, which in the period between the 32nd and 33rd meetings was nearly 37% per annum in nominal terms.

27   Banco Central do Brasil. Comitê de Política Monetária. "Atas do Copom: 34ª reunião." 14 de abril de 1999. Since the previous rate-setting meeting, the goal for the nominal interest rate had already been reduced from 45% to 39.5% per annum by means of the use of the monetary policy bias. The definition of the bias for the interest rate is a mechanism by which the Monetary Policy Committee indicates a direction—an increase or decrease—for a potential change in the goal for the interest rate, delegating to the president of the Central Bank this prerogative until the next meeting.

28   Banco Central do Brasil. Comitê de Política Monetária. "Atas do Copom: 33ª reunião." 4 de março de 1999.

over which it held practically absolute control—monetary policy—to signal to the rest of the state apparatus what else would be necessary to control inflation, namely the so-called fiscal austerity. The fiscal policy then had to be austere to pay for the rigid monetary policy. This also revealed a contradiction between the monetary policy and the alleged need for fiscal austerity, which became compromised precisely by the rise of spending on public debt interest (see figure 13).

The objective of inflation control that had been pursued since the so-called re-democratization attained its most long-lasting success with the *real*; after becoming threatened in early 1999, it earned an important institutional framework. At that time, the nominal anchor, which had been the exchange rate, came to have a monetary nature. The policy that allowed interest rates as high as needed to control inflation that had been implemented since before the Real Plan gained important legal support. This responded to one of the demands of finance that academic economists defend with the axiom that economic policies should be based on rules and not on the discretion of policy makers. Since then, the government came to set, explicitly and formally, commitments to given levels of inflation. In this way, the interaction between the state and finance via the Central Bank reached a special format, with inflation targeting as the monetary regime that protected real financial income and the prices of financial assets.

According to the presidential decree that established the new regime, monetary policy had to obey the following guidelines: (i) the National Monetary

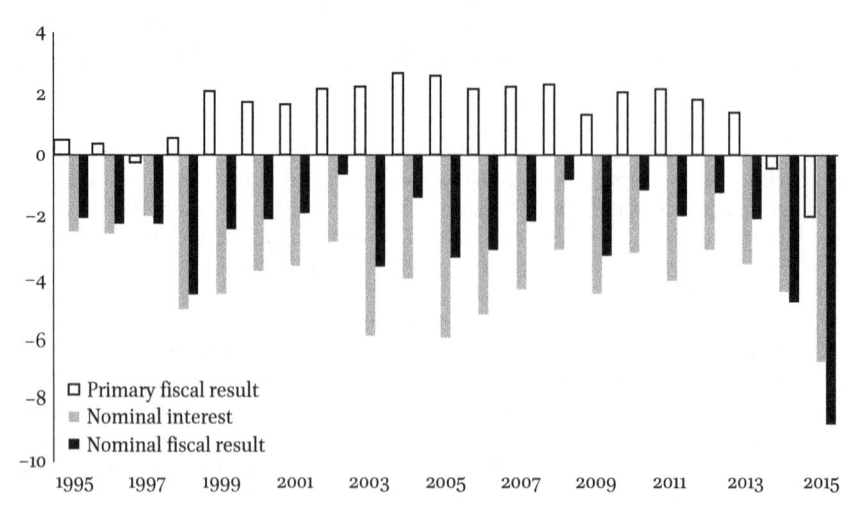

FIGURE 13   Central government borrowing requirement, Brazil, 1995–2015
Note: percentages in relation to GDP.

Council (Conselho Monetário Nacional in Portuguese) became responsible for setting the inflation targets; (ii) this had to be done up to eighteen months before the year to which the target refers; (iii) the Central Bank of Brazil was given the authority to execute the policies needed to meet the target for inflation; and (iv) in case it were not met, the Central Bank president must report, in an open letter to the Ministry of Finance, the reasons for the lack of compliance, the measures needed to meet the inflation target, and the estimated time required for this to occur. The decree focused on that which official discourse usually defines as transparency, and also involved a commitment from the government or a strong signaling to economic agents about how it would behave in relation to this issue. In sum, a legal determination was thus established that allowed the monetary authority "to execute the policies necessary to comply with the targets set [for inflation]."[29]

The signals of inflation targeting were aimed at all the economic agents, which, however, did not mean that the new regime was favorable to all of them. To the contrary, this was one more institutional mechanism with a clear class character. With its support, finance was the main fraction favored in the repartition of the surpluses garnered through the state fiscal apparatus.

Upon concluding this subsection, I highlight that this analysis makes no consideration about whether the targeting regime was effective. This polemic does exist, for example, in the debate between analysts concerned mainly with monetary stability and those with economic growth. I understand that this debate is less important here. What matters to my argument is to investigate how this mechanism was articulated with others—for example, the delinking of federal revenues, which I analyzed in the previous subsection, and the Fiscal Responsibility Law, which I will analyze in the next—that shaped the financial-class character of the Brazilian state.

3.3 *So-called Fiscal Responsibility*

Over history, certain terms gain impressive ideological strength. The objectives that they evoke can guide actions of individuals and organizations, including state entities, as if they were universal values. For analyses of the post-World War II period, we can select terms such as economic development or full employment. For those under dictatorship, we can mention democracy; a bit later, our choice could fall on inflation control. What all had in common were their presentations to society as if all social classes and their fractions would be equally benefitted by their realization. Currently, one term that appears to

---

29 Brasil. Presidência da República. "Decreto n. 3.088, de 21 de junho de 1999." Art. 2º.

follow this logic is 'responsibility.' It was precisely the alleged lack of fiscal responsibility that was used as a pretext to give a legal varnish to the coup staged within the Brazilian capitalist state in 2016 in the effort to return the macroeconomic policy to the course desired by finance (see the book's afterword).

At times accompanied by adjectives like social, environmental, or socio-environmental, the term responsibility has served as an important propaganda tool for various business or state organizations. Since it is now imperative to be 'responsible,' the state sector must also be so. If a company should be socially responsible—whatever this has meant—and if we should all be environmentally responsible, the state, in addition to all these responsibilities, should also be fiscally responsible. After Brazil's so-called re-democratization in the late 1980s, having passed through monetary stabilization in mid-1990s, the state was then pressured to promote certain institutions particularly important to capitalism in its current stage. Based on the neoliberal presumption that the state, in addition to spending too much, spends poorly, new institutions would be needed that could contain this impetus. This was the foundation of the discourse of so-called fiscal responsibility.

Along with other measures, the Fiscal Responsibility Law deserves special attention in our search to reveal the state's class character. Since being enacted in 2000, it has been celebrated by the corporate press, by financial economists and those in the academy, and by many others based on the intentionally simplistic discourse that the state spends too much and poorly. I say simplistic because these analyses often fail to consider, for example, on what that state spends; or, even more importantly, to analyze *for whom* it spends and *from whom* it extracts what it spends. These biased analyses about the theme thus wind up privileging certain aspects of the law without addressing a fundamental issue, which is precisely its class character. In this sense, the understanding about how classes operate in relation to this specific point of fiscal affairs can result from the analysis not only of what the law does, but also of what it does not do, which in fact is another mode of doing.

Primarily, the Fiscal Responsibility Law declared that its main objective was the establishment of norms for the responsible administration of public finances. Fundamentally, this was understood to be compliance with the goals for fiscal results and obedience to debt limits. To do so, the Fiscal Responsibility Law determined that the Budgetary Directives Law (Lei de Diretrizes Orçamentárias in Portuguese), which is a yearly law that sets the guidelines for the following year's budget law, must establish goals for revenue, expenditures, nominal and primary fiscal results, and debt limits. The Fiscal Responsibility Law determined that if in a given moment total revenue were expected to not comply with the goals for fiscal results, spending should be cut as needed to attain equilibrium. However, this spending cut could not include expenses related to constitutional and legal obligations, which include—and this is what is most important to my argument—those aimed at payment of public debt services.

Two points call special attention in this configuration. The most obvious is the proviso of the Fiscal Responsibility Law that no limits be set on spending for debt services. This effectively and explicitly granted privileges to the creditors of the public debt. If the state has financial difficulties, these lenders will not see their share in fiscal allotments be sacrificed, at least in the first moments. This is similar to establishing a type of competition among creditors, to which the Fiscal Responsibility Law places finance in first place on the line of potential recipients. Of course, according to the law, alongside the rentiers would be the social fractions that receive state monies linked to constitutionally mandated spending. However, as we saw previously, the delinking of federal revenues mechanism weakened the guarantees of social welfare spending. An implicit goal of the Fiscal Responsibility Law was to avoid potential obstacles for the state to fulfill its obligations towards finance.

Another and less obvious point in the distributive configuration that the Fiscal Responsibility Law promoted was the target for the primary fiscal results, which is composed of all non-financial revenues minus all non-financial expenditures. Since the enactment of the Fiscal Responsibility Law, the goals for primary fiscal results, as well as those for nominal results, came to be established in each year's Budgetary Directives Law.[30] Nevertheless, the treatments given to these two types of results were not the same. In one edition of the Budgetary Directives Law, the Brazilian government clarified that

> each year's goals are established for the primary result to guarantee the continual solvency of the public debt. In turn, the nominal result and the outstanding public sector debt are *merely indicative*, given [that] they suffer influence from a series of factors beyond the government's direct control.[31]

In practice, the government did more than this to attain the fiscal primary surpluses. In every Budgetary Directives Law for the years from 2001 to 2014, the goal was to maintain a surplus in the primary result—the most important according to the government statement quoted above—with an annual average

---

30 Brasil. "Lei complementar n. 101, de 4 de maio de 2000." Art. 4º, § 1º.
31 Brasil. "Lei n. 11.768, de 14 de agosto de 2008." Anexo IV; emphasis added.

for the federal government equivalent to 2.3% of GDP.[32] In contrast, in none of these years did this occur with the goals indicative of the nominal results, for which the forecasts were always for deficits.

It is certain that the goals for surpluses in the nominal results also serve the interests of finance. After all, once these goals are attained, all the commitments would have been paid. But governments rarely operate in fiscal equilibrium. Capitalism in general, and financial capitalism in particular, depend on fiscal deficits. If the conditions forecasted for the economy and for public finances indicate *nominal* deficits during preparation of the budget—the process of parliamentary discussion and negotiation, from the proposal of the bill by the executive branch until it is signed into a specific law that guides state spending—the goal of a *primary* fiscal surplus is one way to set aside a given flow of interest payments. This was precisely what took place, as shown in figure 13. During nearly the entire 1995–2015 period, the central government reached fiscal primary surpluses (at an annual average of 1.4% of GDP), which were outweighed, however, by the nominal interest on the public debt (which averaged 4% of GDP), leading to recurring nominal deficits (2.6% of GDP).[33]

We saw in the previous subsection that the period that began with implementation of the new currency, the *real*, is divided into two subperiods according to the respective means for inflation control. The change in monetary policy also revealed changes in fiscal policy. During the first subperiod (1995–1998), the primary results had averaged annual surpluses equivalent to 0.3% of GDP. In the following subperiod (1999–2015), this average rose to 1.6%, which took place to contain the advance of the public debt caused by increased interest. These increases, in turn, took place because of rises in the benchmark interest rate in the economy, which was adopted as a nominal anchor to the *real* soon after the collapse of the exchange rate pegging. As a result, the annual average of nominal interest on the federal public debt rose from 3% of GDP in the 1995–1998 period to 4.3% in 1999–2015.

The importance of the difference between the primary result and the nominal result is not merely an empiric issue, which in Brazil's economic situation was characterized by the maintenance of *primary* surpluses and *nominal* deficits. There is a relevant theoretical aspect here, which is that the very existence

---

32   For fiscal year 2015, the Budgetary Directives Law established a goal for a primary surplus that at the end of the year was converted into a deficit by an amendment to the original law (Brasil. "Lei n. 13.080, de 2 de janeiro de 2015"; "lei n. 13.199, de 3 de dezembro de 2015"). The federal government encompasses federal state-owned companies, the national treasury, the social security system, and the Central Bank.

33   The central government is comprised by the national treasury, the social security system, and the Central Bank.

of the concept of primary result makes it an instrument for favoring finance. To understand this issue, let's look at the public budget as an arena in which political agents are moved by interests that determine class struggles (O'Connor 2002). When the goal for primary fiscal results is a surplus, the state announces in advance that the corresponding portion in the fiscal budget will no longer be the object of dispute. In this case, the dispute has already taken place, and the winning class or fraction is already known. The difference between the concepts of nominal and primary fiscal results makes this point clearer. As I mentioned in the subsection on the delinking of federal revenues, the primary result is equal to the difference between non-financial revenues and non-financial expenditure. Thus, the reaching of a primary fiscal surplus means that total revenues have exceeded total expenditure, excluding the interest on public debt.

The existence itself of the concept of primary result also reveals a class option. Furthermore, it reveals the contradiction between the discourse of fiscal responsibility idealized in the Fiscal Responsibility Law and the actual state practice in the fiscal realm. At this point, the most that can be said of that law in terms of 'responsibility' is that it indicates towards *which classes* the fiscal management has been responsible. The combination of the primary fiscal surpluses and nominal fiscal deficits shows that the Brazilian state has been responsible from the perspective of finance. It is for this reason that demands on the composition of the budget in the name of fiscal responsibility are often political weapons that reflect the power of the strongest agents to defend the absolute levels they want by imposing compositional restrictions on weaker agents.[34] The primary fiscal result omits interest on the public debt from the political debate and creates a competition between classes over the rest of the economic surpluses collected by the state. The debate and dispute are thus restricted to the levels of the non-financial revenues—which are predominantly composed of taxes—and non-financial expenditures, in a movement towards a reduction in these expenditures and an increase in taxation.

The Fiscal Responsibility Law established a belief that Brazil had entered a phase of greater care for public finances because of the imposition of restrictions—and penalties as well—on governments in the execution of spending. In the words of Maria Loureiro and Fernando Abrucio (2004), the law inaugurated a political culture of fiscal responsibility and since its enactment, they add, it became more difficult for state officials to adopt populist and irresponsible fiscal practices. This, however, is an at least incomplete analysis, which is revealed by that which the government decided to tighten and

---

34 I owe this passage to Erik Olin Wright (personal correspondence).

that which it decided to loosen through the same law. In fact, the Fiscal Responsibility Law is manifestly biased about the type of spending to be limited and the type that cannot suffer any limitation. For example, it set explicit limits on spending for civil servants' salaries and benefits, and determined that mandatory spending of an ongoing character should be accompanied by a demonstration of the origin of the resources for this spending, which nevertheless "does not apply to spending on debt services."[35] That is, servicing the public debt, which is mandatory and has an ongoing character, does not depend upon the disclosure of the origin of the resources for the spending on debt.

The reality is that the state spends more than it collects in revenue, which, after all, is a feature of the capitalist state that appears to deepen in times of financialization. In Brazil, the state spent more than it collected in tax revenues to a large degree because of interest on public debt. Thus, fiscal responsibility has assumed a more rhetorical than factual character in light of its effects. These included a recurrent increase in taxes and the continual turn to debt. The declared objective of the Fiscal Responsibility Law to induce fiscal management committed to equilibrium in public finances was accompanied by the requirement that state agents obey the limits and conditions for public indebtedness. Although the law determined that the government should establish debt limits, they were only set for states and municipalities, while the federal government—which has been the largest debtor—faced no legal limit of this kind. In relation to the little that exists in the budget process in relation to the debt, the passage from the Budgetary Directives Law for 2009 mentioned previously makes clear that "the outstanding public sector debt [was] *merely indicative*."[36]

In this way, the ideology of fiscal responsibility legitimated the virtual establishment of goals for interest payments at the same time that it gave the impression that public finances were managed in an austere manner. The recurring nominal deficits and the growing public debt are evidence of this. Since the spending limit is basically determined by tax revenue plus the change in debt, if either of the latter two is increased accordingly, a rise in the spending limit would be virtually granted. Figure 14 displays some evidences that this is what took place during the time of 'fiscal responsibility.' The average federal tax revenue—not including social contributions for retirement and other pensions—which in 1990–1999, that is, before enactment of the Fiscal Responsibility Law, was equivalent to 11% of GDP, rose to 15% in 2000–2015. This took

---

35   Brasil. "Lei complementar n. 101, de 4 de maio de 2000." Art. 17, art. 19.
36   Brasil. "Lei n. 11.768, de 14 de agosto de 2008." Anexo IV; emphasis added.

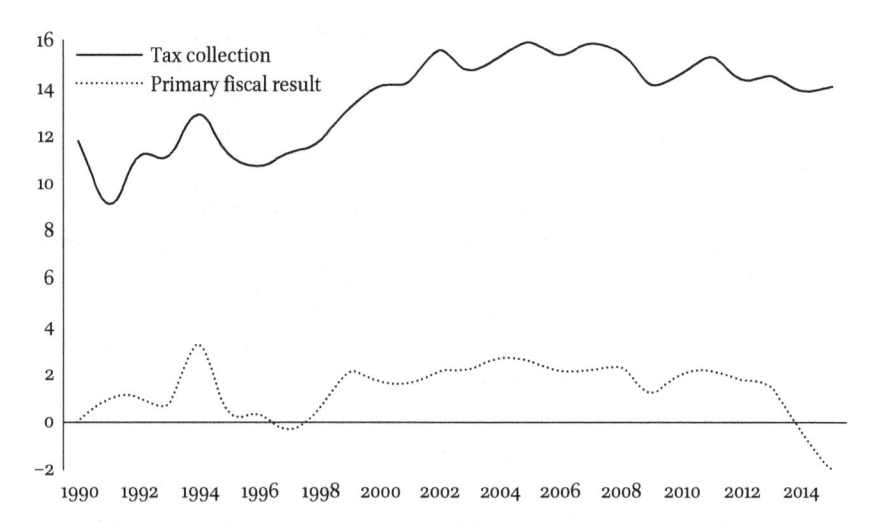

FIGURE 14 Tax collection and primary fiscal result, Brazil, 1990–2015
Notes: (i) percentages in relation to GDP; (ii) tax collection includes social contributions, except those for retirement and other pensions.

place largely to sustain the expansion in the primary fiscal surplus, whose average rose from 0.9% to 1.6% of GDP between these periods. Fiscal responsibility, in this sense, is behavior that is not restricted to limiting spending to tax revenues; it is also possible to be fiscally responsible by collecting in tax revenue the precise volume needed for a given volume of spending. Which route to take depends on the struggle that classes take in the fiscal arena.

For this reason, Jorge Garagorry (2007) was correct to affirm that the Fiscal Responsibility Law established a set of mechanisms designed to generate fiscal results aimed at payment of interest on public debt. This is revealed, Garagorry adds, by the imposition of limits and conditions on non-financial spending concomitantly to the prohibition on placing any limit on financial spending. This distinction between spending that *must* be and spending that *cannot* be limited also points out which classes or fractions either ceded or appropriated the economic surpluses levied by the state. More than revealing the class character of the state, the Fiscal Responsibility Law evidenced the privilege granted to the hegemonic fraction of capital in its stage of financial expansion.

The very text of the law reveals the effort made to avoid ambiguities concerning the priority for servicing the public debt. This appeared in a difference between the text of the bill as approved by the legislature and the final version signed into law by the executive branch. The legislature had proposed that "the budgetary directives law … [should] establish … a referential limit to the amount of expenses for interest, based on a percentage of the net current revenue." But this was vetoed by the Brazilian president at the time, who alleged that "the introduction of a limit on spending on interest, even as a reference, would be susceptible to the interpretation that the objective was the non-payment of interest, which presents a quite different character, if not one opposite to the tone of the ... law."[37]

Octavio Ianni (2004 [1989]) once made the fine observation that when the interests of big capital overwhelmingly predominate, the government does not dedicate itself to discoursing to public opinion, to the people. In the case of the Fiscal Responsibility Law, with the particular clarity made explicit in the veto mentioned, the government discourse was aimed at finance, which was then awarded a law that would not impose any limits on interest payments. In this way, the Fiscal Responsibility Law itself is evidence to supplant the incorrect notion that it sought to decrease political influence over fiscal issues. A law, like any decision of the state, is the result of the disputes that classes engage in over the potential results. Thus, its idealized universal character is empirically supplanted by the class character of capitalist society that is inescapably reproduced in the state apparatus and action.

---

37   Brasil. Presidência da República. "Mensagem n. 627, de 4 de maio de 2000."

institutional apparatus—law, sovereign risk, economic bureaucracy—assure finance profits, liquidity, and risks very often not available in the productive sectors of the economy.

1   The Financialization of Class Exploitation

The term class tends to steer our attention to the old Marxist distinction between the two fundamental classes of the capitalist mode of production: the owners of the means of production and those who own only their own labor-power. This route, however, expands due to the complexity that characterizes the contemporary class structure. While this phenomenon is not exclusive to current times, there is now a significant presence and relevance of other agents in the relationship between direct producers—workers—and capitalists. Bureaucrats, service providers, managers, consultants, scientists, financiers and a series of other non-productive agents—"productive … are all those who contribute in one way or another to the production of the commodity" (Marx 2000 [1863]: 156–157)—multiply as claimants to the surplus-value. In times of financialization, the class fraction formed by those who are neither owners of the means of production nor sell their own labor-power gains importance. They are those who own capital in the form of money who, through interest, appropriate a part of the surplus-value.

Max Weber (1964 [1922]), upon defining the property-owning class—that in which differences in property determine the class situation in a primary manner—indicated that the rentiers, including money lenders, were the favored portion of society, while the borrowers were within the disfavored portion. We cannot fail to observe that the Weberian concept is problematic, because, as Marx said (1990 [1890]), the roles of the lender or borrower result from the simple circulation of commodities. Thus, the notion of exploitation assumes a different nature, which Marx (1972 [1850]; 1991 [1894]) referred to as secondary exploitation.[1] Nevertheless, Marx himself also observed that "the class struggle in the ancient world … took the form mainly of a contest between debtors and creditors, and ended in Rome with the ruin of the plebeian debtors, who were replaced by slaves" (Marx 1990 [1890]: 233).

---

1   Despite the pejorative connotations of the term, the concept of capitalist exploitation refers only to the appropriation of surplus-labor of one class by another (Roemer 1982a, 1982c; Therborn 1999). Thus, the term exploitation is important not as an ethical category, but as an explanation for capitalist accumulation (Roemer 1982c).

But if that specific struggle remained in the past, struggles of another nature, which now take place in financial markets, have deepened. In this realm, important means for the appropriation of surpluses have developed, making these markets particular loci of class struggle. In Brazil, as we have seen in Chapter 1, much of the financial market developed along with the increase in the public debt, which, upon being converted from foreign to domestic, and from contractual to securitized, contributed to the financial expansion of the economy. Allied to this, the anti-inflationary fundamentalism and the search for foreign capitals provided finance opportunities to count on interest rates that were among the highest in the world. These were accompanied by sustained increases in the tax burden for the sake of an alleged fiscal responsibility, which actually served to support the growing spending on the debt servicing. This pointed to an approach to the relation between debtors and creditors as a class relation involving expropriation of surpluses produced by labor that, nevertheless, takes place beyond direct labor relations. It involves an *expropriation* that, however, can cause a rise in the rate of *exploitation* of others' labor.

According to classic Marxist thinking, capitalist exploitation is based on the relation between owners of the means of production and those who own only their own labor-power, who are both 'free' to meet in the labor market and establish contracts there. In a first moment, no exploitation takes place, and both capitalists and workers have the option to decide to accept or not the conditions of the contract. However, after the worker is hired, the relations move inside the point of production, where labor-power is converted into labor whose resulting value exceeds the value of this labor-power, which in turn gives origin to surplus-value. When the fruits of labor are exchanged for money in the commodity market, that surplus-value is realized as the profit of the capitalist, who thus appropriates in the form of money the relevant portion of the value of others' labor. In this sense, the entire capitalist process, including both production and circulation, indicates a concept of class based on the notion of exploitation, which takes place within a corresponding class structure.

In previous modes of production, slave masters exploited slaves and lords exploited serfs; in the current mode, capitalists exploit workers. Thus, although Marx recognized the existence of other classes, the fundamental distinction is between exploiter and exploited (Johnston and Dolowitz 1999). It is thus understood that social classes "are groupings of social agents, defined principally but not exclusively by their place in the production process, i.e. in the economic sphere" (Poulantzas 1978a: 14). Although it is in the point of production that the fundamental process of capital develops, the economic sphere must be understood in a broader sense. This sphere "includes not only production, but also the whole cycle of production-consumption-distribution" and, as such, encompasses all forms of capital: "productive capital, commodity capital, money capital" (Poulantzas 1978a: 18). This notion of production and of economic sphere in a broad sense also applies to the notion of class.

If we limit our analysis to the modes of production in the abstract, we see that in each of them there are two fundamental classes: masters and slaves in the slave mode of production; lords and serfs in the feudal mode; and the bourgeois and workers in the capitalist mode of production (Poulantzas 1973). However, in a concrete society, Poulantzas adds, the social formation involves more than two classes. Although these other classes may not be fundamental, they can assume a leading position in accumulation processes, depending on the historical conditions of capitalist development. This occurs because certain events can have a special relevance in the reproduction of capital, at least for some class or fraction of class in its pursuit of accumulation or, more precisely, to centralize capital in its hands. This is what took place, for example, under financialization of the economy, which led financial organizations and mechanisms, and their corresponding assets and debts, to reach levels that placed finance at the top of the hierarchy of those who earn profits (Duménil and Lévy 2011).

This reveals the importance of the fractions of class for understanding the current regime of accumulation. Bourgeois domination operates by means of an alliance between its fractions—industrial, commercial, financial—that are all dominant and share political power (Poulantzas 1973, 1978b). But this alliance, Poulantzas adds, can only function regularly under the hegemony of one of these fractions, which unifies the power of class under its leadership. It is broadly recognized that in the past approximately four decades this hegemony has been held by finance. This, as we have seen in Chapter 1,

> refer[s] to the upper fractions of capitalist classes and to financial institutions in any social arrangement in which these fractions of capitalist classes control financial institutions ... . Finance ... is not a separate industry. Instead, it combines class and institutional aspects.
> DUMÉNIL AND LÉVY 2011: 13

This very concept calls our attention to the possibility that the current hegemonic fraction and the related financial processes might alter the terms under which surpluses are generated and distributed, thus influencing the entire process of capitalist exploitation.

Exploitation means "that one category of economic agents works more than is necessary for their own reproduction and that the fruits of their surplus labour are appropriated by another" (Therborn 1999: 9–10). In an approach that highlights the relational character of exploitation, Erik Wright states that "the welfare of the exploiter depends upon the *effort* of the exploited" (Wright 2000: 10; emphasis in original). According to Wright, this notion of dependence is what distinguishes exploitation from oppression, given that exploitation involves a dependent relation of one social agent towards another, which does not occur in relations of oppression. The end of an oppressive relation does not impose any material loss on the oppressor, but the end of an exploitive relation imposes material loss on the exploiter. In this way, a coalition is exploited when the complementary coalition, that is, the exploiter, depends on the relation between them to earn its income (Roemer 1982c). This distinction is in some way present in Poulantzas's (1978a) framework for the structural determination of classes, which is brought about by relations of economic exploitation and also by relations of ideological and political domination.

The distinction that Erik Wright makes between oppression and exploitation is useful for understanding on an abstract level how the accumulation of capital occurs. For Poulantzas, these social relations appear in an integrative way, and thus serve an empiric need in the effort to understand the current regime of accumulation, to which finance has been organic to the entire accumulation process. As the hegemonic fraction of capital, finance imposes its own social logic on production. It is for this reason that the organization of work and relations of labor display a limited analytical framework, given that the extraction of value takes place by means of a variety of mechanisms internal or external to the point of production (Appelbaum, Batt, and Clark 2013). Therefore, both Wright's and Poulantzas's approaches allow an understanding of the exploitation process in a broader social scope. For example, they each allow considering the possibility that exploitation rates are influenced by developments that take place in the capitalist superstructure, such as the financial sphere, the state, or even through an association between them.

This does not mean that exploitation can occur without actual material production, but that it may have its terms altered by what takes place outside the point of production. As Bob Jessop recalls, "capital accumulation has major *extra-economic* conditions of existence in other social forms, institutions, organisations and social practices" (Jessop 2013: 7; emphasis in original). This is the case of the relations that develop in financial markets, where money operates as a commodity whose corresponding form of revenue is interest. They are extra-economic because "in the case of interest-bearing capital the return ... is simply the result of a *legal* transaction" (Marx 1991 [1894]: 470; emphasis added). This steers our attention to the role of the state and its economic apparatus in the process of financialization. As in the preceding Fordist regime of accumulation, the state once again assumed a central position in the corresponding mode of regulation.[2]

In the Fordist regime of growth, the main structures of contradictions were associated to wage relations and money forms, with the latter regulated through the steady expansion of both credit and state spending, and wage relations regulated through mass production and mass consumption reinforced by the Keynesian welfare state (Jessop 2013). In that regime, the state exercised strict regulation over finance—including the general supply of credit, interest rates, and financial operations—to create mechanisms aimed at full employment and to limit business-cycle fluctuations (Duménil and Lévy 2001). Later, under neoliberalism, the main role of the state became to create and maintain an institutional framework characterized by the strengthening of individual private property rights and promotion of free markets (Harvey 2005). Compared to Fordism, the regime of accumulation dominated by finance made money the most abstract expression of capital, disembedded in the space of worldwide flows; and portions of the social wage were privatized or reconverted into commodities, including private consumer credit (Jessop 2013).

Financialization thus expanded the relative importance of the circulation of money-capital, upon which restrictions were removed to facilitate the search for more profitable outlets throughout the world-system. Like money, debts and financial assets became central to the accumulation process, and inflation became a critical issue, given that it had been one of the mechanisms for distribution of the costs of both Fordism and the welfare state (Jessop 2013). Inflation control became a priority in the neoliberal era, conferring it a strong class character and, for this reason, more than an economic problem, it became a political question (Duménil and Lévy 2011; Krippner 2011). In the realm of monetary policy, finance was assured that inflation would not be tolerated (Papadatos 2013). The main result was that this class fraction of capital gained prominence in the appropriation of surplus-value, which came to take place mainly by means of revenue extracted from the income from labor in the form of interest.

---

[2] Mode of regulation is "an ensemble of norms, institutions, organisational forms, social networks, and patterns of conduct that can temporarily stabilise an accumulation regime through its *régulation-cum-governance* of specific structural forms despite the conflictual and antagonistic nature of capitalist social relations" (Jessop 2013: 8; emphasis in original).

2   Exploitation beyond Labor Exchange

In the previous section I called attention to means of activation of, or influence over, capitalist relations—including the distribution of the fruits of these relations—that are conducted in spaces that extend beyond the sphere of production. Given that capital only reproduces in motion (Harvey 2010), the sphere of circulation is essential to the analysis of the integral process of exploitation of others' labor. Yet the capitalist mode of production, unlike others, conceals the exploitation of direct producers. In feudalism, for example, the exploitation was clearly seen in the portion of production of the serf that was appropriated by the lord; in capitalism the product is not shared between capitalist and worker, but is rather taken to the market (Cohen 1979). There, a variety of relations can affect the division of surpluses, which, in addition to making the exploitation of others' labor less obvious, signals a potential rise in ulterior rates of exploitation. The fact that the output is taken to the market also adds processes of appropriation and agents who were previously absent.

According to Marx,

> the separation of sale and purchase makes possible not only commerce proper, but also numerous *pro forma* transactions, before the final exchange of commodities between producer and consumer takes place. It thus enables large numbers of parasites to invade the process of production and to take advantage of this separation.
>
> MARX 2010 [1859]: 334; emphasis in original

Due to a series of superstructural arrangements, these agents present themselves as recipients of portions of surplus-value to be redistributed through markets, including the financial one. The functioning capitalists who earn profits—industrialists and merchants—are joined by other unproductive agents, like the state, which collects taxes, by money capitalists, who earn interest, and by all sorts of professionals, bureaucrats, middlemen, and brokers who receive salaries, commissions, fees, etc. Rephrasing a proposition by Gerald Cohen about capitalist exploitation, it can be affirmed that "the proletarian produces the whole product, but the capitalist [and other unproductive agents appropriate] part of the value of the product" (Cohen 1979: 358).

This argument does not deny that the object of capitalist exploitation is the labor of others; it rather affirms that the terms of exploitation can be modified by relations that develop beyond those in the sphere of labor. This hypothesis was defended by John Roemer who argued that "even the Marxian class structure can be produced without any institution for labor exchange" (Roemer 1982b: 263). Moreover, he affirmed that even exploitation could take place without this institution. Roemer did not refute the idea that class exploitation is bound to labor, which he actually used as the criterion to distinguish exploiter from exploited. For Roemer (1982b, 1982c), the exploited is someone who works more than is socially necessary and the exploiter is someone who works less than is socially necessary. What Roemer sought to demonstrate was how exploitation could take place based on inequalities that were not necessarily related to the *sale* of labor-power. To make his point, he envisioned three hypothetical economies: a competitive market, where there would be unequal ownership of the means of production; a labor market; and a credit market.

For Roemer, all of his hypothetical economies would be capable of producing the Marxian class structure, even without the existence of the sale of labor-power. In the first, all the producers would work in their own facilities, all having the same needs, using the same technologies, and distinguished from each other only by their initial endowments. The latter characteristic would give to the richer the option to produce goods whose market value would allow them to work less time than the poorer ones. In this way, market conditions would create a structure of exploitation because they would force an agent to work more than socially necessary and allow the other to work less than this, even if no labor relation were established. The result would be an indirect appropriation of the fruits of the labor of others, mediated by the market. Roemer's second hypothetical economy—the labor market—differs from the previous solely by the existence of the option each producer has to buy or sell labor-power.

The third hypothetical market is especially important for one of the arguments of this section because it involves the social relation of debt. This type of economy—the credit market—would also be capable, according to Roemer, of producing the Marxian class structure even without the existence of the sale of labor-power. In this model, labor-power is substituted by capital to be loaned by the potential exploiter to the potentially exploited. These statuses of exploiter or exploited and their class positions are defined by means of interest on debt, which would allow the exploiter to work less and would require the exploited to work more than the socially necessary time.

Marx had made a similar analogy by saying "that money, and likewise commodities, are in themselves latent, potential capital, i.e. can be sold as capital; in this form they give control of the labour of others, give a claim to the appropriation of others' labour" (Marx 1991 [1894]: 477). Referring to what he called secondary exploitation in France of 1848–1850, he said that the exploitation [of peasants] differs only in *form* from the exploitation of the industrial proletariat. The exploiter is the same: *capital*. The individual capitalists exploit the individual peasants through *mortgages* and *usury*; the capitalist class exploits the peasant class through the *state taxes*.

MARX 1972 [1850]: 111; emphases in original[3]

Despite the controversies related to Roemer's approach, it is possible to note that the relations of exploitation can extend beyond the point of production (Dymski 1992).[4] This broadens the sociological meaning of exploitation by recognizing that it may have its terms altered by social phenomena that develop outside production, such as in the realm of financial markets. This idea appears when Bowles and Gintis (1990) criticize precisely Roemer's idealization of markets in equilibrium, which they affirm are all empirically improbable. Upon developing the concept of contested exchange, Samuel Bowles and Herbert Gintis affirm that transactions are contested in either labor or credit markets, that is, there are no guarantees that agents will fulfill the terms of the contracts. For example, even if a given amount of time to be devoted to work might have been contracted, the effective realization of its quantities and qualities cannot be guaranteed a priori. Similarly, although the conditions of a loan can be contracted, future actions of the debtor, or of others capable of influencing the probability of payment of the loan, cannot be guaranteed a priori.

It is thus perceived that financial markets, like any others, are not spaces in equilibrium. Moreover, they are spaces of class struggle. Therefore, individuals' class locations are not only defined according to social relations developed in production; they go farther, due to relations that also take place in financial markets (Williams 2001). Money capitalists, for example, in addition to possessing loanable capital, are capable of extracting extraordinary revenue through their positions relative to the financial system (Lapavitsas 2013). The critical point in this relation is interest on money, which is itself a commodity

---

3 "The working class is ... exploited by the petty trader who supplies the workers with means of subsistence. This is a *secondary* exploitation, which proceeds alongside the *original* exploitation that takes place directly within the production process itself" (Marx 1991 [1894]: 745; emphases added).
4 Roemer's model has been severely criticized by other Marxists. For Gary Dymski (1992), Roemer cast exploitation aside by dispensing with the notion of effort and basing himself entirely on the differentiation of the agent's ownership of productive assets. Michael Lebowitz (2005) went even farther by accusing Roemer of placing Marx's presuppositions within an anti-Marxist framework, namely that of methodological individualism.

circulating in this system. It must be emphasized that, in the same way that surplus-value does not come from the mere circulation of commodities—the origin of surplus-value is productive labor—it also cannot originate in the mere circulation of money-capital moved by debt. Nonetheless, interest on this debt serves to establish class relations that develop beyond the limits of the realm of direct production of surpluses.

In qualitative terms, interest is a mechanism for redistribution of surplus-value and can also be a monetary expression of additional effort to be carried out by workers. Interest is "nothing but a part of the profit, i.e. the surplus-value" (Marx 1991 [1894]: 493). It does not arise from objective conditions underlying the essential characteristic of capitalism—the separation between the owners of only their own labor-power and the owners of the means of production—but from the circumstance in which not only capitalists who run productive activities have access to money-capital (Hilferding 2006 [1910]). However, even if the capital that Marx (1991 [1894]: 732) characterized as interest-bearing "has capital's mode of exploitation without its mode of production," the fact that money is not only in the hands of the functioning capitalists allows finance, by feeding off others' labor, to interfere in employment, in wages, and in the forms of domination over labor (Salama 1998). In this sense, financialization has a clear class content established by its potential to deepen the exploitation of others' labor in a situation constructed to confront a regime of accumulation—Fordism—that had revealed its limits.

At the end of the 1970s, when capital accumulation experienced mediocre and precarious growth, capitalists found new sources of profits via financial markets (Lapavitsas 2013). This was made possible, in part, by stagnation or even retraction of real wages, including the social wage, which led workers to increasingly rely on borrowed money to meet basic needs for reproduction (Lapavitsas 2011; Santos 2013). This created opportunities for modes of *appropriation*—or expropriation—of surpluses that assumed a character of *exploitation* to the degree to which they developed through an organic relation between material production and finance. This character of exploitation by the part of finance also highlights the Marxian distinction between secondary and primary exploitation. Primary exploitation "involves the direct extraction of surplus labor" and secondary exploitation "occurs in distribution and exchange, and rests on capitalists property power alone" and can take on forms such as "housing rent, interest, dividends" (Dymski 1992: 295). The appropriation of surpluses via financial processes can thus engender a potential deepening of the rates of labor exploitation to the degree that workers are led to turn to borrowing to meet the insufficiency of their wages. This is the case of consumer or mortgage credit, whose exploitative social content is given by the fact that the respective "interest-payments are generally made from subsequent wage-receipts by borrowers" (Santos 2013: 94).

3 Public Debt, Taxation, and Redistribution of Surpluses

Expropriation or exploitation can involve different institutional arrangements according to the regime of accumulation. We saw that the potential exploitation inscribed in financial relations may take place in the very context in which workers are pushed into debt and to eventually transfer part of their wages to finance in the form of interest. In both the processes of exploitation, which takes place through labor relations, and of expropriation that takes place in debt relations, the parties are relatively visible to each other. Even if it is not possible to empirically determine the magnitudes involved, it is owners of the means of production who exploit waged workers, and it is creditors who expropriate debtors. At the level of class, owners and workers, creditors and debtors meet each other in their respective markets—namely of labor or of credit—and there they enter into contested exchanges. In their respective struggles, they see with reasonable clarity their class adversaries, towards whom they make their claims.

The factors that confer this class character to social relations in the financial sphere are present in another mechanism critical to financialization. This is public debt, which can also assume an exploitative character by demanding additional effort—materialized in interest—from the debtor. Nevertheless, there is a characteristic that singularizes the public debt as a mechanism that has potential to expand ulterior exploitation. This is the presence of the state in the relation. At the same time that the state's intermediary role reduces tensions between classes, this state's role contradictorily makes viable redistributions of surpluses between them. The state is responsible for the visible part of the decisions about who cedes and who appropriates, and those concerning the amounts redistributed through its intermediation. Therefore, these decisions take place without sufficient clarity about the place of each class in this process. When the state goes into debt, various versions about who benefits are plausible. It can be said that the borrowed monies will finance public goods and services that benefit society in general; or that they will be invested productively and thus generate jobs, growth, and more tax revenue.

Any of these discourses may or may not be true, but what is certain is that the state finances can connect expropriators and expropriated at the same time that, contradictorily, it hides one group from the other. This phenomenon raises an analytical challenge. Wealth, which had been more visible as it circulated in industry and commerce, now perhaps draws less attention by circulating in significant sums in the financial realm (Pinçon and Pinçon-Charlot 2007). In this dynamic, the public debt reveals the class character of the state. Committed to stabilizing social relations, the state also serves to reduce tensions in the type of social relation materialized by its debt. This takes place, however, in a subtle manner, without the need for adjudications like those that at times the state is led to issue about disputes between capitalists and workers or between private debtors and creditors.

We see in historical capitalism that the state has always performed mediating roles in the processes of accumulation. Since the welfare of one class takes place at the expense of another, the relation between them is necessarily conflictual (Johnston and Dolowitz 1999). Nevertheless, difficulties in identifying adversaries make the disputes more complex. It is thus up to the state apparatus to provide the material means to connect the classes "in an asymmetric relationship of domination and exploitation" (Therborn 2008 [1978]: 220). By doing so, it hides exploiter and exploited from each other, decreasing the chances of conflict. It thus performs the process of mediation that Göran Therborn (2008 [1978]) calls displacement or canalization, which designates the intervention by means of which the state is capable of displacing contradictions and disguising exploitation. One of the reasons that this is possible, Therborn affirms, is that the central position of the state frequently leads to supposing that it and its leaders do not know about the exploitation, nor are they immediately responsible for it. This has also been essential to the financial type of expropriation that has been taking place during neoliberal financialization.

In terms of capital accumulation, "the main achievements of neo-liberalism have been redistributive rather than generative" (Harvey 2006b: 43). Here arises the contradiction inscribed in the fact that the income redistribution from working people towards the ruling classes undermines the legitimacy of the redistributive system itself. Nevertheless, since the consequences of this contradiction require time to be revealed, until this takes place capitalists can continue to profit. In the regime of accumulation under the hegemony of finance, capital depends both on the legitimacy of the state and on the ambiguous position that the state occupies in relation to the classes that it connects. In terms of state legitimacy, to paraphrase Gramsci, the state contributes to having those who are exploited—or expropriated—consent to their condition. In terms of the state's ambiguous position, by being relatively autonomous from particular classes, it enjoys the legitimacy to present itself as an agent of the interests of the entire society in the redistribution of surpluses collected through taxation. The state therefore acts not only as a buffer of class conflicts generated by financial expropriation, but also supports the redistribution of surpluses. Let's examine how this functioned in Brazil beginning in the mid-1990s.

Neoliberalism raised taxation as one of its most important targets and, following the rhetoric that defends reducing the role of the state in the economy, advocated the reduction of taxes on property. The logic was that this would stimulate private investment—which neoliberals affirm is the most efficient type—that would consequently stimulate economic growth, leading to increased tax revenue. Yet tax reductions are not automatically converted into investments when capitalists are free to decide what to do with the retained surpluses, which can be steered to production, but can also simply be consumed (Przeworski 1985). Thus, Adam Przeworski adds, when tax reductions are not coordinated with systems of fiscal incentives that condition investment, the latter would be only one possibility, with the sole guarantee being the increase of the wealth available to the propertied classes. As Thomas Piketty (2014) showed, the countries at the center of capitalism that, between 1980 and when he wrote, made the steepest reductions in their top tax rates were also those where the top earner's share of national income increased the most.

This was one more neoliberal fallacy, which in practice meant a reduction of taxes for the most wealthy and an increase for the most poor, leading to a deepening of economic inequality. Moreover, the economic growth that would theoretically spring from reduced taxes on capital did not occur. While economic growth does not guarantee universal improvement in living conditions, a lack of it imposes even greater restrictions on the lower income classes. What is curious in this situation is that taxation in general was not reduced. According to Matías Vernengo (2007), globalization and what he calls the conservative revolution were only able to check the rate of growth of the state, but not reduce its size. Actually, if we take taxation as an indicator of the representativeness of the state to the economy, we reach the conclusion that the state's participation in this realm expanded. This was also true in Brazil. The point is for whom the tax burden changed and in what direction (I shall discuss this later).

Without the state's creditworthiness found in some central countries, and without sufficient military power to borrow money with lower restrictions from lenders, the Brazilian state had to offer, in addition to high interest, guarantees that it would be able to pay them back.[5] To do so, it assembled a fiscal

---

5 In a study conducted with managers of the largest U.S. investment funds with an international scope, Mosley (2006) concluded that they required from governments of emerging countries a much stricter observance of indicators of inflation, the fiscal situation, debt, labor regulations, and composition of state spending than they did in developed countries.

complex that guaranteed tax levels high enough to securely support the interest due on the public debt. The goals for primary fiscal surpluses became a part of this complex, which in practice guaranteed that substantial portions of tax revenue increases were steered towards creditors. The complex is as simple as that described by Marx in his study about primitive accumulation of capital, of which "the public debt [is] one of the most powerful levers" (Marx 1990 [1890]: 919). Since the debt is supported by state revenues, which must also cover the interest payments, "the modern system of taxation was the necessary complement of the system of national loans" (Marx 1990 [1890]: 921).

In Brazil, as figure 15 displays, there were increases of both public debt and the federal tax burden, which rose largely to support that debt. During most of the 1990s, its level was kept relatively stable, and federal tax collection was lower than in following years, which also had high debt levels. The annual average debt of the central government, which was equivalent to 26% of GDP in the 1991–1997 period, jumped to 51% in 1998–2002; the average federal tax revenue rose from 11% to more than 13% of GDP between these same periods. The latter period coincides with the eruption of various financial crises—in Southeast Asia, Russia, and in Brazil itself—that pushed the Brazilian government to raise interest rates and consequently spending on interest on the public debt (see figures 3 and 13). The level of indebtedness began to fall in 2003, and several years later, so did the level of taxation, movements that were interrupted in 2014–2015, when the Brazilian economy entered another crisis.

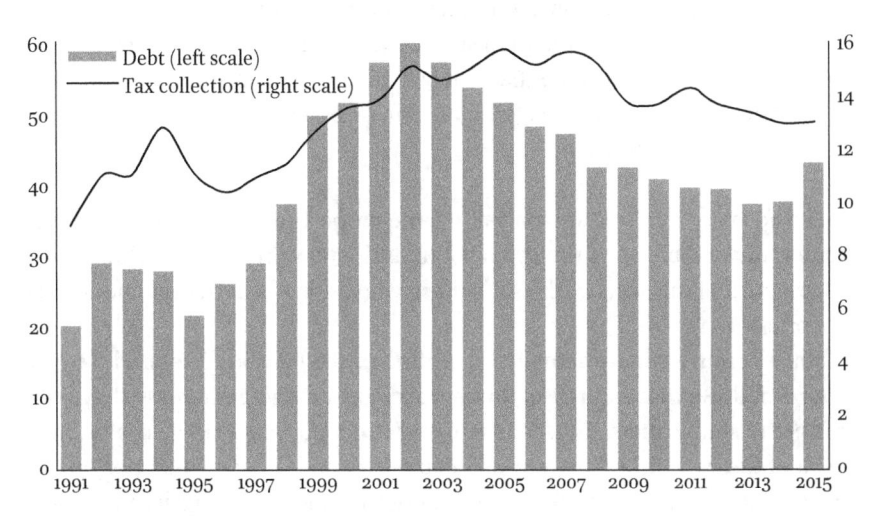

FIGURE 15   Public debt and tax collection, Brazil, 1991–2015
Notes: (i) percentages in relation to GDP; (ii) debt: monthly averages in each year of the outstanding domestic federal securitized debt held by the public plus gross external debt of the central government; (iii) tax collection includes social contributions, except those for retirement and other pensions.

This configuration guaranteed the sustainability of the public debt at levels suitable to both the state's capacity to service it and the need for the appreciation of money-capital loaned. From a fiscal perspective, both the debt and interest rates on it had to be low enough so that the debt services could be supported by the budget. From a class perspective, debt and interest had to be high enough to continue to nurture finance with satisfactory yields on the monies loaned to the state. This is why finance sought to sustain both fiscal deficit and public debt. Thus, the response is clear to the rhetorical question raised by Hall Wilson (2002): why would anyone give up charging extortive interest to an entity that cannot go bankrupt when all that is needed to perpetuate this situation is an outstanding debt high enough to not be significantly reduced by the instruments available to such an entity? Marx had already said that "*public credit* rests on confidence that the state will allow itself to be exploited by the wolves of finance" (Marx 1972 [1850]: 40; emphasis in original).

Taxes, like profits, interest, and rents, are forms of appropriation of surplus-value. All of them are means for capturing the values of surplus-labor, which assumes one or another form according to the role of each appropriator in the process of capitalist circulation. Marx also affirmed

> that the 'social need' which governs the principle of demand is basically conditioned by the relationship of the different classes and their respective economic positions; in the first place, therefore, particularly by the proportion between the total surplus-value and wages, and secondly, by the proportion between the various parts into which surplus-value itself is divided (profit, interest, ground-rent, taxes, etc.).
>
> MARX 1991 [1894]: 282

Thus, the tax or its abolition "only alters the proportion in which that surplus-value is divided between the capitalist himself and third persons" (Marx 1990 [1890]: 658). In this way, workers are those who always bear the economic burden of taxation.

Since surplus-value—actually the entire exchange-value—is produced by labor, it follows that capitalists do not carry any *actual* tax burden; they only *transfer* to state coffers, under the name of tax, a portion of that surplus. As a result of the struggle among workers, capitalists, and the state, that portion no longer belongs to the first two, at least until the following struggles take place in the fiscal realm. Nevertheless, it cannot be affirmed with certainty that taxes levied in the present are exclusively deductions from past profits, nor that these taxes cannot be deferred to future production cycles. Workers cannot put

FISCAL SUPERSTRUCTURE, EXPROPRIATION, AND EXPLOITATION 99

off their needs for reproduction, but individual capitalists can reallocate capital from present activities towards alternative outlets in the future. They might do this by steering money to financial assets to substitute productive investments they consider unsatisfactorily profitable in the present. Figure 16 shows a situation in which the changes correspond to this hypothesis.

In the period shown in figure 16, three phases can be distinguished based on changes in the gross fixed capital formation, which represents investment in production. A negative correlation is noted between gross fixed capital formation on one hand, and interest rate and public debt on the other. While fixed capital formation fell from an average of 18% in 1991–1998 to 16% in the 1999–2005 period, the domestic federal securitized debt increased from 14% to 41% of GDP, remaining a bit above this level during 2006–2014. In this last period, when the annual average of the real interest rate fell to 5.3%, compared with 10% in 1999–2005 and 22% in 1991–1998, gross fixed capital formation rose to nearly the same level as in the first period. In sum, when the interest rate rose, portions of potential investments in production were steered to what Marx called interest-bearing capital; inversely, investment in production increased when interest rates dropped.

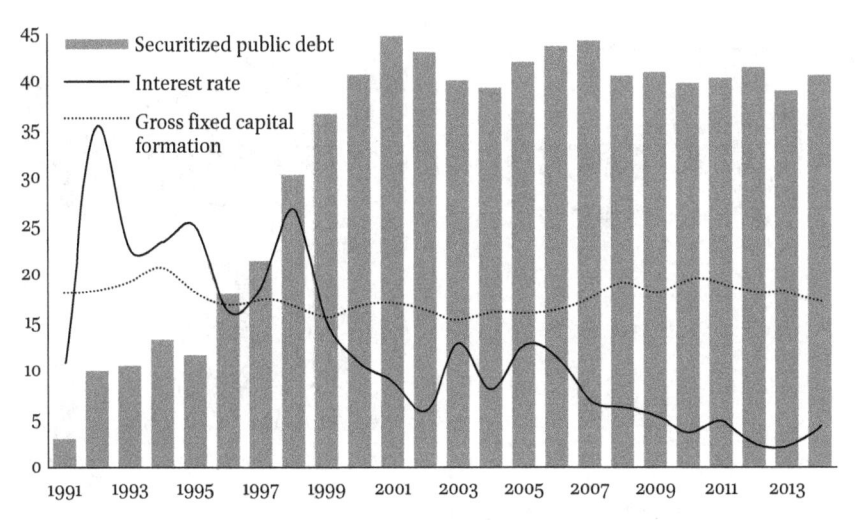

FIGURE 16   Securitized public debt, interest rate, and investment, Brazil, 1991–2014
Notes: (i) percentage scale; (ii) ex post real interbank interest rate; (iii) securitized debt: monthly averages in each year of outstanding domestic federal securitized debt in relation to GDP; (iv) gross fixed capital formation in relation to GDP, whose data were retrieved from the System of National Accounts reference 2000, in which 2014 is the last year in the series.

Taxes levied in the present can engender ulterior exploitation of others' labor to the degree that capitalists are able to defer the apparent tax burden to future production—we recall that capitalists just transfer a portion of surplus-value to state coffers. Even more clearly than displayed in figure 16, this takes place to the degree to which tax systems are regressive, that is, when the burden falls with greater intensity on those with lower incomes. As stated previously, the total tax burden is ultimately levied on workers, but there always exists the possibility that this burden be expanded through changes in the tax structure. When indirect taxes like those on workers' consumption are a larger portion of total revenues than direct taxes, the working class supports a burden heavier than that supposedly levied on capital. This actually involves a movement that concentrates either income or wealth in two manners, because while waged laborers transform nearly all their income into consumption, the propertied classes retain a portion of theirs to increase capital, which is the source of this same income (Furtado 2007 [1959]).

Figure 17 shows that indirect taxation in Brazil was significantly higher than direct taxes and contributions, which are those levied mainly on income and property. While the annual average of indirect taxes increased 2.1 percentage

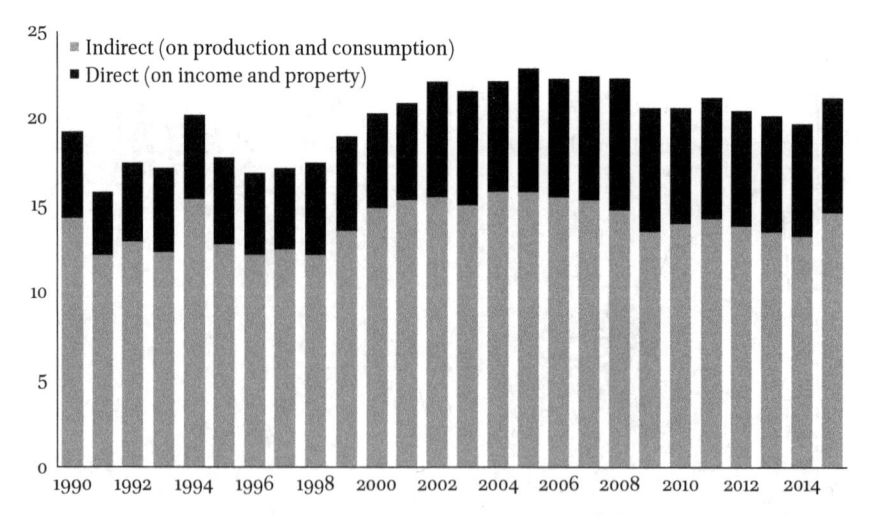

FIGURE 17 Indirect and direct taxes, Brazil, 1990–2015
Notes: (i) percentages in relation to GDP of total revenue from federal taxes and social contributions, not including those for retirement and other pensions, plus countrywide total state sales tax (ICMS in its Portuguese initials); (ii) these taxes averaged approximately 85% of total taxes and social contributions, except those for retirement and other pensions, from all levels of government during the 2002–2009 period (Gobetti and Orair 2010).

points (from 13% to 15.1%) in relation to GDP between the 1990–1998 and 1999–2005 periods, direct taxes increased 1.4 percentage points (from 4.7% to 6.1%). After 2006 the trend reversed. Between the periods 1999–2005 and 2006–2015, the average of indirect taxation fell 0.9 percentage points while direct taxes increased 0.7 percentage points in relation to GDP.

I will not advance much farther on this path to avoid differentiating taxpayers by how much they 'pay'—or how much they transfer to the state—in taxes, which contradicts the fundamental argument that the working class effectively bears the entire burden. This contradiction can be found precisely in the example of indirect compared to direct taxation just analyzed. Nevertheless, I understand that any possible mistake in this analysis is not so serious if we consider that the portion of surplus-value collected through direct taxes affects the propertied classes more than the productive ones, namely workers. Inversely, more workers than capitalists cede surplus-value through indirect taxes, such as those on consumption. This is why it is important to investigate who cedes, how much they cede, and who appropriates the fraction of surplus-value redistributed due to a given tax structure.

Beyond the subtleties subjacent to the differences between direct and indirect taxation, there are measures that eventually grant advantages to the classes that earn interest. This is not to say that the state acts in a totally discretionary manner, with the explicit objective of favoring one class fraction or another. There are apparently technical reasons for fiscal policies, as in the case of regressive tax increases aimed at preventing capital flight (Pastor Jr. and Dymski 1991). However, this does not eliminate the fact that the advantages are held by the propertied classes, and if they are not exclusively guaranteed by state actions, they are by class relations, which includes those of the state. Another measure that can expand tax regressiveness includes fiscal incentives to finance, of which I will mention one significant example.

In February 2006, by means of a provisional decree, which was converted into law in June of the same year, the Brazilian government "reduced to zero the income tax rate on earnings ... produced by public securities ... paid, credited, delivered or remitted to a beneficiary resident or living abroad."[6] The same measure also reduced to zero the tax rate on financial transactions (CPMF in its Portuguese initials) then due on stock purchases. Even if at that time

---

6   Brasil. "Medida provisória n. 281, de 15 de fevereiro de 2006." Art. 1º; "lei n. 11.312, de 27 de junho de 2006." Art. 1º. In Portuguese, the term used for such a 'provisional decree' is medida provisória, which is issued by the president of the republic and has the strength of a law until it is reviewed by the legislature.

there was no pressing need to confront threats of capital flight—although such measures had been taken recently before that, by offering higher interest rates—the practical effect expected was similar, because the elimination of those taxes sought to attract additional foreign financial capitals. According to the state discourse, the measure did not favor a particular class, because it envisioned universal benefits. The justifications presented by the incumbent minister of finance upon presenting the concession of tax exemptions took the same line. He affirmed that

> the possibility of increasing the participation of non-resident investors could result in important benefits in the administration of the federal public debt and in saving in spending on interest. This is because the greater participation of foreign investors can help to decrease the perception of risk associated to debt and thus to decrease the premium paid by the national treasury when issuing its securities. ...
>
> The improvement in the profile of the public debt, as is well known, has the potential to induce positive implications in various areas, including in the productive sector. The lower financial volatility and the expansion of the effects of monetary policy, which can come from the measure, are only the most direct effects. The improvement tends to be transmitted to the entire fixed-income market, favoring a drop in costs, an increase in maturity and the expansion of the opportunities for private companies to raise funds. The reduced cost of the productive investment is an important ingredient for the creation of jobs, the increase of income, and economic growth.
>
> In the medium-term, with the strengthening of the capital market, it can be expected that households will expand their access to credit, particularly medium- and long-term credit—as is the case with the residential loan—leading to an increase in the level of social well-being.[7]

I would not dare to evaluate these outlooks since it is virtually impossible to know whether they were fulfilled or not; it is even harder to know if any eventual result was caused exactly by the very measures that the outlooks had served as a justification for. Nevertheless, it is important to emphasize at least one point. According to the justifications given by the government, it forecasted for the year 2006 a reduction of interest spending of approximately

---

7 Brasil. Ministério da Fazenda. "[Exposição de motivos] EM n. 00017/2006 – MF." 14 de fevereiro de 2006.

1.2 billion Brazilian *reais* and tax exemptions of about 152 million *reais*.[8] The point is that the exemptions were enacted—the law was signed—while the reduction of interest was only a hypothesis. This hypothetical character of the reduction in interest expenses indicates the continuity of the dispute for the surpluses appropriated by the state.

It is important to note that, due to the tax exemptions, part of the dispute was momentarily resolved by the law's determination of who would not 'pay' a given amount of income tax. According to the minister of finance "the cost of implementation [of the provisional decree would be] compensated by the increased revenue ... resulting from the expansion of the tax base ... beyond that initially forecasted for 2006."[9] In Marxist terms, it could be supported by the increase in the rate of surplus-value brought about by increased taxes. In the next section I discuss how the rise in the rate of surplus-value can take place in more structural terms.

4 Public Debt and the Rise in the Rate of Exploitation

Taxation has always been critical to the superstructure of capitalism but became even more relevant with the advent of neoliberal financialization. Governments, as well as businesses and households, have been thoroughly financialized to the degree that finance became able to create and market legal claims to portions of all sorts of future income flows, including those from taxes (Radice 2010). Joint efforts by state and finance led to the creation of financial mechanisms that combined with the tax system in an organic complex of expropriation and exploitation of the labor of others. Thus, beyond taxation as a form of redistribution of surplus-value, I now raise the hypothesis that taxation can increase the very magnitude of ulterior surplus-value. I follow the track signaled by Göran Therborn (2008 [1978]) who indicates that, in the dynamics of any specific mode of production, the working class has to generate surpluses for its exploiters and *additionally* fund the state's domination over the working class itself.

For Erik Olin Wright (1999), due to the weight of the legitimacy of the state, it is reasonable to suppose that the working class might accept a level of taxation on wages higher than the corresponding wage cut that would otherwise

---

[8] Brasil. Ministério da Fazenda. "[Exposição de motivos] EM n. 00017/2006 – MF." 14 de fevereiro de 2006.
[9] Brasil. Ministério da Fazenda. "[Exposição de motivos] EM n. 00017/2006 – MF." 14 de fevereiro de 2006.

occur in a hypothetical context in which these taxes did not exist. One of the explanations for this would be that, "owing to the distance of the state from … the immediate exploitative process …, it is usually easier to increase the amount extracted for 'public' purposes than it is directly to raise the profits of individual members of the ruling class" (Therborn 2008 [1978]: 227). For this reason, "a rise in taxation has tended to encounter less resistance than rent increases or wage-cuts" (Therborn 2008 [1978]: 227). If this argument is correct, "taxation can thus be seen as, in part, a weapon in the class struggle by which the state appropriates a certain amount of surplus labor that is *unavailable* to private capitalists" (Wright 1999: 129; emphasis in original).

Wright thus opposes the thesis that capitalists would invariably appropriate the presumable amount of tax that might be dispensed in a hypothetical situation without taxation, that is, that in this case capitalists would already have reduced wages to the minimum required for the reproduction of labor-power. For Wright, this reasoning is at best dubious if real wages and taxes are seen, at least partially, as results of class struggle instead of results of extraction of a part of a wage supposedly higher than that necessary for the reproduction of labor-power. To summarize, "taxation … has the capacity to increase the aggregate rate of surplus value" (Wright 1999: 129). In this way, Wright affirms that exploitation also takes place in the sphere of circulation, as do John Roemer and other scholars. Costas Lapavitsas, for example, uses the term "financial expropriation" to "[avoid] confusion with exploitation at the point of production," but he also warns that "this does not preclude the existence of exploitative processes in circulation" (Lapavitsas 2013: 33).

Considering the legitimacy that the state has to tax, it is reasonable to suppose that it also has legitimacy to steer to the exploiters—in the form of interest, for example—part of the surplus-value garnered. Through taxation, the state indicates potential rises in the rate of surplus-value, which can occur to the degree that the public debt is capable of leading to rises in the level of taxation itself. The ability to borrow can increase the power of taxation if we consider that when the state goes into debt, it is effectively collecting the amount correspondent to spending that exceeds total tax revenue. In the same sense that "interest-payments are generally made from subsequent wage[s]" received by workers who were led to substitute credit for wage insufficiencies (Santos 2013: 94), tax increases to be used to pay interest on the public debt can also have an exploitative character. These increases can alter the terms of labor relations in ulterior production processes, raising the rate of exploitation to recover a certain profit level expected to be reduced—or that was already reduced—by taxation.

Increasing taxes is one of the options available to the state to finance its spending, in addition to issuing money or taking loans. The latter is politically cheaper than raising taxes, which tends to encounter resistance from taxpayers. Of course, borrowing money will lead to increased taxes in the future, but by taking a loan the government garners extraordinary resources without taxpayers immediately sensing this (Marx 1990 [1890]). Printing money, given the potential inflationary effects, is no longer a common practice, particularly since monetarist theory became politically relevant. The adoption of one or another, or a combination of financing alternatives would depend on the correlations of forces between those who dispute space to influence economic policies. This is a class relation whose contradiction is revealed in the doubt about to what extent the satisfaction that the state gives to the lenders of the public debt compromises satisfying the concerns of taxpayers (Moore 2004).

The public debt is not only a temporary substitute for taxes that cannot be collected in the present. It signals a real increase in taxation in the magnitude of the real interest to be paid. There are certainly alternatives, like reducing spending, printing money or borrowing, as we have seen, but they are not mutually exclusive. Nonetheless, no source of state revenue, not even the most efficient tax system, has the capacity that borrowing does to quickly raise large sums of money (Moore 2004). In Brazil, as figure 18 shows, the increases in federal tax collection since the Real Plan were generally exceeded by nominal fiscal deficits, that is, by needs for financing through borrowing. While the annual average increase in federal tax revenue was equivalent to 1.6% of GDP in the 1995–2015 period—the only year with a reduction was 2009—the annual average of the nominal fiscal deficits was 2.7% of GDP. In sum, borrowing was by far the state's most effective means for obtaining extra funds.

Tax increases most often depend on parliamentary approval, and when they occur do not always produce immediate effects, as in the cases in which constitutional rules establish a time lag for them to be charged. This does not apply to borrowing, which the executive branch in Brazil has the discretion to undertake. This combines with a false debate about the magnitude of the tax burden, in which the hegemonic opinions are generally that it is very high and should stop growing or even decrease. Capitalists and workers united around this idea, based on the belief that lower taxes would lead to both higher wages and higher profits, which would come from a supposed economic growth. However, to say that the tax burden is high, without the necessary qualifications, tends to hide one class from the other.

When we analyze the public debt considering the interest and tax revenue to support this interest, an important sociological implication arises from this

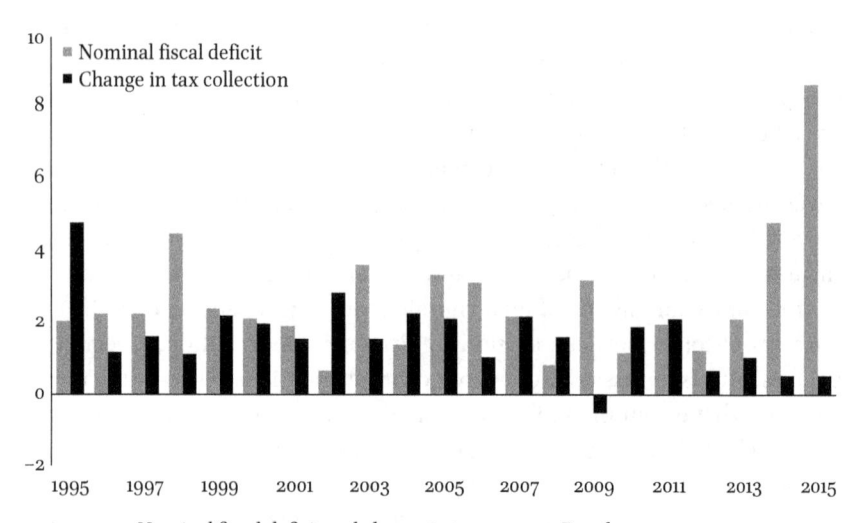

FIGURE 18 Nominal fiscal deficit and change in tax revenue, Brazil, 1995–2015
Notes: (i) percentages in relation to GDP; (ii) changes in total revenue from federal taxes and social contributions, not including those for retirement and other pensions; (iii) deficits, as such, could correctly be shown as negative numbers in the scale, but are displayed in absolute values to allow visual comparison to changes in tax collection, most of which were positive.

dynamic. As in the allocation of resources collected through taxation, debt exercises a similar function when it allows the transfer of surpluses through interest. In a situation of increasing interest concomitant with a rising tax burden, it is reasonable to suppose that the latter occurs to some degree to accompany the higher interest. Moreover, the interest on the debt functions as a sort of tax on workers, and simultaneously as a negative tax for the class of appropriators composed of bondholders. It is this aspect that leads to the need for greater clarification of the apparent unanimity about whether taxes are high or low. From a perspective of classes, it is not possible to think of *the* tax burden, but of tax *burdens*. For this reason, we must always ask: are the tax burdens high or low for *whom*?

It is symptomatic that even within the business class, which we may suppose is unified in the struggle for lower taxes, there is not a consensus about this issue. As Therborn (2008 [1978]) recalls, taxation, like other state forms of extraction, is a source of dispute both between classes and within the ruling class. In periods of financialization, this is revealed by at times conflicting positions between industry and finance. For those who accumulate capital by means of material production, taxes tend to be seen as an obstacle to investment and to their potential profits; for those who appropriate surplus-value and centralize money-capital through interest, the defense of reductions in the tax burden tends to be less emphatic. An example of this was seen in 2007 when the Brazilian Senate was discussing a proposal to prolong the tax on financial transactions, which had been scheduled to be extinguished in the following year. Defending the termination of the tax, the then president of the Federation of Industries of the State of São Paulo affirmed that

> the tax reform proposals being discussed do not mention tax reductions; so our only chance to have reductions is to comply with the law and the Constitution and do away with the [tax on financial transactions] on December 31, 2007, opening the door for the tax reform, but reducing taxes ... at a time when Brazilian society does not accept, under any hypothesis, additional increases in the tax burden ... Therefore, [committee] chair ..., senators, here is an appeal from the Brazilian society: let's do away with this.[10]

Meanwhile, the president of the National Confederation of Financial Institutions, who at the time was representing the president of the Brazilian Federation of Banks, was more restrained. While stating that he considered as valid the data and arguments used by the industrialist to defend the extinction of the tax and to assure that the government budget would be able to support such a loss in revenue, the banker's proposal was similar to that defended by the government, which was to maintain the tax. Referring primarily to the argument of the representative of São Paulo industry, the representative of finance stated that

> this is all unquestionable; I have no corrections to make ... but we live in a world that has many twists, changes occur, and we thus need to act with a certain prudence ... I think that prudence would recommend that, even with all of the defects that the [tax on financial transactions] has, it could continue ... but clearly with a trajectory towards reduction.

A bit earlier, the banker had said that

---

10   This statement and the two following ones were recorded in audio by the author during the meeting of the Brazilian Senate Committee of Constitution, Justice and Citizenship on October 31, 2007. The Committee was then holding the second public hearing concerning the instructions for proposed constitutional amendment n. 89, which originally sought to prolong both the Delinking of Federal Revenues and the tax on financial transactions.

> the reduction of the tax burden ... could spark potential growth in the Brazilian economy because private investments would be stimulated ... Therefore, some suggestions that I make here to you ... would be that the prolongation of the [tax on financial transactions] should be accompanied by a commitment, to a consistent trend towards reducing the taxation, or to a reduction of the [tax on financial transactions] itself. Thus, we could ... with the hypothesis of making a gradual reduction ... in taxation ... terminate, at the end of a period of six or seven years, with a residual rate.

We saw previously that the Brazilian tax structure is more burdensome for the working classes than for the propertied ones because indirect taxation is higher than direct taxation (see figure 17). But this regressive character is not confined to the tax realm and can be extended to the broad scope of the fiscal structure. In the period being analyzed, the Brazilian state operated a complex of redistribution of surpluses that, by combining taxation and public debt, became even more regressive than the tax system on its own. This hypothesis had already been raised by Marcelo Medeiros (2003), for whom it would not be an exaggeration to affirm that the Brazilian state favors the rich. According to Medeiros, this is due to the regressive character of state spending, mainly that not regulated by any legislation of an egalitarian character, such as that concerning social spending. Meanwhile, financial spending, which was among the highest portions of the federal budget and was appropriated by a minority, made the state an agent that deepened the inequalities in favor of the wealthy, Medeiros concluded.

Figure 19 presents evidences of what I call the regressive fiscal structure, which resulted from a specific and class-referred combination of taxes and interest on the public debt. It also reveals that federal tax revenue did not grow to the degree that an aggregated analysis—that is, one that does not consider *who* supports the burden—would indicate. Beyond the fact that capitalists effectively do not *bear* any actual tax burden—they only *transfer* this portion of surplus-value to state coffers—the amounts that they effectively delivered to the state might have been even lower than is claimed to have been paid.

During the 1995–2015 period, total gross federal taxation corresponded on average to 13.5% of GDP, a ratio that falls to 9.5% after subtracting from total taxes interest on the public debt, which in fact functions as a negative tax. Considering only direct taxes on income and property, these indices represented 6.2% and 2.2% of GDP respectively. The difference between gross taxation and net taxation was 4% of GDP, which is how much interest on the public debt represented on average during this period. It turns out that interest works

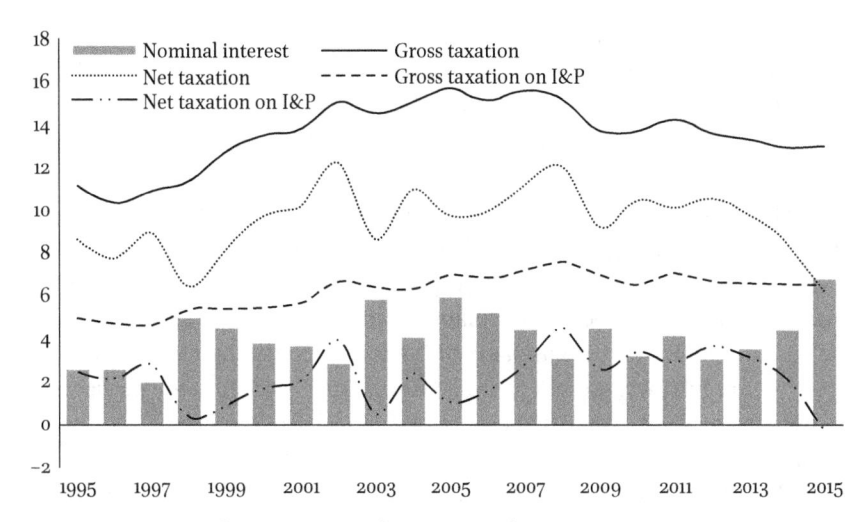

FIGURE 19 Gross and net taxations, and interest, Brazil, 1995–2015
Notes: (i) percentages in relation to GDP; (ii) total revenue from federal taxes and social contributions, not including those for retirement and other pensions; (iii) I&P refers to income and property.

as a negative tax on capital, since the state returns it to the very class that holds public debt securities. As interest is paid to bondholders who also 'pay' taxes on income—including on the income from this interest—finance was the class fraction that received the greatest fiscal benefit.[11]

Figure 19 also shows that the net taxation—gross taxation minus interest—changed more significantly in moments of crisis. This reinforces the thesis that crises tend to create opportunities for the propertied classes to increase their earnings. In 1998, a year of currency crises; in 2003, the first year of the leftist Lula government; and in 2015, a year of deepening of the economic and political crises that led to the toppling of the Dilma government, there was a pattern related to what I call the debt-taxation-finance nexus. In those years, there was nearly no aggregate net taxation on income, property, and capital gains due to the interest on public debt that the state paid to finance. The financial crisis of 2008, whose deepest consequences were observed in 2009, also had a result compatible with this hypothesis, because it interrupted the trend of rising net taxation on income, property, and capital gains that had begun in 2005.

---

11 During the 2000–2015 period, investment funds, banks, and other financial companies held an average of nearly 90% of the domestic federal public debt bonds, and non-financial companies and individuals held approximately 10%.

When recognizing that interest on the public debt is a negative tax; and that this tax is negative for the propertied classes; and mainly when we recall that the effective tax—that which sustains state spending—originates from the productive classes, the complex of public debt and taxation reveals its potential to raise the rate of exploitation of the labor of others. But this expansion in exploitation does not occur as a compression of the socially necessary labor and the corresponding expansion of the surplus labor carried out in an already concluded production process. The expansion rather takes place through the class struggle in the sphere of circulation, which nevertheless signals a potential rise in the rate of surplus-value in the future. It may be higher—or even lower—not only because of economic factors sensu stricto—the production of exchange-values—but also because of political aspects related to disputes between classes in which the state is the main intermediary.

In Brazil, macroeconomic policies, especially fiscal and monetary ones, have followed a global pattern of favoring finance capital in detriment to the working classes. As we saw in Chapter 1, the first objective of the neoliberal prescriptions was not to redistribute income or wealth, at least not from the wealthy towards the poor. Precisely the opposite was seen. Even so, the essential lines of neoliberal credo reached Brazil as a solution to the country's economic backwardness. This marked what in late 1994 the then recently elected and future president of Brazil claimed would be a break with the Vargas era.[12] On the eve of assuming the presidency, then Senator Fernando Henrique Cardoso stated that

> a part of our past policy remains that still obstructs the present and delays the advance of society. I refer to the legacy of the Vargas era—to its autarchic development model and its interventionist state. This model, which in its time assured progress and allowed our industrialization, began to lose steam in the late 1970s. We crossed the 1980s blind, without realizing that the conjunctural problems that tormented us—the fallout from the oil and foreign interest crises, the decadence of the authoritarian regime, the hyperinflation—disguised the symptoms of the structural depletion of the Vargas development model.[13]

---

12   Getúlio Vargas was Brazil's president from 1930–1945 and from 1951–1954, when the country experienced important economic transformations towards industrialization under government guidance.
13   Fernando Henrique Cardoso. *Diário do Congresso Nacional*. Seção II, ano XLIX, n. 160. 15 de dezembro de 1994: 9187.

This meant that the economic growth model anchored by direct action of the state should give way to a model that would supposedly let market agents lead the process. The belief was that macroeconomic stability and Brazilian integration to the world economy, through deepening of the commercial and financial openings, privatizations, termination of state monopolies, floating exchange rate, inter alia, would lead to economic growth and development. Nevertheless, considering what was seen since then, the alleged break with the Vargas era led to contradictory results in terms of development. The average annual real growth in GDP per capita, which had been nearly 4% in the 1931–1980 period, and virtually zero in 1981–1994, was only a bit more than 1.6% in the 1995–2013 period.[14]

As we saw previously, it was in this last period that finance rose to the top of the hierarchy of appropriation of economic surpluses, which was made possible by high real interest rates. These rates led to financial profits at the expense of reduced profits in production, compromising wages and thus raising the rate of labor exploitation (Oliveira 2006). According to Armando Boito (2007), this was the reality observed in Brazilian industry since the mid-1990s. It is clear that finance is organic to the process of capitalist accumulation, which, by encompassing the state, also affects the complex formed by public debt and taxation. Thus, this tax-debt complex allows raising the rate of exploitation of labor in a form similar to what private credit does in the context of financialization of workers' incomes.

It is difficult to empirically grasp the capacity of the complex formed by public debt and taxation to raise the rate of exploitation, which is a hypothesis that, until here, I have discussed in abstract terms. We are not able to specify how much of the surplus redistributed refers to socially necessary labor, how much refers to surplus labor, and mainly, how much the latter could have been expanded in ulterior production cycles. Nevertheless, if it is correct to assume that taxation itself can raise the rate of ulterior exploitation, even if it is not possible to determine precisely by how much, at least the general trend can be grasped. In Brazil, after the launching of the Real Plan, in the mid-1990s, for nearly a decade there was an expansion in favor of capital in the gap between capital's and labor's share in the appropriation of the total output, as displayed in figure 20. This supports the claim that, "judged by its own class objectives, neoliberalism was an unquestionable success" (Duménil and Lévy 2011: 25).

---

14   Any data presented in this chapter with no source reference are based on the author's calculations from standard databases. Technical aspects or sources not made explicit will be communicated upon request.

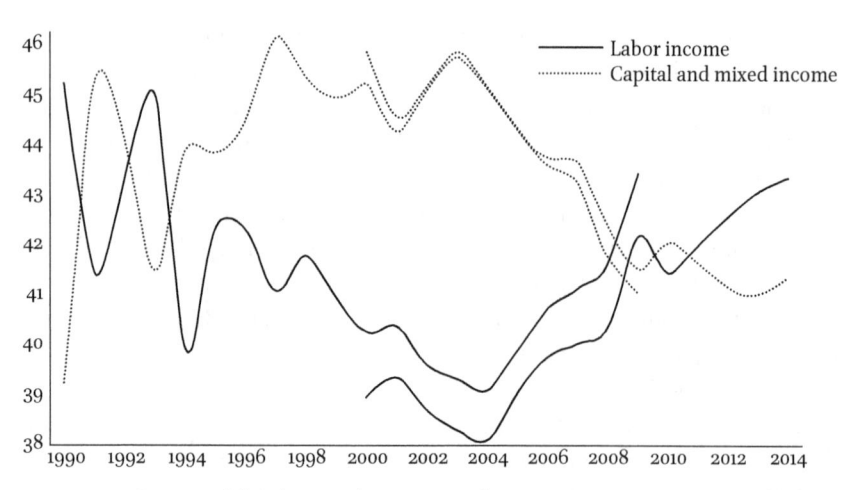

FIGURE 20 Functional distribution of income, Brazil, 1990–2014
Notes: (i) percentages in relation to GDP; (ii) not considering taxes on production and imports, which represented and annual average of some 15% of GDP in the period; (iii) the lines that begin in 1990 correspond to data from the System of National Accounts reference 2000, and those that begin in 2000 are based on data from the System of National Accounts reference 2010; (iv) Labor income comprises wages or salaries and related mandatory social contributions; (v) Capital and mixed income comprise profits, dividends, rents, interest, other capital gains, and mixed income, which is that not identifiable as arising exclusively from labor or capital.

Figure 20 shows that in the first years of the 1990s labor and capital alternated in terms of which class appropriated the largest portion of output, represented by GDP. After the launching of the Real Plan (1994), this did not occur again until 2008. During the 1994–2008 period, the income of property-owners and mixed income combined exceeded labor's share by an annual average of 3.8% of GDP (or 5.3% in the 2000–2008 period if one considers the GDP data in the System of National Accounts reference 2010). I emphasize that interest on the public debt, which is eventually transformed into income to money capitalists, averaged 4% of GDP in the 1995–2008 period (see figure 13). Declines in labor income and systematically high real interest to some degree signified the rise of the rate of exploitation of others' labor through finance. This whole movement confirms Samir Amin's (2008) analysis of how high interest rates and oligopolistic financial markets have allowed finance to appropriate significant portions of value—roughly GDP minus labor income—in the last several decades.

This phenomenon cannot be totally explained by the joint increases in interest and taxation that occurred with the financial expansion of the Brazilian economy, but these increases have a share in the explanation. In situations of

FISCAL SUPERSTRUCTURE, EXPROPRIATION, AND EXPLOITATION   113

rising interest rates, agents seek to adapt their decisions. Companies, for example, require higher returns on investments and seek these returns in shorter time periods (Krippner 2011). To attain this, they tend to increase pressure placed on labor to be able to extract profits not only at the rates sought by functioning capitalists; profit rates must now be high enough so that an additional portion can be appropriated by finance. Even if functioning capitalists do not steer money-capital to financial assets, they rely, to some degree, on finance to activate production. In addition, given that interest rates tend to function as the opportunity cost for both capital invested in production and capital steered to financial assets, any rise in interest rates will increase the profitability expected from material production. The way in which functioning capitalists seek to reach this objective is by making labor-power cheaper. And, as Marx explained, "the worker becomes an ever cheaper commodity the more commodities he creates" (Marx 1973 [1844]: 107).

As shown in figure 21, productivity of labor in Brazilian industry, measured through the ratio of industrial sales to hours worked, rose consistently throughout the period analyzed. We can see that these revenues grew at considerably accelerated pace in relation to the amount of hours worked. While working-hours declined by 22%, sales revenue rose 93% from the beginning to the end of the series, peaking, however, above 115% in 2013, when there already were signs of the crises that culminated in the ousting of the Dilma government. A similar trend had been found by Pastor and Dymski (1991) who noted a

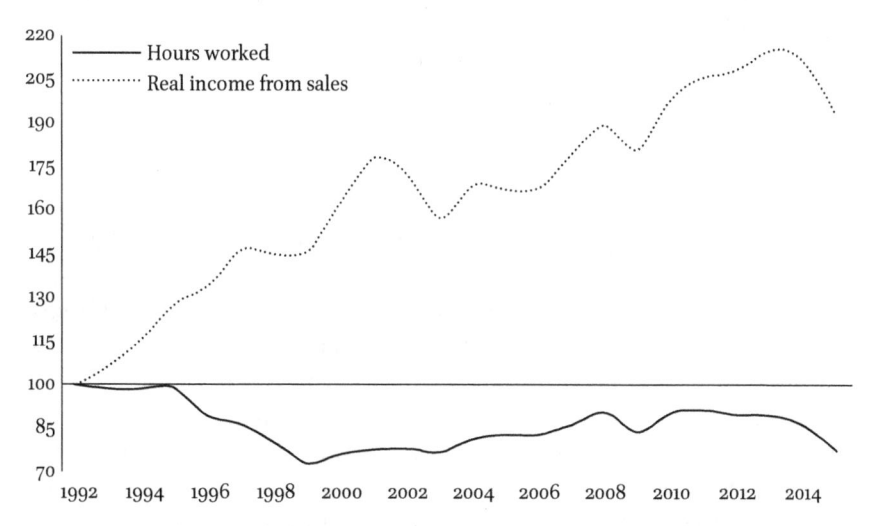

FIGURE 21   Productivity of labor in industry, Brazil, 1992–2015
Notes: (i) scale in index number; (ii) 1992 = 100; (iii) monthly averages in each year.

positive correlation between increased interest on the external debt and a reduction in the ratio of wages to industrial output, in various Latin American countries, between the mid-1970s and the mid-1980s. And since the mid-1990s, Brazil came to follow a fiscal strategy that had first spread through the center and then reached the periphery of the world economy. Due to this strategy, in various parts of the planet

> the working classes, directly through wage repression to boost international competitiveness, and indirectly through tax increases and public sector cuts, should pay for the crisis and for the restoration of the economic viability of capitalist control over the financial system.
> ALBO AND EVANS 2010: 286

Fiscal policy is thus an issue in dispute between producers and various types of appropriators, not only those who are owners of the means of production. And the results—that is, if the state will reduce (or expand) spending or taxation, how it will, who will cede surpluses, and who will appropriate the surpluses in dispute—from the struggle will depend on the correlation of forces that act on the state budget. The latter can then be characterized as a subfield of the economic field, which, according to Pierre Bourdieu (1997), is a socially constructed field of action where agents confront each other. There they count on different endowments, and the objectives and effectiveness of actions will depend on the position of each one within the structure of capital distribution. The budget, more than a mere technology for managing resources, represents a political arena, where classes dispute surpluses transitorily appropriated by the state. This is what I investigate in greater detail in the next section, to reveal how these surpluses were used in the past nearly twenty years.

5 State Spending and Appropriation of Income

The neoliberal discourse, in addition to the fallacious objectives that it proclaimed, namely growth and development, and the real aim it disguised, namely restoration of profits compromised by Keynesian policies, also defended reducing the state's direct intervention in the economy. In structural terms, the latter did not happen, as we saw previously. But in some specific aspects this reduction was visible, as in the case of privatization of state companies and of the transfer to the private sector of services until then predominantly provided by the state. Since the early 1990s a type of induced consensus claimed that that the state would be an inefficient administrator and irresponsible spender, while private agents would be precisely the opposite. Another discourse that gained strength was that the state spends too much and this would be one of the causes of the economic stagnation observed in the developing world since the early 1980s (Vernengo 2007).

The potential solutions were then delineated in such a way as to reduce state presence and spending, although with a clear bias about which areas suffered reforms. Those selected included state intervention in production, civil servants and social security, upon which the following measures were applied in Brazil: (i) in 1996, implementation of fiscal adjustments and financial restructuring of the states through financial support from the federal government to states committed to the control and reduction of spending on civil service, privatization and concession of then state-provided services, control of state-owned companies, commitments to fiscal control, and reduction and control of debt; (ii) between 1996 and 1998, privatizations of the state-owned companies Light Serviços Elétricos, Companhia Vale do Rio Doce, and Sistema Telebrás, and the concession of the railroad network run by Rede Ferroviária Federal; (iii) in 1996–1997, termination of some 170 thousand public sector jobs, dismissal of more than 27 thousand non-tenured employees, extinction of special leaves of absence and of the right to promotion during retirement, institution of a voluntary dismissal program in federal public service, and limitation of advantages and benefits for employees of state-owned companies to the minimums determined by law; and (iv) extinction of retirements based on special laws, review of rules for calculation and concession of retirement pensions to both reduce benefits and delay retirement among private sector workers.[15]

But it was precisely at this time that a certain spending came to be one of the main contributors to the fiscal deficits, however, gaining virtually no attention in the public debate. This was interest on the public debt, which along with the financial liberalization begun at the end of the Sarney government (1985–1989), intensified in the Collor government (1990–1992) and accelerated even more in the Cardoso governments (1995–2002), led the Brazilian state to important monetary and fiscal restrictions. What Morais, Saad-Filho, and Coelho (1999) define as a fundamental contradiction between fiscal and monetary policy was established, which is that monetary tightening in a situation of high debt automatically leads to fiscal loosening via increased interest

---

15   Banco Central do Brasil. "Boletim do Banco Central do Brasil." Relatório 1996 (Vol. 33); Relatório 1997 (Vol. 34); Relatório 1998 (Vol. 34); Relatório 1999 (Vol. 35).

payments. This movement was similar to those observed in countries of the center, which since the early 1980s had their fiscal deficits deepened by high interest rates (Duménil and Lévy 2001, 2004a).

Those developments revealed how and why the issue of public spending was discussed selectively, nearly giving the impression that the state simply wasted economic surpluses. In an ideologically guided discussion, no time was spent by mainstream analysts in debating all the objects of state spending. But when this is analyzed under a dialectic that makes clear who pays and who receives the public monies, one reveals concerns for a specific distributive configuration, which tends to favor a specific class or fraction of class. Since the funds managed by the state can cause expansion of the exploitation of the labor of others, the analysis that focuses on one of the sides—state spending—favors those who benefit from this act, namely the recipients of that spending. This is done by omitting from the debate the large appropriators of state spending. As John Roemer recalls, "exploiting and exploited coalitions are always complements of each other" (Roemer 1982c: 285). I have already mentioned that the exploited coalition includes the working classes; I also argued that it is they who occupy the place of real debtors of the loans taken by the state. This is because they are responsible for producing enough surpluses to feed a tax system for which one of the functions is to service the public debt.

On the other side of this social relation is the exploiting coalition that at other times I refer to as finance. I am now giving this term a broad meaning, to include all those who earn interest, whether or not they are legally classified as financial companies. In the period covered in figure 22, banks and other

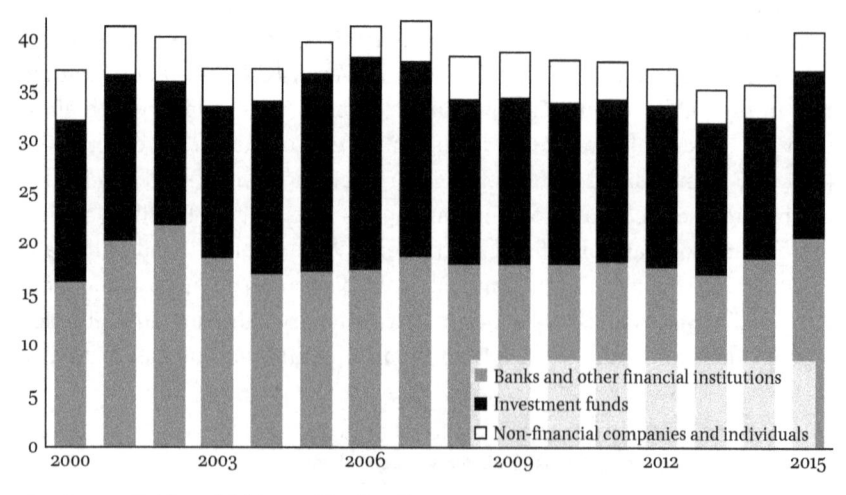

FIGURE 22 Holders of debt securities, Brazil, 2000–2015
Notes: (i) percentages in relation to GDP; (ii) monthly averages in each year.

financial institutions were creditors of 48% of Brazil's domestic federal public debt, which was equivalent to 18% of GDP. Investment funds—most of which are administered by banks—held 42% of the debt, equivalent to 16% of GDP. These two groups combined thus detained nearly 90% of the total domestic debt, with the rest held by non-financial companies, for example, pension funds. These figures show that finance was the main beneficiary of the public debt and of the economic policies that sought to maintain the trust of lenders in the state's capacity to pay back its commitments.

As I have discussed, the division of surpluses is the result of class struggles or even struggles within classes, that is, between class fractions. There are various mechanisms by which this took place in Brazil, and what I highlighted was the fiscal complex formed by public debt and taxation. This complex has another mechanism that was also used by the Brazilian state in its role as stabilizer of class relations that resulted, however, in expropriation and signaled an expansion of capitalist exploitation in ulterior production cycles. This was the primary spending, which is state spending not including any financial expenditures, mainly interest on public debt. Primary spending, like tax revenues, depending on the direction they take—who receives and who 'pays,' respectively—can change the levels of expropriation, the potential exploitation, and thus material inequality.

With the advent of neoliberalism, a nearly consensual belief was promoted that the state spends poorly and excessively, which strengthened the clamor for reductions in public spending. This did not occur, as we saw, and a simple look at the increases in the tax burden, even gross revenues, and of the public debt leave few doubts about this (see figures 15 and 19). But here, when analyzing the highest level of the statistical aggregations, we risk reaching incorrect conclusions. One of them would be that the reductions in state spending sought by the ideologues of the fiscal crisis did not take place. Yet these claims had a specific target in terms of what kinds of expenditure should be reduced. For example, no argument was made to reduce spending on interest on the public debt as emphatic as the demands to cut spending on civil servants or social security. For example, according to the president of the Central Bank during nearly all of Cardoso's second term in office,

> the debt grows because the government has a certain primary result, surplus or deficit, which is steered to interest payments. But beneath this given primary surplus, as Brazil has had, or deficit, as at some times in the past, there are important components. ...
>
> One important subcomponent, but not nearly the only one, is the component of public servants [salaries and related mandatory spending]. We could show a few others. ...

I view with great concern, for example, the approval … [of an attempt by the legislature] to do away with the social security factor and other measures that increased public spending even more, mainly for that which is not investment.[16]

I know that the reality is difficult, the pressures are enormous, the country is needy, this is all sad, but the fact is that this all has a price as well. That is, it is not possible to keep taking one measure after another without this influencing other variables, which in my view winds up reducing our capacity to deal with these social issues, which are so pressing.[17]

The affirmation that the state spent too much for retirement pensions could be as true as that it spent too much on interest or on anything else. This depends, for example, on the point of view, or even the interests, of the one who is issuing the opinion or even the so-called 'technical' analysis. Nevertheless, there does not seem to be much doubt among mainstream analysts about what kind of expenditures must be reduced in any measure aiming at fiscal equilibrium. Examining increases in the minimum retirement age and deindexation of pensions promoted by the United States, Canada and Sweden in the mid-1990s, Herman Schwartz (1998) found that the greater the public debt, the higher the probability of reducing spending on social welfare. Schwartz clarifies that, while the welfare transfers essentially represent an implicit property right—they are secured by law—the public debt is an explicit property right. When there is conflict between them, it is nearly always the first to be sacrificed in name of maintaining a state's creditworthiness. In Brazil, it was precisely retirement and other pensions—the most substantial portion of public spending—which suffered important reforms in the period of deepening of the financial logic.[18]

---

16 The social security factor (fator previdenciário in Portuguese) is a rule for calculating retirement pensions whose fundamental goal is to induce workers to retire later by granting them higher pensions if they retire at an older age.

17 Brasil. Câmara dos Deputados. CPI—Dívida Pública. "Transcrição ipsis verbis: reunião ordinária n. 2129/09." 18 de novembro de 2009: 5–7. If a source was not available in English, its respective reference was used in its original language, namely Portuguese. Any reference that may not provide enough information to locate the source will be provided in detail upon request.

18 Two constitutional amendments, one in 1998, during the Cardoso government, and the other in 2003, during the Lula government, promoted deep changes in the retirement and other pensions regimes, with the first reform being more significant for private sector workers and the second, for civil servants. The most important changes included the rise in the minimum ages for retirement, limits on the amount of retirement and other

FISCAL SUPERSTRUCTURE, EXPROPRIATION, AND EXPLOITATION 119

If we consider spending for retirement and other pensions and social assistance in relation to GDP we see, as shown in figure 23, that since the Real Plan this spending has increased, which could contradict Schwartz's conclusion. Nevertheless, this does not mean that these benefits have not been affected by spending limits, which would be better revealed if they were considered not only in relation to GDP, but rather to the number of people who benefited from them. I do not have enough data to specify how many people benefitted from each type of spending displayed in figure 23. However, it is certain—and this is

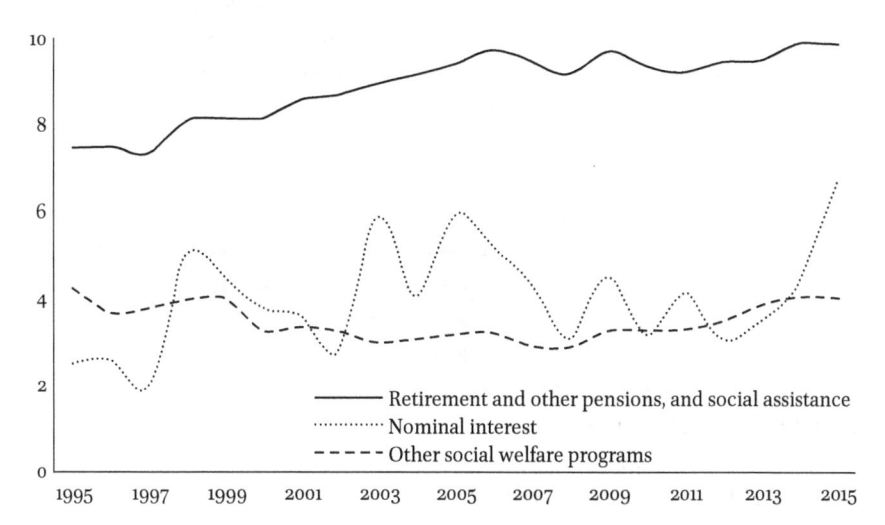

FIGURE 23 Selected expenditures by the central government, Brazil, 1995–2015
Notes: (i) percentages in relation to GDP; (ii) other social welfare programs comprises spending on healthcare, sanitation, education, culture, housing, urban projects, and labor, with the latter mainly for unemployment benefits.

---

pensions benefits, and the requirement that retired civil servants and pension recipients contribute to their social security plans (Brasil. "Emenda constitucional n. 20, de 15 de dezembro de 1998"; "emenda constitucional n. 41, de 19 de dezembro de 2003"). In 2005, a new constitutional amendment re-established some retirement and other pensions benefits for civil servants that had been suppressed by the reform of 2003 (Brasil. "Emenda constitucional n. 47, de 5 de julho de 2005"). In late 2014, soon after Dilma Rousseff was re-elected to a second presidential term, the government changed some rules for granting labor and social security benefits, limiting access to pensions for the death of a spouse, illness assistance, unemployment benefits, and the annual bonus equivalent to the minimum wage for workers with monthly income up to two minimum wages (Brasil. "Medida provisória n. 664, de 30 de dezembro de 2014"; "medida provisória n. 665, de 30 de dezembro de 2014"; "lei n. 13.134, de 16 de junho de 2015"; "lei n. 13.135, de 17 de junho de 2015").

sufficient for the objectives of this analysis—that retirement and other pensions and social assistance, as well as the other expenditures that compose the social wage, were aimed at many more people than spending on interest. Relatively few finance capitalists appropriated interest paid by the state. We have already seen that banks, investment funds and other financial companies detained nearly 90% of the federal public debt securities on average in the 2000–2015 period (see figure 22).

On the other side of this relation was the majority of the population—workers, their families, and the most poor—that depends on state spending for social security, unemployment benefits, education, healthcare, and other programs. As figure 23 reveals, the annual average of these expenditures combined—excluding those for retirement and other pensions, and social assistance, which are shown separately in the chart—fell from 3.9% of GDP in 1995–1999 to 3.1% in 2000–2010, rising to 3.7% in the 2011–2015 period. In contrast, the average spending on interest rose from 3.3% to 4.2% of GDP between the 1995–1999 and 2000–2010 periods, reaching 4.4% in 2011–2015. Throughout the entire series, the average spending on interest was 4% of GDP while the selected social welfare spending—not including retirement and other pensions and social assistance—was 3.5% of GDP.

To summarize, the economic model implemented in the late 1990s, in which inflation control came to depend largely on high real interest rates, raised spending on interest on the public debt and compromised the leading forms of social welfare spending. The situation shows that in Brazil some of the results of the policies associated to this model were an increased public debt, a selective increase in taxes in such a way that it most affected the ruled classes, and a reduction or limitation on the main forms of welfare spending. Echoing Camara and Salama (2005), it can be affirmed that regardless of how debt services are funded, the effects are increasingly more profitable for finance and for small portions of the population, and disastrous for the majority, particularly the poorest segments. Beyond its redistributive and economic effects sensu stricto, this situation would not have been possible without a political structure that, under the guise of capitalist democracy, manifested precisely the contradiction between democracy and capitalism, which deepened with the financialization of the economy. This is the hypothesis that I investigate in the next chapter.

CHAPTER 4

Macroeconomic Policy and Economic Democracy

Economic power confers political power. Where ancient empires deployed their armies, for modern empires it is enough to deploy their bankers.
JOSÉ CARLOS MARIÁTEGUI

∴

If at the end of the Brazilian industrialization process the external debt conferred to multinational companies, foreign banks, and governments of imperialist countries the capacity to influence domestic economic, social, and political processes (Ianni 2004 [1989]), more recently, the domestic public debt has combined with the external debt to expand the power of finance. Regardless if the creditor is foreign or domestic, debt has always originated in relations of class and political power (Chesnais 2005a), placing the state at the mercy of private property owners (Marx and Engels 1982 [1846]). Without insinuating that this influence makes the current capitalist state less democratic today than it had been in its history of mutual reproductive relation with capital, my argument is that this anti-democratic character now assumes a version based on financial logic. Samir Amin (2008) correctly affirmed that the new plutocratic capitalism of the financialized oligopolies is the enemy of democracy, draining it of substantive content.

Critics of neoliberalism say that the state became subordinated to financial markets. This, however, would only be plausible if we conceived these realms to be autonomous from each other. Markets are social constructions over which the propertied classes have ascendance, as they also do over the capitalist state. Markets do not act, do not decide; it is people who are in relation to each other, either in collaboration or in dispute, who do act or decide. Nevertheless, markets have been reified to the point that the phenomena observed within them are used to justify important state decisions in the economic field. Government officials have confidently affirmed that they are on the right path, even a democratic one, when their decisions follow market standards. Popular thinking has also absorbed the near conviction that society should be regulated by free markets. The idea that markets would resolve that which the

Keynesian model was not capable of sustaining became hegemonic and, evoking dogmas of a new liberalism, mainstream analysts came to treat democracy and free markets as complementary to each other, if not as synonymous.

But the freer markets are, the farther they are from what can be called democracy. The capitalist market, for example, instead of facilitating a decision-making process based on a public spirit, tends to destroy it, because it does not promote relationships between agents as fellow citizens, as members of the same community, but as mere factors of processes of production and exchange of goods (Elson 1988). The antithesis between market and democratic politics is clearly revealed when individuals have the opportunity to obtain in this same market private solutions to problems that, nevertheless, concern the collectivity (Bowles and Gintis 1986). When they turn to the capitalist market in search of private solutions to healthcare, education, public safety, etc., they wind up reproducing insufficiencies in these sectors. On one hand, these individuals free the state from the pressure to supply services that are still public, on the other, they create spaces for the wealthy to appropriate social resources that could potentially be allocated to pay for such public services.

These initial comments indicate that I do not limit the concept of democracy to its liberal characterization, although the very existence of liberal democracy appears to make it seem more real than the radical concept of democracy. Yet it is an egalitarian and participatory perspective that inspires this analysis. This study is interested in those criteria that distinguish *capitalist* democracy from that which I define as a *genuine* type of democracy. These criteria are economic equality and egalitarian social participation in decisions that affect life in society. Another point to be stressed in the theoretical path chosen is the importance of keeping in perspective the notion of degrees of democracy, in both space and time. Certain societies can be more or less democratic than others, and each can be more or less democratic at one period or another. They can also be more or less democratic in terms of a particular issue or issues. This also indicates the need to recognize advances and setbacks in the direction of the democratization of society even under the rule of the capitalist mode of production.

While bourgeois democratic institutions serve more the reproduction of capital than substantive movements towards social justice, they are not free from being challenged by effectively democratic movements. This can occur to the degree to which the ruled classes become more politically active. If in theoretical terms democracy and capitalism are each on a different pole, in empiric terms the economy and politics are located between these extremes. That is, even within capitalism, there are democratic movements—although they are still marginal and under constant threat—whose evolution can lead to the overthrow of capitalism. The central idea is that the establishment of a democratic order, and the elimination of the main institutions of the capitalist economy are requirements for the expansion of the capacity of people to govern their own personal lives and their social histories (Bowles and Gintis 1986).

1 Capitalism *or* Democracy

The idea that capitalism and democracy have a dependent relation to each other has become hegemonic; that for a society to be democratic it has to be capitalist and, being capitalist, it would be democratic. The experience of actually existing socialism, by combining non-private ownership of the means of production and centralized economic planning with totalitarian forms of government, played a fundamental role in the consolidation of this belief. The comparison of actually existing socialism with the group of countries ruled under the combination of private property and economic coordination through markets, all supported by liberal democratic political systems, helped to build a clear opposition: on one side capitalism and democracy and on the other, socialism and totalitarianism. Thus, the immediate reaction of Western commentators to the collapse of the Soviet regime was to declare that its downfall ratified the permanent triumph of both capitalism and liberal democracy (Hobsbawm 1995).

But it is also a fact that the authoritarian statism of the actually existing socialism led to great skepticism about a model of socialism based on centralized state planning (Wright 2013). Yet what happened is that these countries overthrew their capitalist states but remained under the rule of capital (Mészáros 2011). This led to what would be the central problem for socialism in the moments following the Soviet experience, namely to show that societies could develop some form of self-government that combines social equality and political liberty (Weffort 1992). Not even the fact that this did not take place following the Soviet collapse was sufficient to question the belief that capitalism was a democratic economic system and socialism was not. Defeating an empire does not imply that better institutions will be established, as shown precisely by the post-Soviet experience of Russia (Block and Evans 2005; Evans 2008). Like most post-communist societies that threw themselves directly into liberal democracy and capitalism, Russia actually experienced economic failure as a result (Žižek 2008).

Despite the erratic path those moves have taken, they served an ideology that has been functional in supporting the maintenance of the political legitimacy that capital needs to reproduce itself, even if in an increasingly more unstable manner. On the other hand, this ideology has also been disproved in some historical phases, which were generally brief, but when capital was able to develop without liberal democracy. This was seen in Brazil during the Getúlio Vargas dictatorship (1937–1945) and the most recent military dictatorship (1964–1985), both periods of significant economic growth in the Brazilian economy. It is not inappropriate to recall the alliance between the large Western capitalist powers and Stalin's Soviet Union whose Red Army was responsible for the victory over Hitler's Germany (Hobsbawm 1995).

But a market economy can only develop under certain democratic conditions, just as certain social structural conditions for a stable democracy can only be established under a developed market economy (Offe 2004 [1991]). In the long-term, capital requires that the political system be organized under a bourgeois type of democracy, because a state apparatus that is too strong can create other types of threats to capital. Moreover, it is essential that capital be able to remove governments that are incapable of responding to its class needs (see the book's afterword).

For Joshua Cohen and Joel Rogers (1983), just as a capitalist democracy is not purely capitalist, it is also not purely democratic, because the political rights—those of expression, association, and voting—to which citizens have access are more formal and procedural than substantive. For example, the application of these rights do not consider the inequalities in the distribution of resources that decisively affect the exercise of political rights and, thus, limit the power of expression. As Pierre Bourdieu (2001) observed, all political agents do not have the same level of access to the instruments needed to produce their own opinions, either in terms of autonomy or in terms of interests linked to a particular position. Thus, Bourdieu continues, voting is not the true universal suffrage that it intends to be, unless the conditions for access to the universal are universalized. And economic conditions—such as wealth, income, and control over capitalist production or circulation—are definitely essential to making substantive political participation viable.

On the other hand, as Cohen and Rogers (1983) argue, capitalist democracy also differs from pure capitalism, because the same formal political rights just mentioned, as well as a series of actions in the political arena, allow workers to interfere in state policies and thus influence the behavior of capital. These rights, according to Cohen and Rogers, even without guaranteeing results, make capitalist democracy more favorable to material gains of workers than other capitalist regimes, such as fascism or bureaucratic authoritarianism. In addition to uncertainty about the results of a possible revolution—which could discourage such a movement—the possibility for some immediate material gains or compensations leads the ruled classes to consent to keeping their demands at a level that is safe to capital (Cohen and Rogers 1983; Przeworski 1985). The class compromise between capital and labor, which is required to maintain the peace and tranquility that are so important to capitalist accumulation, is thus constructed (Harvey 2005).

An emblematic example of this compromise can be seen in Brazil during the Lula governments (2003–2010). According to Chico de Oliveira, although the Workers Party had been historically linked to resistance against the military dictatorship (1964–1985), and encouraged debate about poverty and inequality, when it ascended to political power, it brought something new to the relationship between the rulers and the ruled: the terms of the old Gramscian equation 'coercion + consent = hegemony' changed in such a way that coercion disappeared and consent had its direction inverted. It was no longer the ruled who consented to subordinate themselves, but the ruling classes who came to consent to be apparently 'led' by representatives of the ruled classes (Oliveira 2006). Meanwhile, the consent of the ruled classes was attained through the incorporation of popular movements to the Workers Party-led governments and with public policies aimed at the poorest, such as income transfer programs, expansion of bank consumer credit and substantial increases in the minimum wage (Braga 2015). To give just one example, during Lula's governments (2003–2010) the minimum wage grew about 66% in real terms.[1]

Even so, despite concerns for alleviating poverty, little was done to substantially alter the structure of government spending. The rates of class expropriation sustained by the monetary and fiscal policies, for example, were higher during the Workers Party-led governments than during the previous governments of President Cardoso's Brazilian Social Democratic Party (PSDB in its Portuguese initials). To give just two examples, both of which synthesize much of those macroeconomic policies, we return to some data related to debt and social welfare spending. Under the Workers Party governments, in the 2003–2015 period, nominal interest on the federal public debt was equivalent to an annual average of 4.4% of GDP, compared to the 3.3% observed in the 1995–2002 period, under Cardoso (see figure 13). Meanwhile, the annual average of total federal spending on housing, urban infrastructure, labor—mainly for unemployment benefits—education, culture, healthcare, and sanitation, which was 3.7% of GDP in the period 1995–2002, fell to 3.3% in 2003–2015 (see figure 23).

---

1 Any data presented in this chapter with no source reference are based on the author's calculations from standard databases. Technical aspects or sources not made explicit will be communicated upon request.

But this was not a new problem, because there has always been great difficulty for the Marxist tradition to deal with the paradoxical phenomenon of democracy as "a regime in which the exploiting minority rules by means of a system of legally free popular elections" (Therborn 2008 [1978]: 248). The solution to this difficulty involves the finding that the political system does not impose itself on capital; it is rather capital that conditions the political system and its fundamental institutions, including formally free elections. Capitalists have power over governments because governments foresee a loss of popular support if they act against the interest of capital (Barry 2002). It is the capitalists who have the prerogative to make decisions about investment, and one of its clearest expressions is in capital flight. Its potential realization warns members of a certain society that companies will move their production on a global scale in such a way that minimizes expected future costs; the employment outlooks in each country will then depend on the ability of each nation-state to create an attractive business environment; and the ability of any ruling political group to remain in office will largely depend on the employment situation in the period preceding elections (Bowles and Gintis 1986).

Once again, the first Lula government serves as an example. Given the signs that the monetary and fiscal policy of the then new government, inaugurated in 2003, would continue to follow the tight fiscal and monetary policies that had been in force since the Cardoso governments (1995–2002), sectors of the Workers Party rose up in protest. Some demonstrations wound up leading to the expulsion of some party members, while others left the Workers Party voluntarily. But the Letter to the Brazilian People issued by then candidate Lula on the eve of his election in 2002 had already warned that if he were elected his government would maintain the ruling macroeconomic model. For example, Lula committed himself to primary fiscal surpluses to service the public debt at the levels considered by finance to be needed and satisfactory. And this is what his governments did during most of Lula's two terms in office (see figures 10 and 13). The letter was not a mere strategy to win the presidential election; its proposals would be made part of the government program if Lula's party won.

The Letter to the Brazilian People showed that in the capitalist system, despite some variations—such as the election of governments not totally aligned to the values of this system—the tendency is that only groups who fulfill certain minimal requirements safe to capital qualify to exercise state power. Anything that differs from this standard provokes reactions that seek to return the system to 'normality,' even if they turn to methods opposed to the ideals of liberal democracy. This was the case of the dictatorships that spread through Latin America during the 1960s and 1970s, which were supported by alliances between capitalist and military elites supported by the U.S. government. A more recent example was the Collor government (1990–1992), which was removed from power because the implementation of its 'modernizing' agendas was not sufficiently careful with powerful interests (Morais and Saad-Filho 2003) and because it did not meet the expectations of finance (Garagorry 2007). The removal of Dilma's government in 2016 fits this pattern. For the first time since 1998, in 2014 the central government had ran a primary fiscal deficit, which was repeated in 2015, on the eve of the parliamentary coup that removed the Workers Party from the federal government.

It would not be an exaggeration to argue that on this point Marxists and liberals, although with different value perspectives, tend to agree about the mutual relation between capitalism and liberal democracy. Liberal democracy is a safe harbor for capital, because no competitive party system has been able to lead to any distribution of power capable of altering the logic of socioeconomic power generated by capital (Offe 1984b). More than just a safe harbor, liberal democracy is a fundamental political requirement of capitalism, considering that the economic infrastructure cannot reproduce without a political superstructure that is suitable to it. Liberal democracy and capitalism are not two essentially distinct and discontinuous orders, because the relations of production take the form of legal and political relations that are not merely secondary outcomes, but rather constituent elements of productive relations (Wood 1981). In sum, in the contradictory coexistence between capitalist economy and liberal democracy, the private character of class exploitation can only be maintained under the bourgeois-democratic form of organization of political power (Offe 1974).

But this form of political organization is anti-democratic by nature, for at least two reasons. The first, curiously, is revealed in the contradiction inscribed in the very idea of liberty present in liberal thinking, which supports itself by using the individual as the fundamental analytical category. According to Claus Offe (2001), this notion of liberty creates an ambivalent distinction between my liberty and your liberty, because it is capable of having the latter appear to me as the liberty of someone who does not truly deserve it. The solutions that Offe presents for this type of tension—a tension that can result from the exercise of individual and democratic rights, and those to social welfare—involve attitudes such as tolerance, trust, and solidarity. These are all socially referenced values. For this reason, in true democratic practice, there is no distinction between the individual, the social, and the political; all individual activity is also a social activity with political effects (Pogrebinschi 2007).

Liberty does not exist for an individual who is compelled to submit to another, as is the case of those who are owners of only their labor-power when they face the owners of the means of production. Jean-Jacques Rousseau had said that for civil freedom to exist, it is necessary "that no citizen shall be rich enough to buy another and none so poor as to be forced to sell himself" (Rousseau 1968 [1762]: 96). In the same way, democracy is a relationship between free people, and economic dependence is the antithesis of liberty (Bowles and Gintis 1986). This was recognized even in the narrow concept of democratic politics found in Weberian theory. While his thesis that only wealth can make a person economically independent (Weber 1982 [1919]b) is by no means correct, it is true that poverty makes any man or woman dependent. Thus, it can be said that at most, in a class society, liberty exists for some individuals who nevertheless exercise it at the expense of the liberty of others.

Among those who have their autonomy compromised are precisely the "workers who in the formal sense voluntarily, but actually under the compulsion of the whip of hunger, offer themselves" (Weber 2003 [1919–1920]: 277). This is why the liberty defined by liberal theory is a false liberty, given that it stems precisely from the absence of collective action (Bowles and Gintis 1986). As Karl Marx said "it is not the consciousness of men that determines their existence, but their *social* existence that determines their consciousness" (Marx 2010 [1859]: 263; emphasis added). Thus, freedom of choice, considered by capitalist ideology as its main moral virtue, tends to be only partial in this mode of production, because its inequalities impose limits to true liberty (Wright 2006b). After all, "men make their own history, but they do not make it just as they please; they do not make it under circumstances chosen by themselves, but under circumstances directly encountered, given and transmitted from the past" (Marx 2010 [1852]: 103). This leads to a second reason why capitalism is incompatible with genuine democracy: inequality.

Economic inequality is one of the fundamental characteristics of capitalism, which, in turn, creates restrictions to the political capacity of individuals or classes to influence their own destinies. Capitalism limits democracy, for example, because of the fact that private property impedes collective access to decisions about important domains of economic activity (Levine 1995; Wright 2006b). Thus, a truly democratic order cannot evolve with liberty and equal conditions when decision-making about the allocations of the surplus of social production is monopolized (Cohen and Rogers 1983). The concentration of economic power subverts democratic principles by granting the propertied classes a disproportional capacity to influence political results—through the financing of politicians and their organizations, control over large media organizations, contracting of bureaucrats and politicians when they leave government, and the ability to persuade government officials—that will nevertheless have effects on the collectivity (Wright 1994a, 1994b, 2005).

For example, because it involves inequality and is supported by state intermediation, the public debt has a character antithetical to democracy, as do capital relations sensu stricto. Especially at the periphery of the world economy, public debt allowed financial organizations to increase pressure for greater financial liberalization and to obtain monetary policies favorable to finance (Chesnais 1998). This took place without the issue undergoing significant discussions in broad political and social arenas. In Brazil, the concentration of portions of financial capital under the control of a few organizations (see figure 22) generated specific interests about macroeconomic policies, leading to a situation in which a few agents can influence government much more than other social forces (Minella 2007). Thus, if on one hand the concentration of economic power in capitalists' hands does not totally invalidate the democratic benefits of political liberty—of expression, association, vote, and the like—on the other hand, it is the rich minority that this form of democracy favors (Glaser 1999).

The logic that came to dominate most economic policy decisions was that the only route to be followed in neoliberal state practice should be that dictated by the economic apparatus. Introduced by the economic technocracy and promptly assumed by political representation, this dogmatism had been preceded by another one, according to which the market came to be considered the only space capable of granting rationality to economic activity. This thinking appeared to forget that markets are, firstly, social constructions, and therefore are not capable of operating without the (visible) human hand, which, actually, would be logically impossible. To accept as true the discourse that calls for a market that 'acts' on its own leads to disguising the fact that the market is operated by those who do not allow it to function with greater degrees of autonomy. Precisely because people cannot enter markets as equals, it is difficult to see how and why this space should be considered as their guardian and savior (Corbridge 1993).

Economic policies in general, and fiscal or monetary policies in particular, thus require an institutional apparatus guided by a logic of action as if there were no alternative. This logic would be guided by a supposed market in which the phenomena that develop there are all self-justified. Thus, considering what we have seen until now, we can suppose that the implementation of policies tends to be based on the exclusion of many points of view and by the reinforcement of others. This, as well as the aspect of inequality, steers our attention to the questioning about how political practice in a supposedly democratic environment can be profoundly anti-democratic. This aspect is especially important for the discussion in the next section, where I analyze how certain issues—macroeconomic policies—were systematically excluded from the democratic debate in the period that followed the implementation of the *real*, in 1994.

2 Depoliticization of Economic Policy

The specific form that a democracy assumes is contingent on both the socio-economic conditions and the state practices and structures of a country (Schmitter and Karl 1991). In Chapter 1 of this book I argued that in the context of liberalization of the economy, finance became the hegemonic fraction of capital, first at the center of the capitalist system and later in Brazil and other countries of the periphery. This took place with the state performing a central role in attaining the reform measures. The whole process deepened the anti-democratic character of capitalism by expanding economic inequality via rising rates of labor exploitation and containment of public provisions on which the working classes and more poor social fractions depend. However, measures with anti-democratic contours in procedural terms were also necessary to the reforms that placed finance in the hegemonic position. As Adam Przeworski summarized,

> since the neoliberal "cure" is a painful one, with significant social costs, reforms tend to be initiated from above and launched by surprise, independently of public opinion and without the participation of organized political forces. ... The political style of implementation tends toward rule by decree; governments seek to mobilize their supporters rather than accept the compromises that might result from public consultation. In the end, the society is taught that it can vote but not choose; legislatures are given the impression that they have no role to play in the elaboration of policy; nascent political parties, trade unions, and other organizations learn that their voices do not count.
>
> PRZEWORSKI 1992: 56

I also argued earlier in this chapter that, although capitalism and democracy are mutually exclusive theoretical constructs, in historical terms, capitalist democracies are organized in gradations of both capitalism and democracy. Economic equality or inequality are not absolute in capitalist democracies, and political power is not completely centralized or decentralized. Nevertheless, economic inequality must be sufficient to include the few and exclude the majority from the decision-making processes that affect the living conditions of an entire society. This also indicates that power, contrary to Michel Foucault's assertions about its microphysical character, is not a manifestation that is impossible to locate. It is capitalists—and they are not many, in relative terms—who rule over production and investment and, for this reason, exercise influence on the economic policies of the state, with broad consequences for society as a whole (Bowles and Gintis 1986).

Nevertheless, there are no guarantees that economic inequality would be sufficient to maintain itself and the political system that allows this inequality. Given that capitalism depends on liberal democracy, movements in the direction of a democratic configuration that exceeds the limits set by this liberal democracy can make politics less secure for capital. The greater involvement of society in decisions that concern it influences political decisions in a way that imposes on them a dialectic that, by expanding the space to new parties interested in influencing the decisions, places limits to the realization of interests present until then. If this process is effective, we can then envision a tendency towards a more egalitarian allocation of economic surpluses, given that more agents share the decisions. It is important to keep in mind that this movement would find resistance by the part of those who stand to lose from it, because, as Adam Przeworski recalls, "democracy inevitably threatens 'property rights'" (Przeworski 1992: 53).

We have now reached the point at which the other democratic requirement—the first I discussed was economic equality—that I want to highlight also reveals itself to be incompatible with capitalism. This requirement involves egalitarian participation, direct or by means of representatives, in the decisions that affect social life, which, in an effectively democratic reality, would be broadly encouraged. The incompatibility between capitalism and economic democracy is due to the fact that participatory models of organization of productive activities of the state, which seek to increase the administrative capacity to serve social needs, would be inadequate to the capitalist character of the state (Offe 1975). This is because, Claus Offe adds, these models "tend to crystallize conflict and protest and can thus easily become *subversive* of the balance between the state and the accumulation process" (Offe 1975: 143; emphasis in original). Offe distinguishes from productive activity the activity of state allocation, which refers to the power to redistribute resources via government policies. One example is the tax system; another is the execution of economic policies, such as monetary or fiscal policy.

While Offe specifically emphasizes the incompatibility between a state's productive activities with participatory models, this is no less true for activities of allocation. In addition to the democratic limits to the participation of the ruled classes imposed by the socioeconomic structure, institutions are configured in such a way as to impose limits on political debate by society as a whole.

If class exploitation is not maintained without a certain political configuration and if, more specifically, this configuration tends towards the radicalization of democratic practices, inequality itself—which implies the advantage of one class over another—would be threatened. It is for this reason that institutions tend to limit the exercise of democratic politics in activities of allocation, as they do in production as well. We live under that which Jacinda Swanson (2008) calls the depoliticization of the economy, which is manifest in at least two related ways, which are the conceptual naturalization of economic practices and the limited political control over them.

Absolute truths are established in this context. Economic issues are sterilized from some—that is, not from all—political influences and legitimated by certain forms of technical knowledge, despite the existence of others. These economic issues are then presented to society as if there were no alternatives to neoliberal prescriptions. Here it is also seen that the state is not weakened as is understood by this ideological belief or even contemporary political theories. This is because it still has the legitimacy to issue discourses about 'truths.' As Bourdieu (2011 [1996]) defined well, the state, which has the means to impose and instill lasting principles of vision and division according to its own structures, is the place par excellence of the concentration and exercise of symbolic power. In this way, if the level of democratization of a society refers to the scope of its decisions that are subject to democratic control, which goes beyond the extension of political equality (Wright 1994b), depoliticizing the economy lowers this level.

The exclusion of certain themes from political debate is not accidental. It is part of the arsenal of the institutional arrangements developed in the realm of the state to safeguard its primordial function of maintaining the mode of production and specific forms of regulation of accumulation. According to Offe, the capitalist state is governed in such a way that policies are selectively generated in a process of choice configured by "institutionalized exclusion rules" (Offe 1974: 36). These rules of selection compose the internal structure of the state apparatus and define its class character in two ways. Firstly, the selectivity operates via positive action of the state, which formulates policies that coincide with the collective interests of capital, that is, those that avoid interests of particular fractions capable of compromising accumulation. In a second form of selectivity, the state acts negatively, not allowing either the development of conflicts or the articulation of anti-capitalistic interests. In synthesis, in this form of selectivity the state does not place anti-capitalistic themes up for debate.[2]

---

[2] I owe this passage to Erik Olin Wright (personal correspondence).

Given that the commitment of the state is to the collective interests of capital; and recognizing, however, that the accumulation process takes place under the hegemony of one of the fractions of the ruling class, the selectivities referred to by Offe are also based on this restriction. That is, both the positive and the negative selectivities of policies can refer at some time to the interests of the hegemonic class fraction, which, however, does not mean that they address the interests of particular capitalists. Thus, the way that fiscal and monetary policies in general, and the public debt in particular, were administered in Brazil since the new currency—the *real*—was created corroborates Offe's thesis, particularly the negative form of selectivity. These issues, whose main results tended to favor the financial fraction of capital, were not submitted to debates that could potentially be anti-finance. Protected from broad social scrutiny, the probability that they would have been objects of conflict was thus relatively low.

The selection mechanisms defined by Offe compose a system of filters by means of which government policies are defined. They can be identified on the levels of: (i) structure, at which the entire system of political institutions has a radius of action that determines which social questions are open to political treatment, that is, which will or will not be objects of state policies and actions; (ii) ideology, which makes the system of ideological and cultural norms the promoter of the selective perception and articulation of social problems and conflicts; (iii) process, where regulations, like those of parliamentary deliberation or of bureaucratic planning and administration, are not mere procedural formalities, but determinant of the possible contents and results of the process, because they create conditions for the issues, groups, or interests to be favored or excluded; and (iv) repression, which makes the police and judicial entities the final stage for the restriction of the scope of possible political events (Offe 1974).

Selection mechanisms were visible in the administration of Brazilian macroeconomic policies. This was seen in the various attempts to distinguish economy and politics, more specifically in such a way that fiscal and monetary policies would be strictly economic issues and that, for this reason, should be handled technically. In these issues, the discourse was that of liberal social theory that bifurcates into a liberal political theory that does not address the economy, and into a liberal economic theory that ignores politics (Bowles and Gintis 1986). A sample of this was given by the Brazilian minister of finance in early 2010—the year of a presidential election—by proposing what he called the "sustainability pact." He affirmed that it was necessary to "*shield* the Brazilian economy from the elections." On the side of government this meant a "*commitment* to maintain solidity (fiscal and monetary) and the same responsible conduct as in the non-electoral period." On the side of business that pact meant "maintaining normal performance, not accepting provocations, not believing in distortions," and "demanding a commitment to the maintenance of the solid foundations and the successful growth policies."[3]

The idea of democracy as state power subordinated to social power, and as social power as a constraining force on state power (Wright 2005)—Gramsci (2004 [1932]) referred to this as the government with the consent of the governed—thus did not find significant empiric expression in the execution of Brazilian economic policies since the Real Plan was launched, in 1994. This confirmed David Harvey's (2005) thesis that neoliberal theorists are suspicious of democracy, because to govern under majority rule would be a threat to individual rights and constitutional liberties. For this reason, Harvey adds, neoliberal solutions involve a preference for governance exercised by specialists and elites, and for decisions taken in the realm of the executive and judiciary branches, instead of those produced by a legislature. It also involves insulating key institutions, such as the central bank, from democratic pressure. This is an example of what Bob Jessop (2010) called the fetishism of the separation between the economic and political moments of capital. Moreover, it is precisely in this separation, as in the idea of a citizenship separated from its social interests and from the struggle over the accumulation of capital, that the fetishism of the state is manifest (Costilla 2000). This fetishism raises the state to the extreme of being precisely a political institution responsible for depoliticizing the economy. For this reason, Ellen Wood (1981) keenly affirms that perhaps there is no greater obstacle to a socialist project than that imposed by the separation between economic and political struggles.

3   Selective Bureaucratic Insulation

One of the phenomena that makes macroeconomic policies important expressions of the contraction of democracy is the shrinking of spaces of debate and decision-making. Beyond the objections about the effectively democratic character of the legislature of a capitalist state, democracy can become even more limited when spaces of action are left to hegemonic occupation by the

---

3   Brasil. Ministério da Fazenda. "Apresentação do ministro da Fazenda 'Brasil: preparado para crescer,' realizada durante o 'Seminário LIDE—Grupo de Líderes Empresariais.'" São Paulo, SP. 2 de fevereiro de 2010; emphases in original. If a source was not available in English, its respective reference was used in its original language, namely Portuguese. Any reference that may not provide enough information to locate the source will be provided in detail upon request.

executive branch. It is precisely this that political parties do vis-à-vis the state bureaucracy when the economic apparatus assumes centrality within the state (Poulantzas 2000 [1978]). In Brazil, these movements occurred, for example, during the industrialization of its economy (Ianni 2004 [1989]) and also with the more recent fiscal and monetary stabilization measures (Diniz 2004). The preponderance of the executive branch is not a particularity of the periphery of global capitalism; the United States, France, Great Britain and the former West Germany are examples where this has taken place at the center of global capitalism (Arendt 2006 [1972]; Mills 2000 [1956]; Poulantzas 2000 [1978]).

In most countries, the executive branch has near total control over policies for investment, exchange and interest rates, loans, social spending, taxes, fiscal incentives, international and domestic trade, and public debt (Costilla 2000). This preponderance caused Brazil to have what Décio Saes (2001) calls limited democracy, which led to the emergence of a civil authoritarianism whose greatest evidence is the removal of the power to legislate from the legislature through institution of the provisional decree (medida provisória in Portuguese). Issued by the president of the republic, it has the immediate strength of a law until it is reviewed by the legislature. According to Saes, Brazil never even reached the stage of a bourgeois democracy in which the legislature would have the real function of government and share the work with the executive bureaucracy. This contraction of democracy also had important material effects for society as a whole. This is because "the inability of democratic bodies to control the movement of capital undermines the ability of democracy to set collective priorities over the use of social resources, especially the social surplus" (Wright 2005: 199). The fact is that investment is a decision that is essential to a broad array of social objectives (Wright 1998). Because it is the only guarantee of the future of a society, if investment decisions are not open to social deliberation, democracy is fundamentally restricted and incomplete (Cohen and Rogers 1983).

An example of the restriction to participation of society in the fiscal question was seen in 2001 when the Brazilian Chamber of Deputies created the Participatory Legislative Committee. The original objective of the committee was to facilitate popular participation in "suggestions for legislative initiatives presented by associations and professional entities, unions, and organized entities of civil society."[4] However, when it set norms for the deliberation of measures in its budget committee, the National Congress prohibited that 'participatory' committee from presenting amendments to the budget bill proposed

---

4 Brasil. Câmara dos Deputados. "Resolução n. 21, de 2001." 30 de maio de 2001. Art. 1º.

by the executive branch.[5] Another example is in the so-called Fiscal Responsibility Law, which determined the creation of a "fiscal management council, constituted by representatives of all branches and spheres of government, from the public ministry [the public prosecutor's office], and technical entities representative of society." Its attributions would be to "permanently accompany and evaluate ... the policy and operationality of fiscal management."[6] In late 2000, the year the Fiscal Responsibility Law was enacted, the Brazilian president drafted a bill to create the fiscal management council.[7] By the time of this writing, the proposal was still being considered in the Chamber of Deputies, and the council has not yet been created.[8]

Another manifestation of the insulation of economic decisions can be seen in the highest regulatory institution of the Brazilian financial system, the National Monetary Council (Conselho Monetário Nacional in Portuguese). Created in 1964, under the military dictatorship, one of its objectives is to "coordinate the monetary, credit, budget, fiscal, and public debt policies."[9] It clearly has a substantial role considering how its decisions can reflect on the economy and living conditions of society in general. In the sense of a substantive democracy, it would be reasonable for this council to include representatives of various social segments. In addition, it would also be reasonable that, with the termination of the military dictatorship (1964–1985), the National Monetary Council would undergo a similar opening to broader social participation. A move in this direction was initiated in the Sarney government (1985–1990) but, after being interrupted in the Collor government (1990–1992), it took a reverse direction during preparations for the Real Plan (1994).

The evolution of the National Monetary Council's composition is an important example of how a state institution can become even less representative of the diversity of classes in society. This evolution occurred in such a way that, created and expanded under the dictatorship, it ironically became more insulated precisely under the first government elected by direct vote since the Council was created, that of Fernando Collor (1990–1992). Figure 24 displays compositions of the National Monetary Council at selected moments since its creation, in 1964, until 2015. From those moments I highlight the radicalization

---

5   Brasil. Congresso Nacional. "Resolução n. 1, de 2006-CN." 22 de dezembro de 2006. Art. 43; Anexo.
6   Brasil. "Lei complementar n. 101, de 4 de maio de 2000." Art. 67.
7   Brasil. Poder executivo. "Mensagem n. 1658, de 7 de novembro de 2000." *Diário da Câmara dos Deputados*. 11 de novembro de 2000: 56381.
8   Brasil. Poder executivo. "Projeto de lei n. 3744/2000." *Diário da Câmara dos Deputados*. 13 de março de 2009: 07660–07662.
9   Brasil. "Lei n. 4.595, de 31 de dezembro de 1964." Art. 3º.

Selected event	Year	Number of members	Composition
Creation of the Council	1964	9	Minister of finance, presidents of two state-owned federal banks, and six appointed members.
End of the most recent military dictatorship	1985	24	Ministers of finance, planning, industry and commerce, agriculture, and the interior; presidents of six state-owned federal banks, the Central Bank, and of two regulatory agencies; the director of the foreign commerce portfolio of the state-owned Bank of Brazil; and nine appointed members.
End of the Sarney government	1990	27	Ministers of finance, planning, industry and commerce, agriculture, interior, urban development and the environment, and labor; presidents of five state-owned federal banks, the Central Bank, and of two regulatory agencies; the director of the foreign commerce portfolio of the state-owned Bank of Brazil; ten appointed members; and *one representative of workers*.
End of the Collor government	1992	17	Ministers of finance, planning, agriculture, and labor; presidents of four state-owned federal banks, the Central Bank, and of one regulatory agency; six appointed members; and *one representative of workers*.
Launching of the Real Plan	1994	3	Ministers of finance, planning, and the president of the Central Bank.

FIGURE 24   Changes in composition of the National Monetary Council, 1964–1994

that took place with the launching of the Real Plan, when the Council came to have only three members vis-à-vis the 27 attained at its peak.

I am not implying that the National Monetary Council had at any time been a forum that was sufficiently representative of the various interests of society. Except for its first five years of existence, it was composed mostly by members of the executive branch, particularly ministers and presidents of official banks. Those who did not have government positions were appointed by the president of the republic. As Ary Minella (1988) indicated, the National Monetary Council was initially composed in a deeply elitist manner, and included important business leaders linked to the military coup of 1964, which gave it a political line that tended to support the interests of the class fraction represented in the Council with greater intensity. The bankers, Minella adds, fought to avoid any representation of workers on the Council as had been considered in the discussions about banking reform prior to the military coup. Workers' representation was only included in 1987, maintained until 1994, and was limited to a single member.

In any case, since the eve of the launching of the Real Plan, the National Monetary Council has only had economic policy-makers among its members. They were the minister of finance, the minister of planning, budget and management and the president of the Central Bank of Brazil. It is interesting to note that the Central Bank president was initially a subordinate of the minister of finance, until 2004, when the presidency of the Bank became a ministerial level position, like the Council's two other members.[10]

The importance of the National Monetary Council to my argument lies in the fact that it has been the decision-making forum responsible for setting inflation targets within the monetary policy regime, which since 1999 was based on the management of the benchmark interest rate for the Brazilian economy. Inflation control, as we saw, came to be a priority of economic policies in the mid-1980s, reaching its greatest strength in the mid-1990s. In the current stage of capitalism, in which financial activities have reached central importance to the economy, the rentier classes could benefit doubly, in particular in Brazil. Firstly, by the protection of the value of money-capital brought about by controlling inflation, the rise of which reduces the real values of money and of loaned capitals. Secondly, finance was benefitted by interest rates that were high enough to both attract capital and control inflation through the targeting regime.

Interest rates have immediate influence on all economic activity, although with different effects between economic sectors and classes. The interest rate is one of the main criteria in investment decisions, making a certain activity more profitable than another depending on the respective rates expected in return. For example, if public debt bonds yield higher returns than the profit rates forecasted in the real economy, the tendency is for productive investment to be sacrificed to some degree in favor of loans to government. As figure 25 displays, this is precisely what took place in Brazil beginning with the first neoliberal movements, inverting the trend observed until the late 1980s. The gross fixed capital formation—investment in the means of production—moved in a direction opposite to the real interbank interest rate. While the annual average of that rate rose from 0.1% in the 1970–1994 period to 10% in 1995–2015, the average of gross fixed capital formation fell from 21% to 17% between these periods.

Returning to the importance of the National Monetary Council at the period of the Brazilian economy analyzed here, I highlight the articulation between its responsibility to set inflation targets and the interest rate policy executed by the Central Bank. I also highlight the consequences of this policy on economic activity and mainly on the redistribution of the economic surpluses. All of these aspects were influenced by decisions taken within the state apparatus and had important impacts on society as a whole. However, despite this scope and importance to the living conditions in society, decisions were made

---

10   Brasil. "Medida provisória n. 207, de 13 de agosto de 2004"; "lei n. 11.036, de 22 de dezembro 2004."

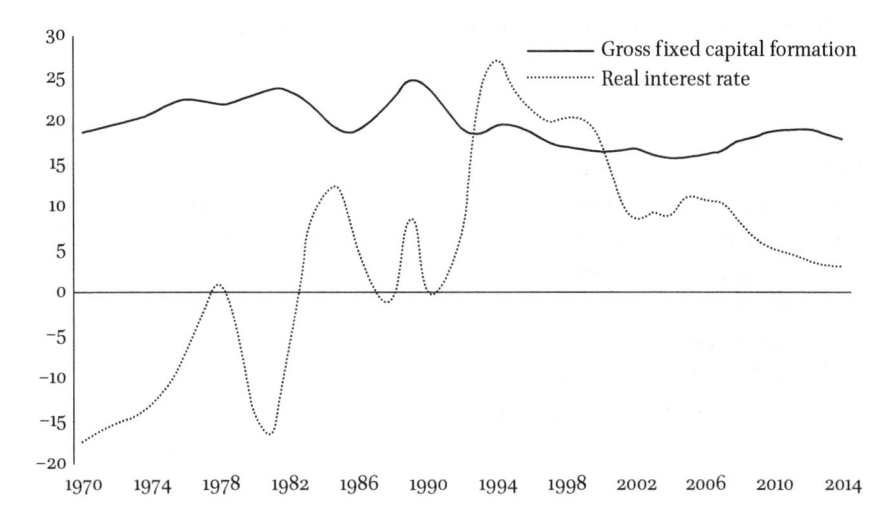

FIGURE 25 Gross fixed capital formation and interest rate, Brazil, 1970–2014
Notes: (i) percentage scale; (ii) three-year moving averages; (iii) gross fixed capital formation in relation to GDP, whose data were retrieved from the System of National Accounts reference 2000, in which 2014 is the last year in the series; (iv) ex post real interbank interest rate.

by significantly limited groups. Thus, the Brazilian capitalist state failed to meet one of the requirements of an effectively democratic society. I am referring to the guarantee that all those interested in the consequences of a decision could participate in the conditions to influence it (Cohen and Rogers 1983).

On this point, I disagree with analyses that affirm that the Brazilian state has an accentuated degree of bureaucratic insulation in relation to the rest of society. I understand that, in the realm of economic policy, the insulation was selective. This adjective is used to indicate that the state apparatus was not isolated from the concerns of *all* of society, but from the concerns of a *part* of that society, which, however, was the majority. With the ruling classes and their fractions, which were numerically minorities but politically and economically hegemonic, the state economic apparatus maintained important connections, was influenced by them, and attended to their desires and demands. These classes included capitalists in general and, among them, with special ascendance, finance and its organic intellectuals. One cannot affirm that the bureaucracy was insulated from finance capital, given that there was a sharing of ideologies between this fraction and economic policy-makers. This was the case of a decision-making body that assumed one of the most important roles for the Brazilian economy, particularly since 1999. This is the Monetary Policy

Committee, formed by the members of the board of governors of the Central Bank of Brazil.

Created in 1996, that committee became responsible for implementing the country's monetary policy. Since 1999, its main tool to do so has been the establishment of the goal for the benchmark interest rate in the economy, the Selic rate. This, in turn, served as a reference for the other short- and medium-term interest rates used in the country. In this way, the committee's decisions influenced the level of economic activity, which is one of the variables to be controlled to contain inflation. This is because, if there is a forecast that consumer-price indices will rise, one way to counteract this is by raising interest rates. This, in addition to making consumer credit more restrictive, may contain the propensity to consume and increase the propensity to save. Moreover, the rise of interest rates tends to attract foreign capital, leading to the appreciation of the domestic currency, which in turn makes importation an alternative to domestic products that may be more expensive. In addition to these impacts on the levels of economic activity and prices, variations in interest rates are reflected in budget expenditures on interest on the public debt.

It is not feasible to estimate to what degree changes in the level of economic activity were due to decisions about monetary policy taken by the Central Bank of Brazil. However, the finding that there was some influence is sufficient to note that this institutional format goes against what I characterize here as economic democracy. It is not difficult to gauge immediate consequences of Central Bank decisions on public finances and thus for society in its various fractions. It is possible to estimate to what degree spending on the state budget was concentrated in the hands of a select few who were not submitted to legislative and social controls, which are so inconvenient to capital. Figure 26 presents a sample of the importance of the decisions of the Bank's Monetary Policy Committee to the federal budget in the past nearly twenty years. The interest is that which the government had to accrue to the outstanding debt pegged to the Selic rate, which was set by the Central Bank's Monetary Policy Committee.

After launching the Real Plan, there was an expansion in the discretionary power of the monetary authority over a significant portion of state spending. Figure 26 indicates, in addition to public debt interest, two other fiscal items on which the government has a high degree of discretion over decision-making. One of them is investment spending, which from 1998 to 2009 was systematically and significantly exceeded by the real interest that was accrued to the outstanding debt as a consequence of the monetary policy anchored to the goal for the Selic rate. The other, which is even more important to my argument, is the amount of the constitutional delinking of federal revenue, which

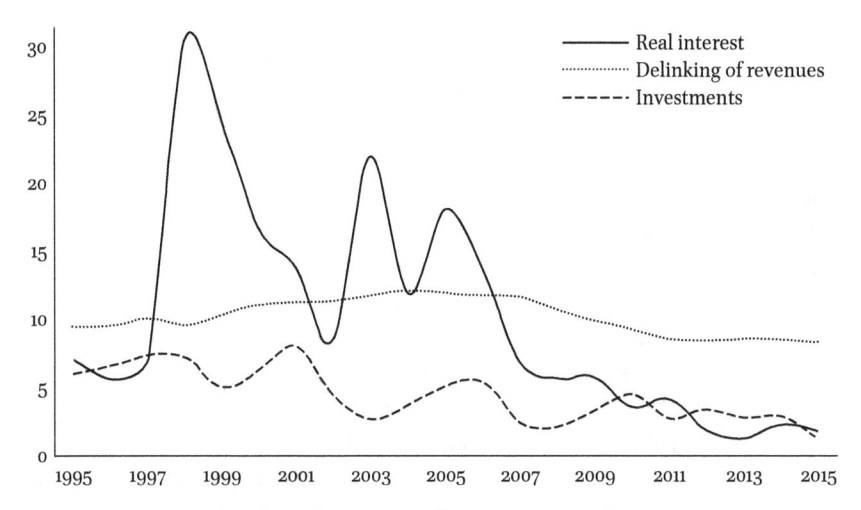

FIGURE 26 Interest, delinking of revenues, and investments, Brazil, 1995–2015
Notes: (i) percentages in relation to total revenue from federal taxes and social contributions, not including those for retirement and other pensions; (ii) real interest estimated by applying the Selic rate, deflated by the consumer price index (IPCA in its Portuguese initials), on the arithmetic average of the current and previous monthly outstanding federal debt whose yield was pegged to the Selic rate; (iii) delinking of federal revenues estimated according to the constitutional amendments that created it, the Emergency Social Fund, and the Fiscal Stabilization Fund.

was initiated during the preparations for the Real Plan. These caused a shift in power in which Congress submitted itself to the economic apparatus of the executive branch, granting it the prerogative to make decisions about the relevant portion of the budget. Let's see how it worked.

We saw in Chapter 2 that a portion of federal revenue was delinked from constitutionally mandated spending on education, healthcare, and other social welfare programs. Part of that which the Constitution of 1988 determined must be used to fund social rights, was released from that obligation a few years later to give the executive branch greater discretionary power over budget spending. As figure 26 also shows, the amount corresponding to this freedom of spending did not reach the amount of revenue delivered—largely because of decisions of the Central Bank—to the propertied classes during most of the period from late 1990s to early 2000s. That is, the portion that was delinked—but which continued to be part of the budget and thus subject to some parliamentary debate—was not as large as the amount of interest due as determined by Central Bank decisions, which, it should be emphasized, were made without any substantive democratic debate. At each rate-setting meeting of the Bank's Monetary Policy Committee, the nine Central Bank governors made decisions, with considerable autonomy from society as a whole, about large interest payments that were eventually made to the financial classes.

The numbers that compose figure 26 indicate that between 1998—the year of the Russian crisis, which in the following year led the Brazilian government to allow the exchange rate to float and to adopt the inflation targeting regime—and 2006, the real interest accrued only on the portion of the debt whose yield was pegged to the Selic rate was equivalent to an annual average of 17% of total revenue from federal taxes and social contributions, not including those for retirement and other pensions. During the same 1998–2006 period, spending on investments made by the federal government averaged 5.3% of tax revenue, while the funds delinked from mandatory expending on education, healthcare, and other social welfare programs averaged 11% of tax revenue. Since 2007, with the first signs of the global financial crisis that erupted the following year, the level of interest in question fell below the level of delinked revenue, remaining, however, higher than investments. In the period 2007–2015, the interest accrued to debt pegged to the Selic rate averaged 3.7% of tax revenue, while investments averaged 2.8% and delinked revenue 9.4%.

This situation shows that the actions of the Central Bank in relation to interest did not take place in a political vacuum. To some degree, they were government choices, thus political ones, even if taken within a context that placed pressure on the government to make those decisions. That context, however, was also a result of decisions taken by finance on a global scale. As we saw earlier, the substitution of the ideology that had seen increasing demand as the stimulus for growth by an ideology that saw rising savings as that stimulant (Przeworski 1998) did not take place merely by chance. For instance, the hike in U.S. interest rates known as 'the 1979 coup' was an explicit decision of that government (Duménil and Lévy 2001). The various Brazilian governments since the mid-1990s also decided to maintain interest rates at levels that were among the highest in the world, even if they had much less political autonomy than that available in countries of the center.

Another important aspect in the role that the Central Bank performed is its class character, which was even more apparent than the class character of the capitalist state as a whole. If the state is an arena where all classes are present for struggle, more than a space *where* this struggle occurs, the Central Bank of Brazil has been one of the *means* that finance capital has for this struggle. Working under an economic logic that made it the state institution closest to the rentier classes, it often acted as a virtual representative of this fraction. The Central Bank could do this because it had the advantage of wielding policy tools that were effectively instruments of political pressure. This took place, for example, in the crisis triggered by the external debt default that Russia experienced in August 1998. That crisis soon hit Brazil and was attacked by the Central Bank with rising interest rates. On one of these occasions, on the eve of the Brazilian Congress's vote on fiscal adjustment measures proposed by the executive branch, the Bank's Monetary Policy Committee, at the same time that it justified its decision to raise the benchmark interest rate—which at the time was the Central Bank rate (TBC in its Portuguese initials)—from 19% to 29% per annum, issued the following warning:

> The previous decision to conduct a gradual reduction of the Selic rate considered the situation in which the National Congress would support the fiscal adjustment measures, which, along with international financial support, would allow that at this meeting the Central Bank rate be restored to a level lower than that of the Selic rate.
>
> Upon analyzing the indicators of the economic conjuncture, it was seen that the agreement for international financial support, in isolation, had still not led to the desired improvement in the situation that was expected at the time the last meeting of the Monetary Policy Committee was held. In certain aspects, a deterioration was even noticed, expressed by the rise in the spreads on the negotiations for the Brazilian [external debt bonds known as] Bradies and uncertainties in terms of the effectiveness of the fiscal adjustment with unfavorable repercussions on investors' expectations.
>
> In this sense, the loosening of the monetary policy, even considering the low elasticity of long-term capitals to the difference between domestic and foreign interest rates, could deteriorate expectations of remaining investors even more. This impact on expectations could affect the stock of [foreign currency] reserves and the evaluation of agents about future developments in the economy.
>
> Therefore, the Monetary Policy Committee could not abstain from maintaining the conservative bias and appropriately accompanying the expectations found in the market. *At the next meeting, with an extraordinary convocation [of the National Congress] and the possibility that the legislature will approve the fiscal adjustment, a more favorable situation could be configured.*[11]

---

11   Banco Central do Brasil. Comitê de Política Monetária. "Atas do Copom: 31ª reunião." 16 de dezembro de 1998; emphasis added.

By "fiscal adjustment measures," the Central Bank's Monetary Policy Committee was referring to the stability program launched by the federal government in November 1998, which proposed goals for primary fiscal surpluses for the 1999–2001 period. The mention of "international financial support" was a reference to the negotiation of an International Monetary Fund agreement that would give Brazil access to borrowing to reinforce its foreign currency reserves.

In December 1998, the legislature had rejected the executive branch's proposal to increase the social contribution for retirement made by federal civil servants, which was one of the fiscal adjustment measures proposed. One notices that in the words of the Monetary Policy Committee, in addition to the declared concern for the expectations of finance, a clear message was sent to the legislature, warning that interest rates would fall if Congress acted to meet finance's expectations. In January 1999, the legislature ceded to those claims, instituting the social security contribution for retired civil servants and creating temporary additional contributions for both retired and non-retired servants.[12] In the same month, the Monetary Policy Committee eventually reduced the Central Bank rate from 29% to 25% per annum.[13]

These decisions of the Central Bank were not separate from the general orientations of the state, which, thus granted significant power to agencies whose actions were aligned to the interests of finance. By removing themselves from certain spaces of the political struggle, the popularly elected representatives thus omitted themselves, ceding an important portion of the power granted to them in the framework of the representative democracy. This space was then occupied by sectors of the bureaucracy that, different than what is usually said in analyses of Brazilian policy, were not simply insulated, but selectively insulated, that is, they were closer to some and farther from other classes or fractions of class. The contradiction is that, under the ideology that affirms that most of the important decisions are technical and not political, legitimated by a science that affirms that it is distant from ideologies, a type of financial clientelism developed in Brazil. Those who had the opportunity to influence economic policies were the beneficiaries of these policies, which is synthesized by interest on the public debt.

---

12   Brasil. "Lei n. 9.783, de 28 de janeiro de 1999." In September 1999, the contributions of retired civil employees and additional temporary contributions were ruled to be unconstitutional by the Supreme Federal Court. A social security reform in 2003 established—as a constitutional amendment—the contribution of retired civil servants (Brasil. "Emenda constitucional n. 41, de 19 de dezembro de 2003"; "lei n. 10.887, de 18 de junho de 2004").
13   Banco Central do Brasil. Comitê de Política Monetária. "Atas do Copom: 32ª reunião." 18 de janeiro de 1999.

All of this was not simply processed by the monolithic action of a state influenced by finance. Even in a limited democracy it is necessary for the popular masses to consent to the policies, under threat that they not be executed. It was thus necessary that certain consensuses be composed, or that dissent be so marginal that it could be disqualified in the political debate. The formation of consensuses, as we saw, requires that those upon whom hegemony is exercised be convinced that the model can bring advantages to them. In the economy, hegemony is only sustained when the material interests of the ruled fractions are met to some degree (Przeworski 1985). Those upon whom the economic hegemony was exercised composed the large majority of the Brazilian population but were not called on to give their opinion about monetary policy. Nevertheless, this majority believed that they were in some way served by the decisions in which they did not take part. They were convinced of the alleged adequacy of the measures largely because of the economic apparatus's legitimacy to issue discourses and recommendations. This is what the secretary of the national treasury did in 2009, when he defended that

> the interest rate is at the level that it is because Brazil opted for an inflation control system in which the interest rate is very important. ... The cost of monetary policy is an option of the country. If the country understands that it must have low inflation and that [inflation targeting] is the best system for inflation control, it will have the Selic [interest] rates that are defined [by the Central Bank's Monetary Policy Committee]. *It is an option. But it is an option of the country.*[14]

Convinced by discourses that presented policies as universal—as the one cited above—the majority in society also conferred legitimacy to the measures. One of the material interests that also concerned the ruled, not only the ruling, classes was inflation control. And one of the elements of the capitalist state, according to the concept delineated by Claus Offe (1975), is precisely legitimation. This is established, in part, when the state is able to present the image that its organization of power considers the common interests of society, or 'of the country,' as in the words of the then secretary of the treasury quoted above. This also denotes the ideological component—selective perception and articulation of social problems—that Offe (1974) defined as one of the mechanisms of selection institutionalized in the political system by means of which public policies are defined.

---

14   Brasil. Câmara dos Deputados. CPI—Dívida Pública. "Transcrição ipsis verbis: reunião ordinária n. 1940/09." 28 de outubro de 2009: 31–32; emphasis added.

4 Monetary Expectations and Inducements

Ideology carefully cultivated in recent decades affirms that societies no longer have an alternative to the neoliberal political-economic paradigm. At least until the large financial crisis that erupted in 2008, it seemed there had been unanimous acceptance of the dogma that the market was sovereign and that neoliberal fundamentals were the only ones that could successfully guide the economy. The dogma also included the evaluation that politics was a sphere foreign, or even damaging, to the 'good' functioning of both markets and the economy in general. A reference that Octavio Ianni made to the period of Brazilian industrialization could fit well in the moment of neoliberal financialization, when it is also true that

> the discourse of power is mainly that of the economy, the logic of capital; and not that of politics, in the sense of leadership, hegemony. That is, the political discourse only covers-up the manipulations of the productive forces, the privilege of capital, the interests of the dominant sectors or classes. The reasons of the state and that of capital combine, become merged.
>
> IANNI 2004 [1989]: 263

The pretension to remove any issue from the political arena—which is nonetheless a political action—dialectically indicates the possibility, if not the intention, to leave it subject to exclusive influence by those classes that continue to act politically on that issue. An immediate result of this is to limit participation in the dispute over surpluses by not inviting the majority of society to the debate. For this reason, the conceptual distinction between the economic and political spheres disguises forms of power and domination created under capitalism and serves as an efficient mechanism for the defense of capital (Wood 2003). However, this distinction engenders a contradiction, which consists in the declared objective of maintaining the economy free of allegedly damaging influence of politics, at the same time that it seeks the non-declared objective of establishing a new hegemony. In issues like economic, monetary, and fiscal policy, what takes place is not the removal of some of them from debate, but rather the removal, or even the barring of entrance, of certain agents from the spaces where these issues are debated. And since not all agents are excluded, it is up to one of the remaining class fractions to exercise hegemony.

If the economy, according to neoliberal ideologues, is such an important realm that it must be treated 'technically' and not politically, we are authorized to ask: what are the techniques? who are the technicians? whose interests do the technicians and their techniques serve? It is necessary to emphasize that in a class society there is no such social category that is representative of universal interests. We are all linked to one or another class or fraction of class at some moment, and this influences our actions. Returning to what we saw about what I have called selective bureaucratic insulation, there were concrete evidences of class influence on the Brazilian state during this era of neoliberal financialization. One of them was a mechanism to hear from agents of finance capital about their outlooks for the economy. The system was developed within the framework of the inflation targeting regime. In political terms, its functioning casts light on the financial-economic apparatus of the state that reveals its anti-democratic character.

Every day since November 2001 the Central Bank of Brazil conducted what it calls a market expectations survey among economic agents. According to the Bank, the tool was designed to "monitor the changes in expectations of the market about the main macroeconomic variables, to provide information to be used in the decision-making process about monetary policy."[15] The survey included questions about expectations for the benchmark interest rate in the economy, changes in GDP, inflation, exchange rate, and fiscal results. Most of the expectations were prepared by financial organizations, which, despite the scope of the Brazilian economy and society, formed a quite small and thus restricted group of interests and with particular perspectives on the issues in question. In late 2004, there were 104 informants, among which 52 were banks, 23 investment fund administrators, nine brokers and distributors, fourteen consultants, and six non-financial companies or professional associations.[16] In late 2016, the number of informants was approximately 120 organizations.[17]

It is important to notice that a few years later the Central Bank of Brazil came to affirm that the survey of expectations sought to "monitor the changes in *consensus* in the market about the main macroeconomic variables, to generate support for the decision-making process about monetary policy."[18] Considering the high level of concentration in what the Central Bank was referring to as *the* market, the Bank's definition of consensus was not completely incorrect. Actually, it was a consensus of the few who, despite their reduced number,

---

15   Banco Central do Brasil. "BCB—Sobre o Gerin." Available at http://www4.bcb.gov.br/pec/gci/port/sobregerin.asp, accessed May 4, 2016.
16   Banco Central do Brasil. "Relatório de inflação." Dezembro 2004 (Vol. 6, n. 4).
17   Banco Central do Brasil. "BCB—Sobre o Gerin." Available at http://www4.bcb.gov.br/pec/gci/port/sobregerin.asp, accessed September 28, 2016.
18   Banco Central do Brasil. "Sobre a Gerência-Executiva de Relacionamento com Investidores." Available at http://www4.BC.gov.br/?FOCUSINTRO, accessed January 17, 2010; emphasis added.

were quite important. In the restricted group formed by those whose expectations were heard and considered, the differences were unlikely to be more than marginal. All of the agents consulted were organically linked to the propertied classes and, among them, nearly all were connected to finance. In addition to having the opportunity to present their opinions about the direction of the economy—and possibly some requests and desires—they were also privileged to be able to exchange ideas with the state economic apparatus. For example, in March 2007, it was revealed that Central Bank of Brazil governors regularly met "secretly with executives of financial institutions to discuss the economy."[19] This report added that,

> officially, the meetings do not exist. They are not on the agenda of the Central Bank. Nor are the results revealed to the press ... According to the Central Bank spokesperson ... the non-reporting of the agendas is a procedure that aims to avoid speculation in the financial market. A prior communication, the spokesperson argues, would create space for interference in business. "In this case, transparency is not necessary. It occurs through (brief) communiques after the meeting of the Monetary Policy Committee, the minutes of the meeting, and the quarterly inflation reports. This is the legal framework of the inflation targeting regime," the Central Bank's spokesperson affirms.[20]

In October 2009, in response to that revelation, a parliamentary investigative commission (CPI in its Portuguese initials) of the Chamber of Deputies requested from the Bank "a complete list of the meetings held between the board of governors of the Central Bank with market analysts."[21] With the response in hand, the deputy who signed the request revealed:

> We have the names and we checked into each one. ... All the large international and Brazilian banks. I can name here: Santander, Morgan Stanley, Votorantim, Bradesco. Whichever one you want is here, Paribas, etc., etc. But what is most important is the percentage of those who define [sic] the interest rate: 51% are associated to the banks and 35% to fund

---

19   Márcia Pinheiro; Sergio Lirio. "A república distante." *Carta Capital*. 28 de março de 2007: 22.
20   Márcia Pinheiro; Sergio Lirio. "A república distante." *Carta Capital*. 28 de março de 2007: 23.
21   Brasil. Câmara dos Deputados. CPI—Dívida Pública. "Requerimento de CPI n. 49, de 2009." 28 de outubro de 2009.

managers. ... The productive sector is 4%, that which should be consulted. The public sector is 1%. And the very International Monetary Fund is consulted ... It's here. Who is the beneficiary of this? ... Those who define also benefit?[22]

This evidences restrictions to participation in the economic debate. However, contrary to what critics say when they complain of the lack of discussion about the decisions that influence the economy, there was debate. The point is that not all those interested in the results, or who were capable of giving an opinion, were invited to take part in the discussions.

The fact that such limited fractions of society could impose their will on other fractions that were so broad made neoliberalism an even more antidemocratic mode of regulation of the economy. Finance capital came to have even more power than it previously had over the ruled classes. Moreover, finance garnered more power than other fractions of the capitalist class. In the words of the Central Bank of Brazil president during nearly all of Fernando Henrique Cardoso's second government, "the issue of sovereignty in relation to the market is a question of difficult practical implementation. There is the market. What can the government do?"[23] A consequence of this was the shift in the debate from a realm that tends to be more clear, like the public budget, to a zone over which the possibilities for social control were practically nonexistent. The contradiction revealed was that, along with the restriction to broad democratic participation, the pretension of the universal character of neoliberal economic policies was reinforced.

The attempt to universalize certain orientations emanating from the ruling classes is also a question of legitimacy. It can be conferred, for example, by science, which is often a tool of political-economic power and has always been intimately linked to capital (Gorz 2005; Ianni 2011). Since the classic authors in sociology, this connection was noticed as fundamental to capitalist development. Both Karl Marx and Max Weber perceived that this development would not have taken place with the intensity observed without the association between production and modern science. Science also has a fundamental role at the level that Marx called the superstructure of capital. Thus, what is seen is not only science contributing to technology (Weber 1982 [1919]a) and both

---

22   Brasil. Câmara dos Deputados. CPI—Dívida Pública. "Transcrição ipsis verbis: reunião ordinária n. 2320/09." 9 de dezembro de 2009: 26–27.
23   Brasil. Câmara dos Deputados. CPI—Dívida Pública. "Transcrição ipsis verbis: reunião ordinária n. 2129/09." 18 de novembro de 2009: 54.

contributing to the expansion of capital (Marx 1990 [1890]); it is also seen that science can establish 'truths' with clear ideological contours. For this reason, economists, sociologists, and political scientists become intellectual servants of power and technicians of social control when they grant scientific legitimacy to policies (Aronowitz 2000). They can do this because theories serve various ways to provide ideological justification to authority; research with bureaucratic purposes makes authority more effective and efficient by providing it with information (Mills 2000 [1959]).

In economics there are theories that are nothing more than rationalizations for the political interests of classes and antagonistic groups (Przeworski 1985)—actually, this can take place in any of the social sciences or other fields. Recent evidence of this was the disbelief that fell on the hypothesis of efficient self-regulated markets and the political prescriptions derived from it that contributed to the global financial crisis that erupted in 2008 (Wade 2008). Long before this Émile Durkheim (2001 [1895]) had indicated that the so-called economic laws were nothing more than maxims for action and disguised practical precepts. And he used as an example precisely the well-known law of supply and demand. For Durkheim, it had never been effectively established that economic relations take place according to this law. Nothing more had been demonstrated, he argued, than that individuals would act in this way if they had a clear understanding of their own interests and that any alternative form of action could be harmful to them. This is what Michel Callon affirmed more recently by stating that

> economics—and this is where it derives its strength—is a constructed, logical discourse based on a number of irrefutable hypotheses. As discourse it can change into a system of beliefs that infiltrate agents' minds and colonize them. For example, neoclassical theory is based on the idea that agents are self-interested. If I believe this statement and if this belief is shared by the other agents, and I believe that they believe it, then what was simply an assumption turns into a reality. Everyone ends up aligning himself or herself to the model and everyone's expectations are fulfilled by everyone else's behaviors. To predict economic agents' behaviors an economic theory does not have to be true; it simply needs to be believed by everyone.
> CALLON 2007: 322

Here we have the concept of performativity of economics. In brief, this idea calls attention to the fact that economic models do not only represent economic phenomena, but also create them (Preda 2007). For example, the use of aspects based on economic theories can make events more probable than the very representation proposed in the scientific description (MacKenzie 2007). Callon clarifies that, given that the realms of economic science and of economic practice are not totally distinct, science does not hold a monopoly on performativity. That is, performativity can also be exercised by the practitioners, including the economic agents and market professionals. Bringing this concept to the focus of this book, my argument is that if the Central Bank of Brazil listened to economists from the financial market to assist in establishing the Bank's analyses or even convictions—central banks do this in other countries that adopt inflation targeting—it seems that monetary policy decisions were influenced by a peculiar type of pressure, namely the opinions of the economists surveyed. This was manifested in the decision-making process described by the Bank's Monetary Policy Committee itself. Some of its meeting minutes reveal that when the Bank set interest rates it considered the expectations surveyed from market professionals.

Considering the period of November 2001, which is when the Central Bank of Brazil began to report the expectations for the goal for the Selic rate expressed by the organizations surveyed, until December 2015, there is a significant correlation between what had been expected and the rate effectively set. Figure 27 presents a comparison between the goals expected by the portion of finance heard by the Central Bank and those goals effectively set by the Monetary Policy Committee. The correlation between them is more than 0.99, that is nearly perfectly positive. During the entire series, the only relatively significant distance between the two lines was from late 2002 through early 2003. This was the period between Lula's election and the inauguration of his government, and in part reflected the anti-creditor rhetoric his party consistently sustained since it was established in the early 1980s. At a first moment, Brazilian financial markets were marked by the instability of the electoral period. However, as the new government gave concrete signs that it would maintain the foundations of the monetary policy inaugurated by the previous government, financial markets regained stability. One of the signs was the continuity of the rise in the benchmark interest rate that had begun in October 2002, when Lula was elected. That rate was maintained for nearly a year at levels higher than those on the eve of Lula's election.

It is important to clarify that I am not referring to the possibility that the expectations gathered by the Central Bank of Brazil from financial market agents came to be self-fulfilling prophecies. Nevertheless, I am emphasizing the convergence of the decisions about interest rate targets made by the Bank's Monetary Policy Committee with the forecasts made by the market agents. These forecasts were made by those who, seeking to protect the prices of their

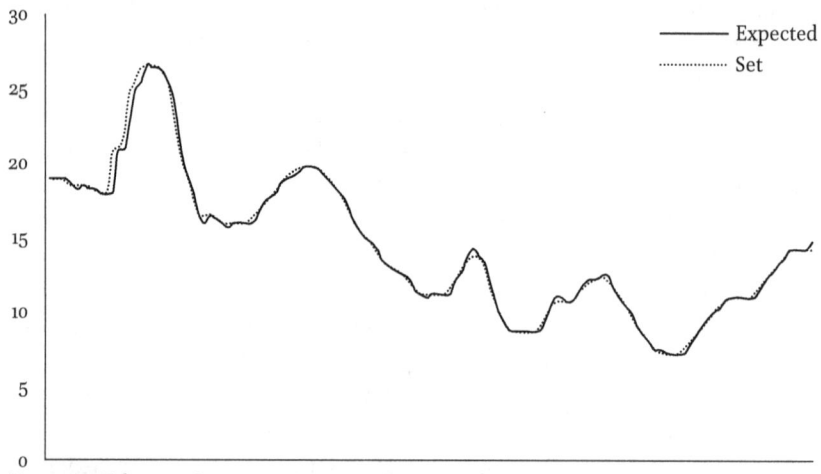

FIGURE 27 Expected and set targets for the Selic interest rate, 2001–2015
Notes: (i) percentage scale; (ii) nominal rate; (iii) expected rate is the median of the daily expectations for the Selic rate target during the period comprised between the dates of the settings of the two last targets in force; (iv) the series covers the period from November 2001 to December 2015.

financial assets, placed subtle pressure so that the antidote to inflation—a rise in interest rates—could be sufficiently effective to maintain inflation and, as a result, the yields of money-capital at levels satisfactory to finance. This on its own indicates a sharing of ideas between members of the state economic apparatus, represented by the Central Bank, and finance, represented by its organic intellectuals—as Gramsci (2004 [1932]) defined those he called intellectuals of industry—namely the economists of the financial institutions heard in the Bank's expectations survey.

It is not odd that these intellectuals made their forecasts considering the context in which they were inserted, and the class interests they represented. After all, this is what those who operate under the logic of capital do. However, the inequalities already existing under capitalism were strengthened by giving voice to one social segment—finance—while denying opportunity for the ruled classes to defend what they thought or wanted, even if everyone in society would experience the impacts of the decisions. If the statistics and tools used to describe a reality have effects on the very reality that they supposedly describe (Didier 2007)—or create?—why were they produced and managed in a process restricted to fractions of class that had obvious interests in the described, or perhaps created, reality?

It would be extremely difficult to empirically test the hypothesis that those economists made their analyses or forecasts based on particular interests. A test would depend, for example, on declarations from those who took part in the processes. But the hypothesis is plausible if it is correct to suppose that agents make decisions according to the convictions forged in the realm where they build their professional careers and their lives, and where they exchange ideas and convictions with peers. If this takes place with bureaucrats in the state economic apparatuses, who, according to Joseph Stiglitz (2002) see the world through the eyes of the financial community, it is reasonable to deduce that this also takes place among agents organically linked to finance. The contrary would be to suppose that there are social segments whose members are endowed with the exclusive ability to analyze a certain reality with sufficient knowledge, objectivity, and impartiality to make them deserving of the public trust to say what is universal and what is correct or not.

I should also make clear that I am not arguing that finance deliberately raised its expectations of inflation to seek automatic rises in interest rates. We must recall the affirmation from Michel Callon cited above that "to predict economic agents' behaviors an economic theory does not have to be true; it *simply* needs to be believed by everyone" (Callon 2007: 322; emphasis added). The adverb 'simply' obfuscates the importance of the legitimacy that a theory—or even a forecast, which is the empirical object of my analysis here— must have to be considered valid and accepted, especially if it is supposed to be taken as a guide for action. Such a theory cannot lack a significant connection with reality, even if this reality has been created with a contribution from that theory. The farther a theory is from that which is supposed to be real, the more difficult it is to believe it. Moreover, forecasts are based on a dialectic in which agents share beliefs about a future that they actually contribute to making more probable. It is thus reasonable to believe that, even if it is far from being a simple inducement, a discourse is tempered with the will of the person who issues it. As Michel Foucault taught,

> it does not matter that discourse appears to be of little account, because the prohibitions that surround it very soon reveal its link with desire and with power. There is nothing surprising about that, since ... discourse is not simply that which manifests (or hides) desire—it is also the object of desire; and since, as history constantly teaches us, discourse is not simply that which translates struggles or systems of domination, but is the thing for which and by which there is struggle, discourse is the power which is to be seized.
> FOUCAULT 1981 [1970]: 52–53

Although it may appear a bit inappropriate to turn to a thinker who conceptualized the microphysics of power (Foucault 1979) and who did not define power as a class issue, what matters is that the conduction of the economy—which also is done with certain uses of certain discourses—can involve a favoring of a particular class or fraction of class. And some can be favored while others can be disfavored to the very degree of existence or not of opportunities for the debate about decisions. As Foucault (1981 [1970]) also observed, not just anyone can speak about any issue in our societies. The economy is perhaps the best example of an issue that affects everyone at the same time that it is debated by very few people who have an effective capacity to influence it.

5 The Talking Shop of Macroeconomic Policy

We saw previously that the Brazilian Constitution of 1988 established a series of social rights to which tax revenues were linked to assure the financing. This is when the universalization of public health was formally established, a specific budget for social security became mandatory, and the minimum wage was set as the minimum value for all retirement pensions. Some of those constitutional determinations caused the executive branch to protest against the rigidity that these constitutionally determined rights supposedly imposed on the administration of government spending. Then, just shortly later, in 1994, the Constitution began to be amended to delink resources from mandatory spending on social policies. This delinking, as we saw in Chapter 2, initially sought to give the government greater discretion to face the increasing difficulties in servicing the public debt expected to be caused by the drop in inflation. The latter, one must recall, works as a source of state financing through the inflation tax.

The delinking was combined with mechanisms that the Constitution had left sufficiently vague and flexible so that decisions about the public debt became concentrated in the executive branch. For example, the Constitution rules that "the president of the republic has sole responsibility ... to submit to the National Congress the pluriannual plan, the bill for budgetary directives, and the budget proposals" of the federal government.[24] It also prescribes that

> the amendments to the proposed law for the annual budget or to the proposed laws that modify it can only be approved if they ... indicate the needed funding, accepting only those from the annulation of expenses, except that for:

---

24 Brasil. "Constituição, de 5 de outubro de 1988." Art. 84, XXIII.

(a) allotments for spending for personnel and related mandatory spending;
(b) *debt servicing*;
(c) constitutional tax transfers to states, municipalities, and the Federal District.[25]

Combining these two constitutional measures, the corresponding institutional framework thus established other restrictions to democracy, even in it its already limited liberal version. They determined that the budget for servicing the public debt that is proposed by the executive branch cannot be amended or changed by the legislature to make room for another expense—except for debt services—that the legislature deemed necessary. This issue was raised in 2009, for example, by an investigative commission in the Chamber of Deputies that examined the public debt. The representatives who addressed the issue unanimously recognized that the debt was not an issue with which the legislature was concerned in the deliberations over the federal budget. I will now present some of the descriptions of the place of the debt in the budget debate according to some of the lawmakers themselves. The first was given by the rapporteur of that investigative commission just before it concluded its work:

> I am inclined to suggest that previous budget authorization be required for the use of resources derived from issuing securities, regardless of how they are issued. ...
>
> At the margin of the budget, at a first moment, the issue of debt [securities] to meet these expenses fattens the gross debt and, in the future, without Congress having any choice, the corresponding mandatory expenses on interest and amortizations of these securities will be allotted in the budget.[26]
>
> In the three years that I participated in the [Mixed Committee for Plans, Public Budgets and Inspection; Comissão Mista de Planos, Orçamentos Públicos e Fiscalização in Portuguese], as party coordinator, as member, every time the debt would be debated, no one debated [and I heard]: "Ah, this is not the place for this." But why not?! If we can't discuss [public debt in this committee], at the time that the budget is being voted, when will we discuss it? ...

---

25   Brasil. "Constituição, de 5 de outubro de 1988." Art. 166, § 3°, II; emphasis added.
26   Brasil. Câmara dos Deputados. CPI—Dívida Pública. "Transcrição ipsis verbis: reunião ordinária n. 0360/10." 14 de abril de 2010:17. By "these expenses," the rapporteur was referring to an issuing of treasury bonds to raise funds for the Brazilian Development Bank in early 2010.

> How many times, I am a witness, did I see a deputy ... wanting to say this to the minister [of planning] ... and even to the president of the Central Bank, and [and the answer was]: "It's not here; no, we cannot discuss [it]; this isn't the issue." But what is the issue?! We're discussing the budget and we cannot discuss the debt?[27]
>
> When the Constitution states, in its first article, ... "that all power emanates from the people, who exercise it by means of elected representatives or directly, ..." we are the recipients of this power that emanates from the people. ... But, if we translate the exercise of power that emanates from the people and is conferred to us into numbers, budget numbers, this power only represents 53% of the actual power, because 47% [sic] of the budget is interest and amortization of the debt, in which we cannot interfere.
>
> The deputy ... may win lots of votes in Bahia, have a million vote[s] for federal deputy, [but he or she] will reach here quietly, miniscule, without power. As the leading senator of the republic, who may have had 20 million votes, cannot ... .
>
> We represent the power that emanates from the people, and it is *said* that it is all power, but in *practice*, from an accounting perspective, that all power is not all the power, it is only a part.[28]

The Brazilian Constitution of 1988 was quite timid in its prescriptions about eventual limits on the public debt. It did nothing more than define that it was up to the Senate to "set, by proposal from the president of the republic, global limits for the total debt consolidated of the federal government, the states, the Federal District and the municipalities" and that it was up "to the National Congress, with the sanction of the president of the republic, to make decisions about ... the total of the federal securitized debt."[29] In May 2000, the so-called Fiscal Responsibility Law determined that the president of the republic submit to the Senate a proposal for the debt limits as established by the Constitution of 1988.[30] Upon doing so, that legislative house approved limits only for states, municipalities, and the Federal District.[31] It should be highlighted that the

---

27 Brasil. Câmara dos Deputados. CPI—Dívida Pública. "Transcrição ipsis verbis: reunião ordinária n. 1233/09." 19 de agosto de 2009: 25–26.
28 Brasil. Câmara dos Deputados. CPI—Dívida Pública. "Transcrição ipsis verbis: reunião ordinária n. 1304/09." 26 de agosto de 2009: 15–16; emphases added.
29 Brasil. "Constituição, de 5 de outubro de 1988." Art. 52, VI; art. 48, XIV.
30 Brasil. "Lei complementar n. 101, de 4 de maio de 2000." Art. 30, I, II.
31 Brasil. Senado Federal. "Resolução n. 40, de 2001." 20 de dezembro de 2001; 9 de abril de 2002.

Senate was relatively fast—it took a bit more than a year—to approve limits for the subnational governments, leaving the federal government without any debt limit.

I previously mentioned that the dominance of the executive branch in the most important decisions made Brazil what Décio Saes (2001) calls a limited democracy, from which emerges a kind of civil authoritarianism. The main evidence of this is the Congress's limited power to legislate due to the capacity of the president to issue provisional decrees that immediately have the strength of a law. Some analysts see in this tool the continuity of the power to issue decree-laws that presidents had during the military dictatorship of the 1964–1985 period (Figueiredo and Limongi 2000). A provisional decree was precisely the instrument used to establish the law that currently authorizes the executive branch to issue public debt securities. In November 1994, the president signed one such decree that came to be re-issued more than eighty times over six years until it was converted into the law that until today rules federal debt securities.[32] In sum, the law that authorizes the executive branch to issue these bonds did not originate from legislative debate, much less from any broader social debate.

That law did not even mention interest on the debt, limiting itself to subjects such as purposes, denominations, forms of issuing, registration, and other secondary characteristics of the securities. It vaguely defined that it is up to the "executive branch [to establish] the general and specific characteristics of the public debt securities."[33] In the following years, by means of another kind of decree, the executive branch defined characteristics such as maturity, yield, interest rates, and forms of adjustment for inflation, among others.[34] For some types of securities it stipulated that it shall be up to the minister of finance to define their characteristics, including interest rates. In sum, the economic state apparatus centralized in its hands an important portion of the decision-making power over the destination of surpluses that were made through public debt. Figure 28 displays a sample of this centralization of power.

Figure 28 indicates the significance to the size of the Brazilian economy of the securities issued under the laws mentioned. It reveals the concentration of decision-making power that was reflected in how a large part of the government budget was spent. In 2000, the value of securities whose rates were defined by the Central Bank's Monetary Policy Committee was equivalent to

---

32 Brasil. "Medida provisória n. 470, de 11 de abril de 1994"; "lei n. 10.179, de 6 de fevereiro de 2001."
33 Brasil. "Lei n. 10.179, de 6 de fevereiro de 2001." Art. 7º.
34 Brasil. Presidência da República. "Decreto n. 3.859, de 4 de julho de 2001."

21% of the GDP; in 2015, it dropped to 10%. During this period, the portion whose interest rates were defined by the Ministry of Finance rose from 11% to 34% of GDP. The decisions about interest were thus concentrated in two agencies of the economic apparatus of the Brazilian state. The Central Bank and the Ministry of Finance combined were responsible for defining the interest rate on an outstanding debt equivalent to 33% of GDP in 2000, which rose to 44% in 2015 and averaged 40% of GDP during this period.

The situation shows that in the years of financial expansion the public debt was not a substantial concern of the Brazilian legislature. The few initiatives to discuss the issue revealed that the state—including the legislature—was moving farther from social control over the economy. For example, the Constitution of 1988 determined that "within one year of [its] promulgation, the National Congress [should promote] ... analytical and technical examination of the acts and facts that generated the Brazilian external indebtedness."[35] In April 1989, a parliamentary commission was established with this objective, which, however, was not attained, since its conclusions were restricted to "legal aspects of debt contracting."[36] Referring to this and other consequences of that commission and alleging that "the National Congress never came to conclude ... any one of the mixed commissions that it established to give complete effectiveness to the constitutional determination mentioned," the Order of Attorneys of Brazil (Ordem dos Advogados do Brasil in Portuguese) filed a suit in the Supreme Federal Court (Supremo Tribunal Federal in Portuguese) in 2004 calling for complete compliance.[37] Until the conclusion of this book, the suit had not been ruled on.

In the first years of the Real Plan, the Brazilian legislature tried to discuss the public debt once again, then focused on the domestic debt. The result, however, was even less significant than the investigation concluded in 1989. In June 1996, the Senate established a special commission with the declared objective of "examining the problem [of the] public domestic debt and ... proposing alternatives for its solution."[38] There were only two meetings, in which no

---

35   Brasil. "Constituição, de 5 de outubro de 1988." Ato das disposições constitucionais transitórias, Art. 26.
36   Brasil. Congresso Nacional. "Relatório parcial da Comissão Mista Destinada ao Exame Analítico e Pericial dos Atos e Fatos Geradores do Endividamento Externo Brasileiro," 4 de outubro de 1989: 2.
37   Ordem dos Advogados do Brasil; Supremo Tribunal Federal. "[Arguição de descumprimento de preceito fundamental] ADPF n. 59." 3–6 de dezembro de 2004: 8. Ordem dos Advogados do Brasil (OAB in its Portuguese initials) is the leading national professional entity for lawyers in the country.
38   Brasil. Senado Federal. Comissão Especial Temporária, criada através do requerimento n. 353, de 1996. "[Notas taquigráficas da 1ª reunião]." 19 de junho de 1996.

Yield	2000	2001	2002	2003	2004	2005	2006	2007	2008	2009	2010	2011	2012	2013	2014	2015
Pegged to the Selic rate, which was defined by the Central Bank's Monetary Policy Committee	21.5	24.5	25.0	25.8	23.4	23.2	17.1	15.0	14.6	15.0	13.4	12.5	8.8	7.4	7.4	10.6
Prefixed rates, understood to have been defined by the Ministry of Finance in public offers	6.2	3.7	0.9	5.3	8.3	12.6	16.4	16.8	13.1	14.1	15.7	15.6	16.4	16.5	16.5	18.4
Pegged to price indices plus interest rates defined by the Ministry of Finance	0.6	1.8	3.8	4.5	5.2	6.3	9.7	11.3	11.5	11.6	11.3	11.8	13.9	13.5	13.8	15.1
Various rates defined by presidential decree or by the Ministry of Finance	4.7	6.3	6.1	3.9	2.3	1.6	1.3	0.9	0.9	0.7	0.6	0.5	0.5	0.5	0.5	0.6
Totals	33.0	36.3	35.8	39.5	39.3	43.8	44.4	44.1	40.0	41.5	40.9	40.5	39.6	37.9	38.2	44.7

FIGURE 28 Decision makers on securitized public debt interest, Brazil, 2000–2015

Notes: (i) percentages in relation to GDP; (ii) the decree that established the characteristics of the securities with prefixed yields did not indicate who was responsible for defining the sales prices, but since these securities were sold through direct issuance or public offer, it is presumed that the decisions about such prices were made by the Ministry of Finance; (iii) the maturities of most federal securities were defined by the Ministry of Finance.

testimony was given by anyone from the executive branch, civil society, or anyone else. The term of the commission was extended four times, but it had no other activity in the extra time and was terminated in August 1998.

The final attempt to debate the Brazilian debt was the formation of a parliamentary investigative commission of the Chamber of Deputies with apparently broader functions than the previous ones. Installed in August 2009, the declared objective of this commission was "to investigate the public debt of the federal government, the states, and municipalities, the payment of interest on this debt, the beneficiaries of these payments, and its impact on the social policies for sustainable development in the country."[39] Originally programmed to conclude its work in December 2009, the parliamentary investigative commission was extended until May 2010. The commission reproduced evidences of a significant portion of the arguments I have developed until here concerning democracy: (i) the virtual inexistence of spaces for popular participation and popular control; (ii) the omission of legislature, even though it was responsible for the investigation; (iii) the hegemony of the state economic apparatus in the executive branch and its disdain for democratic control; and (iv) the sharing between the bureaucracy, the legislature, and finance of concerns and ideologies typical of the neoliberal phase of financial expansion of the economy.

The parliamentary commission was created, in part, because of demands from organizations in society that had been watching the issue for years and which came together in a campaign called Citizen Audit of the Debt. The campaign began in 2001, following a popular, unofficial referendum held in the previous year, in which nearly six million people expressed opposition to continuing payments on the unaudited external debt.[40] The parliamentary investigative commission responded partially to one of the demands of the social movements to conduct the auditing prescribed by the Constitution of 1988. This appeared to create a forum for broad debate about the Brazilian public debt. At one of the moments in which he expressed appreciation for the presence of representatives of social movements, the chairman of the commission raised this possibility: "we will still plan a round-table ... with the entities that have always accompanied and conducted an important movement for the mobilization of civil society around this parliamentary investigative commission."[41]

39 Brasil. Câmara dos Deputados. CPI—Dívida Pública. "Transcrição ipsis verbis: reunião ordinária n. 1304/09." 26 de agosto de 2009: 1.
40 Auditoria Cidadã da Dívida; Rede Jubileu Sul Brasil. "ABC da dívida: sabe quanto você está pagando?" Fevereiro de 2008: 3.
41 Brasil. Câmara dos Deputados. CPI—Dívida Pública. "Transcrição ipsis verbis: reunião ordinária n. 2060/09." 11 de novembro de 2009: 32.

Nevertheless, this only took place on the eve of the termination of the commission's work, outside of its official meetings, and a few days after the rapporteur had already issued his final report.

Another suggestion formally presented to the commission was that it should conduct public hearings in the legislatures of states that were in debt to the federal government. It was also suggested that state secretariats of finance and representatives of civil society entities be invited to the proposed hearings.[42] According to the lawmaker who proposed them, the hearings could help promote and create a popular interest about the issue. During one debate on the proposal, after hearing largely unfavorable opinions, including that of the commission's rapporteur, the deputy who presented the requests for the public hearings asked if there was any "fear of hearing civil society."[43] Nearly one month later, the requests were formally rejected by the commission. The inaction and lack of control from the legislature was also deepened by the difficulties in attaining the quorum needed to vote on requests and by the low attendance of the commission's members during the public hearings.

This situation was in keeping with the spirit of the parliamentary investigative commission, which can be summarized in the words of a deputy who at the time supported the government, and who was named by the rapporteur to prepare a specific report on the domestic debt. This deputy affirmed that

> the country today is in another macroeconomic context in which the public debt is not as agonizing for the Brazilian state.[44]
>
> ... this investigative commission is a bit different than the usual ones, even because its final result is *merely indicative*. It is different than a traditional investigative commission, which has a result: sending the report to the public ministry [public prosecutor's office] for the proper sanctions. In this case it is much more of a *political nature*.[45]

If a legislator understood that the result of work 'of a political nature' would be 'merely indicative,' and if this position was shared by the majority on the commission, it indicates that the depoliticization of economic policy was not

---

42 Brasil. Câmara dos Deputados. CPI—Dívida Pública. "Requerimento[s] de CPI n. 34–37, de 2009." 28 de outubro 2009.
43 Brasil. Câmara dos Deputados. CPI—Dívida Pública. "Transcrição ipsis verbis: reunião ordinária n. 1725/09." 7 de outubro de 2009: 57.
44 Brasil. Câmara dos Deputados. CPI—Dívida Pública. "Transcrição ipsis verbis: reunião ordinária n. 1655/09." 30 de setembro de 2009: 26.
45 Brasil. Câmara dos Deputados. CPI—Dívida Pública. "Transcrição ipsis verbis: reunião ordinária n. 1725/09." 7 de outubro de 2009: 6; emphases added.

revealed only by those I have identified as organic intellectuals of finance. It was also ingrained in forums of party and legislative political struggle.

Another evidence of this effort to depoliticize economic policy was revealed in the investigative commission's resistance to call members of the executive branch to testify, from either the incumbent or preceding governments. A request to testify (known as a convocation in Brazilian law) is one of the prerogatives of any parliamentary investigative commission, and a person called must appear. Nonetheless, not one request of this kind was issued in the original period of the commission; and only one during the extension. Nearly all of the requests made under this format were rather approved as invitations, which meant that the person asked to appear could decide whether or not to do so. According to the legislator who was the author of the request to create the investigative commission for the public debt, a

> parliamentary investigative commission has powers of investigation and convocation. I do not know if it gained this spirit here in the House, and the prerogatives of the House were abandoned long ago. It has been impossible to vote on a request to testify of any person, a minister, an official of the state, in any permanent committee of this House. This is a grave error. This degrades the Brazilian legislature. In the parliamentary investigative commission it is even more grave, because it has much greater power.[46]

This was initially the case of the request for the minister of finance and the president of Central Bank at the time to testify about "the consequences of monetary and exchange rate policies in the formation of the federal public debt, the payment of interest and its amortizations, the beneficiaries of these payments and their impact on financing of social policies, infrastructure, and development."[47] The request was approved as an invitation and the parliamentary investigative commission terminated its original term without either the minister of finance or the Central Bank president being heard. During the extension, given that neither of those invited indicated they would appear, the commission eventually approved the request for mandatory testimony from the president of the Central Bank. The request was only possible because of

---

[46] Brasil. Câmara dos Deputados. CPI—Dívida Pública. "Transcrição ipsis verbis: reunião ordinária n. 1725/09." 7 de outubro de 2009: 4.

[47] Brasil. Câmara dos Deputados. CPI—Dívida Pública. "Requerimento de CPI n. 16, de 2009." 23 de outubro de 2009.

lack of attention by the lawmakers who supported the government during the deliberations. He and the minister of finance appeared to the commission one month before its termination but added little to what had been heard until then. In general, they emphasized issues that in their opinion indicated the success of macroeconomic policy.

Other requests to testify, due to deals among legislators from parties that supported the government of the time and the preceding one, were never even voted on. One of them required that former Brazilian President Fernando Henrique Cardoso be called on to address the investigation about the external debt that he, when he was a senator, reported on in 1987; another requested testimony from the minister of finance during the two Cardoso governments; another sought testimony from the minister of finance during the first two years of the Lula government. This issue is connected to the third mark revealed by the parliamentary investigative commission, which is the hegemony of the economic-financial bureaucracy and its disdain for democratic control.

We saw previously that the bureaucracy has always been the state institution most rebellious against representative democracy (Poulantzas 2000 [1978]), and welcomes a legislature that is poorly informed and thus with little effective power (Weber 1964 [1922]). In a public hearing of the investigative commission, the secretary of the national treasury—who said he was surprised to learn that not all the information requested from him had been sent—was asked the following questions:

> The Ministry of Finance has the legal attribution for financial administration and public accountancy, as well as administration of the domestic and external debts. In this light, how is it possible to explain the fact that *it did not respond to a request we made*, in which we asked for the basic data about the outstanding external debt: the balance, ... amortizations, and interest? We found that *it sent us incomplete data*, for only the period from 1999 through 2008, affirming that the Central Bank would provide the information since 1970, precisely because we had a big shift in the debt in this period, at the beginning of the 1970s.
>
> ... *we did not receive this information*. Second question: in relation to the domestic debt, we asked the minister of finance, in *a request that was not responded to*, to show the factors that led to growth of the domestic debt—the factors—such as the assumption of other debts, variations in the exchange rate, accrued interest. The minister of finance only informed this investigative commission that the Treasury Secretariat only came to prepare and publish the factors of changes in the outstanding debt from 1999 on, ... which is the reason for which data referring to the

previous years are not being sent. Once again, the Ministry [of Finance] affirmed that the Central Bank would provide the information until 1998. *We did not receive this information either.*[48]

This is one more confirmation of Max Weber's (1964 [1922]) thesis that the bureaucratic government, by its own tendency, excludes publicity, and that bureaucracy hides its knowledge and activity from criticism as much as possible.

Upon expanding this analysis beyond the specific issue of the parliamentary investigative commission on the public debt, we see that the administration of the economy as a whole—in which the debt is one of the points of special attention of the economic technocracy—suffered from a similar lack of democratic control. For example, the Fiscal Responsibility Law I mentioned earlier determined that,

> after the conclusion of each semester, the Central Bank of Brazil presents in a joint meeting of the pertinent thematic commissions of the National Congress, an evaluation of compliance with the objectives and goals of monetary, credit, and exchange rate policies, revealing the fiscal impact and cost of its operations and the results displayed in the balance sheets.[49]

According to a former lawmaker who testified to the investigative commission, and who affirmed that he participated in the joint commission meetings held as required by the Fiscal Responsibility Law, the information that this law determined should be presented

> had never been shown. The public hearings of the Central Bank [were] limited here to a large power-point presentation of the economic successes, but a precise evaluation of the costs of economic policy had never been made.
>
> We observed that this entire debate about the financial situation of the Brazilian state is covered up. This debate should be a central debate in the budget committee. This is not done, because the budget committee is merely dedicated to discussing amendments. The primary result is this much, and we have that much revenue ... The non-financial revenue

---

48   Brasil. Câmara dos Deputados. CPI—Dívida Pública. "Transcrição ipsis verbis: reunião ordinária n. 1940/09." 28 de outubro de 2009: 15; emphases added.
49   Brasil. "Lei complementar n. 101, de 4 de maio de 2000." Art. 9°, § 5°.

is this much, non-financial expenses are that much, and the debate [was] limited to this.⁵⁰

This opinion was shared by the rapporteur of the commission, who had also been the rapporteur of the proposed bill for the Fiscal Responsibility Law when it was deliberated in Congress, in early 2000s.

The discretional power that the economic technocracy had to steer, via public debt, surpluses appropriated by the state was also a finding of the investigative commission. This is indicated by declarations made by lawmakers during the work of the commission such as: (i) "the Congress does not assume its competence, which is to discuss the economy under the light of democracy";⁵¹ (ii) "many things are happening by determination of ... the few";⁵² and (iii) "the federal treasury ... practically has absolute liberty to take on debt, to roll it over, to increase and issue government securities."⁵³

The final point that I highlight about the realization of the parliamentary investigative commission is its concern for reaffirming the commitment of the Brazilian state to the interests of finance. The first of these referred to respect for contracts, one of the concerns raised by the then deputy managing director of the International Monetary Fund, who had also been secretary of the national treasury in the Itamar Franco and Cardoso governments, and executive secretary of finance at the beginning of the first Lula government. He affirmed that the investigative commission

> would be an important opportunity to consolidate the creditworthiness of the Brazilian state, reaffirming the respect for contracts and reaffirming the payment of public debts at the various levels of government, in the conditions in which they were contracted; it would be important to support the government policy to raise the primary surplus to 3.3% of GDP, in the following year, and maintain this surplus at similar levels in following years.⁵⁴

---

50 Brasil. Câmara dos Deputados. CPI—Dívida Pública. "Transcrição ipsis verbis: reunião ordinária n. 2320/09." 9 de dezembro de 2009: 9.
51 Brasil. Câmara dos Deputados. CPI—Dívida Pública. "Transcrição ipsis verbis: reunião ordinária n. 1725/09." 7 de outubro de 2009: 54.
52 Brasil. Câmara dos Deputados. CPI—Dívida Pública. "Transcrição ipsis verbis: reunião ordinária n. 2204/09." 25 de novembro de 2009: 38.
53 Brasil. Câmara dos Deputados. CPI—Dívida Pública. "Transcrição ipsis verbis: reunião ordinária n. 2320/09." 9 de dezembro de 2009: 29.
54 Brasil. Câmara dos Deputados. CPI—Dívida Pública. "Transcrição ipsis verbis: reunião ordinária n. 2007/09." 5 de novembro de 2009: 12.

Deputies supporting the then Lula government and others who had supported the previous Cardoso government concurred. According to one of them, the government should act "with impartiality, so we don't transform this [parliamentary investigative commission] into a possibility for ... default."[55] Another lawmaker recalled when, "in the Sarney government, we had no more resources, we had to default on the debt and we took ten years to reposition ourselves in the world market."[56]

Another interest of finance, to which other Brazilian researchers have already referred to as a form of protection of the wealthy, is secrecy about their fortunes (Cattani 2007; Medeiros 2003). This was also a concern of the investigative commission, which even with constitutional investigative powers opted to not discover who were the consignees of the surpluses transferred by the state through interest payments. In light of a proposal to request from the Central Bank of Brazil the names of the creditors of the domestic federal public debt, the interpretation that prevailed in the commission was that this would be "a break in [fiscal] secrecy, which would be flagrantly unconstitutional, as well as an enormous problem that this would cause even of creditworthiness ... for the country ... to raise investments when necessary."[57]

Thus, during the entire parliamentary investigative commission it was sufficiently clear that the majority of its members intended at most to study the origins and situation of the debt until then. It was not their objective to determine who had or had not benefited from the Brazilian debt. In the words of the national president of the party that was leading the governing coalition of the country at the time, in one of his rare appearances—even though he was a member—the commission

> can conduct a history of the debt process of our country since the monarchy, or it can get stuck in a debate, which in my opinion is sterile, about the debt in relation to public spending, which is a debate that is more than completed, redone and consolidated. ...
>
> We are not necessarily discussing here, in this parliamentary investigative commission, economic policy or even about auditing of something for which, in my opinion, there is already enough literature for us to study

---

55   Brasil. Câmara dos Deputados. CPI—Dívida Pública. "Transcrição ipsis verbis: reunião ordinária n. 1304/09." 26 de agosto de 2009: 23.
56   Brasil. Câmara dos Deputados. CPI—Dívida Pública. "Transcrição ipsis verbis: reunião ordinária n. 1655/09." 30 de setembro de 2009: 43.
57   Brasil. Câmara dos Deputados. CPI—Dívida Pública. "Requerimento de CPI n. 67, de 2009." 16 de dezembro de 2009; "transcrição ipsis verbis: reunião ordinária n. 2400/09." 16 de dezembro de 2009: 16.

the origins, errors and correct actions of the macroeconomic administration over the public debt.

Our fundamental issue is to conduct, even for coming generations, a careful survey of the political and socio-economic processes that brought about this situation and what we can do to plan for the future a state that can have the capacity to, yes, take on debt—because there is no problem at all with the state taking on debt when there are sustainable mechanisms for debt financing.[58]

Discussion in the direction opposite to what the government wanted could possibly lead to an approach that sees the public debt as a mechanism for transferring surpluses between classes. By doing this, perhaps some light could have been cast on this portion of the state budget formed by interest on public debt. This same light could perhaps have pointed out who appropriated and who ceded this portion of surpluses. In this regard, the investigative commission preferred to conduct a superficial evaluation about whether the debt was sustainable or not from a fiscal perspective. Here, as I have mentioned previously, the concept of sustainability of the debt refers to a class option, given that it is concerned with the capacity to pay it off, something that is definitively a primary interest of creditors, that is, of finance.

6 Economic Democracy *and* Democratic Socialism

The discussion until here sought to indicate substantive and procedural evidences of contradictions that make capitalism an economic system in which genuine democracy is not viable. This situation has become even more clear in this last phase of financial expansion of the economy. On the other hand, actually existing capitalism and democracy are historical systems that do not fit into discrete conceptual categories, which cannot be used to characterize society as either purely capitalist or purely democratic. Not even the neoliberal version of capitalism is a monolithic system, and different social models and regimes of regulation have led to different neoliberalisms and, therefore, to different possibilities for progressive action (Hadjimichalis and Hudson 2007). The analysis allows envisioning paths that may lead beyond capitalism without, however, losing sight that it is necessary to begin from capitalism itself to abandon it.

---

58 Brasil. Câmara dos Deputados. CPI—Dívida Pública. "Transcrição ipsis verbis: reunião ordinária n. 1588/09." 23 de setembro de 2009: 40–41.

To realize this possibility, it is necessary, although not sufficient, to open paths to the actual democratization of the economy. This involves a dialectic that confronts the phenomena previously identified as structural antidemocratic characteristics of capitalism: economic inequality and the lack of popular participation and social control over economic decisions. These characteristics are mutually reproduced in such a way that modifications in one would influence the other. Changes in economic inequality lead to changes in the concentration of political power and thus to changes in the degree of economic and political democracy. These possibilities leave the door open to another economic-political order: democratic socialism.

Democracy is a socialist principle and, if the term democracy involves subordination of state power to social power, the term socialism involves subordination of economic power to the same social power (Wright 2006b). Thus, by democratic socialism I refer to a system in which the means of production are collectively controlled, investments collectively defined and decisions about the destination of the fruits of production collectively made.

A controversial proposal that sketches a system of sharing of surpluses is the idea of market socialism developed by John Roemer (1994). He defines it as an economic arrangement in which the majority of goods, including labor-power, are distributed by means of a price system and the profits of companies—perhaps managed by workers—are distributed in an egalitarian manner among the population. This proposal, according to Roemer himself, does not discuss democracy and is focused on the issue of economic equality. He also emphasizes that efficiency is a condition for the arrangement to be viable. In this way, his proposal confronts a central issue of capital, which is private property and thus what he calls exploitation. Nevertheless, Roemer does not discuss the political conditions without which neither property nor exploitation would be possible. It is precisely this separation and the absence of political democracy that threaten a project that seeks solely economic equality. As we have seen elsewhere in this book, one cannot exist without another.

It is in this light that Joshua Cohen and Joel Rogers question the viability of Roemer's proposal. On one hand, his proposal can be useful to the construction of a radical democracy, on the other, its egalitarian project lacks popular control over the economy. Even for economic performance—which is essential to Roemer's socialist model—government efficiency, economic development, and the involvement of mobilized citizens and interest groups from civil society with state agencies tends to contribute positively (Block and Evans 2005; Cohen and Rogers 1995; Evans 1996). This involvement can bring about a reduction of costs for monitoring agent-principal relations, for example (Cohen and Rogers 1995). It also can lead to increased efficiency to the degree to which the participants seek to prepare themselves to make good decisions if they have to live with the consequences of their choices (Fung and Wright 2003). Thus, beyond the idea of democracy as a moral question, we can turn to the very need for efficiency in the productive system as a justification for involving society as a whole in economic decision-making.

Even though I have affirmed that economic inequality restricts popular participation in economic decisions, it is not feasible to envision substantial changes in inequality without significant changes in participation. Changes in economic inequality are to some degree politically driven movements that result from changes in the political involvement of classes and other social groups. In this sense, the transformation towards a democratic socialist order would also be determined by the intensity of political involvement of these classes and groups. In a word, transformations in the current reality—capitalist democracy—cannot be based on the illusion that the path begins with a reduction of economic inequality. Nor will this reduction come from a 'natural' functioning of so-called free-market capitalism, as liberals and neoliberals believe to be possible. Since economic inequality is reproduced by a social relation—class exploitation—it is political action that can impose limits on this inequality.

If economic relations and practices are contingent, historical, and socially constituted, citizens are not condemned to conform to oppressive relations or to see themselves as passive victims of an unchangeable system (Swanson 2008). Therefore, in addition to democratic control of property rights, beyond forms of representative and participatory political action, beyond a guarantee of individual liberties in community, democratic control of investments is also a condition for democratic control of the state (Bowles and Gintis 1986). In fact, the well-being of humanity as a whole depends on democratization of the economy. As Cohen and Rogers (1994) recall, it was precisely the lack of democratic control over this realm that has led to current failures such as inequality, unemployment, environmental degradation, and continuous pressure on workers. Although there have been revolutionary challenges to capitalism, the corresponding historical examples did not prove to be capable of sustaining long-lasting democratic institutional processes (Wright 2006b).

The development of a voluntarist theory of construction of alternative emancipatory institutions depends on active, creative empowered participation of ordinary people in a process of deliberation and decision-making (Wright 2006b). This implies that, while recognizing Marx's understanding that people *make* history within certain limits, we should not focus only on the limits, but on the possibility for people to act collectively to change their histories. Collective action should in no way be interpreted as a denial of the importance of freedom, which is so narrowly defined by liberals. As Wright Mills (2000 [1959]) observed so well, freedom is not reduced merely to the opportunity each one has to do what they please, nor to the opportunity to choose between alternatives. For Mills, "freedom is, first of all, the chance *to formulate* the available choices, *to argue* over them—and then, the opportunity *to choose*" (Mills 2000 [1959]: 174; emphases added).

If private property is one of the main constraints to a democratizing change—considering that those who detain property will resist any threat to this institution—a useful starting point can be to democratize decisions about state investments and other spending. Democratic practice in this realm can generate alternative paths to lead society to evolve to some type of democratic socialism. But for this to happen it is necessary to strengthen conditions so that social participation goes beyond that which is allowed every few years by ballot. In this sense, the deepening of experiences of participatory democracy beyond those already existing can serve this proposal. To do so, they should allow deliberations about issues with a broader social scope than those seen until now in the various historical experiences with social participation.

If workers, through the generation of surplus-value, or society in general, through restrictions to access to public services, are called on to support a system for the reallocation of surpluses, a full democracy requires that all have the opportunity to substantially influence state spending. In an effectively democratic economic order organized by means of activity *delegated* by people to the state—and not simply *by* the state action, without popular participation—this spending would be subordinated to social control. In this sense, decisions related to economic policy are not different from any other issue of state administration, however, as I have shown in previous chapters, their relevance in both economic and political terms makes them deserving of special attention. The material consequences of economic decisions for society as a whole are sufficiently significant to justify that control or influence over them do not remain concentrated in a few hands, whether those of finance capital or of its agents in the state apparatus.

Doubts remain about to what degree any issue can be the object of democratic control, in particular those as complex as economic policies. For Archon Fung and Erik Olin Wright (2003), direct participation will not always be useful, given that, in many areas of public life, conventional systems of delegation and representation are sufficient, even if they can be improved. On the other hand, to delegate and elect does not mean to cede power. It means establishing even greater control over issues and those who make decisions. For this reason, it is important to avoid the extremes that this issue usually evokes: on one hand, the argument that power to make decisions about fiscal and monetary policies should be concentrated in a small technocratic elite; and on the other, that decisions should be open to broad and unrestricted debate about the issues. The apparent physical unviability of the latter is often one of the reasons alleged for the insulation of state technocracy, another is that not everyone interested in a certain theme has sufficient technical capacity to make decisions. But like any extremism, these concepts make alternative options unviable.

It can be agreed that not all issues can be subject to deliberations by an entire nation, but this does not imply that all issues should be decided by insulated elites, as it occurs with economic policy today. The other reason alleged for the need for insulation, namely the lack of technical capacity among the broader population, is not merely pretentious; it is motivated by specific interests. Another possible allegation of those who doubt the viability that economic issues can be democratically decided may be that political decisions can conflict with the current insistence on so-called fiscal responsibility. This control, considered by neoliberals to be an unquestionable and universal need, is alleged to be an exclusive virtue of technocrats, whose decisions would be under constant political threat. Contrary to this ideological belief, an empiric study about the correlation between public indebtedness and direct democratic procedures in subnational Swiss governments by Lars Feld and Gebhard Kirchgässner (2001) found smaller per capita debts precisely in those municipalities where fiscal results were subject to popular referendum.

One institution fundamental to democratic control of the economy is the public budget, for which the participatory budget making process can serve as inspiration. Nevertheless, this can only have a chance of being effective if it takes place in a scope broader than those of its best-known manifestations. I refer not only to geographic scope, but also to the objects of the participatory budget. Firstly, the expansion from local to national levels is necessary for an effective democratization of the state budget, because it is at the higher level that large issues are decided in such a way to have bigger impacts for life in society, even in terms of local aspects. For example, there would be little use for a neighborhood to decide to build a school if the resources were committed by decisions taken elsewhere, as when a central government imposes fiscal restrictions on budget allotments for local policies. In Brazil's current federative configuration, with political autonomy of the subnational spheres, but with a significant concentration of resources in the federal government, there are substantial restrictions to local actions.

In terms of the expansion of the objectives subject to popular deliberation, the transformative potential of a budget under social control resides in not being restricted to the role of a simple tool for accommodating conflicts. Like other apparently democratic institutions that have served capitalism by buffering class conflicts, participatory experiences are subject to being used in reformist strategies or those for cooptation. In a study about participatory political practices in Europe, including participatory budget processes, Costis Hadjimichalis and Ray Hudson (2007) identified these risks. However, they also indicated that above all these experiences evidenced struggles for hegemony over questions of local and regional development. In general, Hadjimichalis and Hudson concluded that these experiences could contribute to a long-term educational process capable of strengthening these principles and forging a sense of collaboration through conflict, instead of the values of individual competition and success.

This configuration fits into what would be a democratic economy, which for Bowles, Gordon, and Weisskopf (1990): (i) guarantees all citizens the basic rights to survival; (ii) offers all, directly or by means of elected representatives, the opportunity for participation in economic decisions that affect their lives; (iii) does away with workers' dependence in relation to the arbitrary actions of their employers; and (iv) eliminates the economic dependence of men and women as well as all forms of discrimination in access to work, housing, and the economy as a whole. In sum, in a democratic economy workers and other citizens can more easily become the authors of their own histories. For Bowles, Gordon, and Weisskopf, the need for this alternative is based on the ideas that democracy and equality are values that must be defended on principle and that a more democratic and egalitarian economy would be less wasteful than the current economy.

Other imperatives for a democratic configuration, according to Bowles and Gintis (1986), include democratic economic planning, democracy in the workplace, and common access to the means of production. Democratic planning, they add, refers to the socially controlled determination of the general lines of the economic structure and development by means of collective deliberation and control over investment decisions. According to Jacinda Swanson (2008), it involves politicizing the economy, which means expanding democratic political control over economic relations, placing under deliberation and public review—as opposed to private and elitist control—the discourses and practices that have consequences for the collectivity.

There would of course be resistance to this, because capitalists do not passively watch the state respond democratically to eventual efforts at popular control. Nonetheless, in the field of institutions that are potentially closer to civil society, opportunities for some social control can be found. It is reasonable to believe that legislatures, for example, offer greater chances to be transformed than other capitalist institutions, such as private property, the economic apparatus within the executive branch, or the judiciary. Active legislatures would be needed, particularly those open to all of society, not only to a few groups as occurs in capitalist democracy. It is essential that legislatures be forums for debates and, mainly, deliberations that express the influence of all classes and organized social groups. For this reason it is useful to keep in perspective Bowles and Gintis's (1986) understanding that popular sovereignty is a concept that does not presuppose that the impetus for political action emanates from the people. For them, effective political leadership and innovation by particular individuals or groups are compatible with the ideal of popular sovereignty to the extent that both leadership and innovation are subject to effective deliberation and ex post facto accountability.

One mechanism to hold leaders responsible is of course the vote, but it has proved to be insufficient for the establishment of a genuinely democratic order. Voting, according to Jon Elster (1998), can exercise an anticipation of retrospective control because political representatives know that not addressing the concerns of their constituents decreases their chances of reelection. But Elster also says that this control is quite diluted, given that the voting record of legislators is only one of many factors that determine their re-election chances. In addition, we should recall that elections, although they are central to democracy, occur intermittently and allow citizens to only opt between highly aggregated alternatives (Schmitter and Karl 1991). Thus, any analysis that allows affirming that those who vote have power over those who are elected also requires the recognition that those who detain or control capital have power over those who govern (Barry 2002).

Considering the limits of the possible, including the potential for ideological domination of deliberative democracy (Przeworski 1998), the material limitations of this democracy, and the expected resistance of capitalists to it; and considering the democratic insufficiencies of liberal democracy, including the limited space offered to participation, the insufficiency of the vote as a mechanism for popular control, and the economic inequality; a combination of representation and participation, with a strengthening of the latter's ability to influence representatives, would offer a route towards greater democratization. For Daryl Glaser (1999), a distinct Marxist democratic theory must consider this combination, which Marx and Engels actually found at the Paris Commune, although not accompanied by a systematic theory with democracy as the central category. I mention this to reaffirm the importance of representative democracy, because the efficiency and stability that it tends to provide cannot be abandoned, as long as it is submitted to effective and continuous popular control.

These principles continue to be valid considering what we have seen about the role of the capitalist state, whose economic apparatus has had its political action based largely on financial logic. Perhaps there will be a different logic in the future, and this will depend on the group that is hegemonic in the accumulation process. Nevertheless, the state will remain capitalist as long as the mode of production is capitalist. However, this cannot lead to the conclusion that a democratizing option involves denying the importance of the state in this process, advocating a Marxist-Leninist solution synthesized in the need to dismantle the state (Lenin 2007 [1917]). Democratic socialism involves the preservation of the institutions of representative democracy, although combined with direct, non-elitist, and self-administered democracy. The importance of direct democracy also resides in the threat that simple reforms in the state apparatus of a representative democracy that are left up to this apparatus can lead to an authoritarian statism. In sum, "socialism will be democratic or it will not be at all" (Poulantzas 1978b: 87).

Late Marxian thinking has already moved in this direction by recognizing the modern state as a contract between the governed and those who govern (Engels 1982 [1895]). It would be coherent with this understanding to substitute the Marxist-Leninist idea of the need to smash *the* state machinery by the need to smash the *existing* state machinery, recognizing that an economic democracy requires that another state be constructed in the place of the capitalist state. Just as the capitalist economy requires a capitalist state, a socialist economy requires a socialist state, which would have the function of providing civil society with the institutions—rules and mechanisms of coordination—without which social control over the economy and the state itself would be impossible (Wright 2006b). Equality and democracy are mutually dependent. If control over economic decisions is centralized in the few hands of the capitalist classes, it is because, beyond the control over production and its means, ruling classes can count on the lack of occupation of spaces in the political arena by the ruled classes.

The argument that I have developed until here indicates that all classes and groups must occupy these spaces for the economy and politics to be jointly considered democratic. One contribution in this direction is the normative concept of associative democracy developed by Cohen and Rogers (1995). In summary, their proposal advocates that the democratization of the state takes place through the strengthening of what they call secondary associations—unions, workers' councils, neighborhood associations, parent-teacher associations, environmental groups, women's associations, etc. Democratization is realized when these associations are particularly capable of effectively representing the interest of their members in a process of mediation between state and society. The central idea is that the political groups remain under mutual control by means of an associative policy and, at the same time, collectively contribute to the process of democratic-egalitarian government. This does not mean abolishing the affirmative state, or the insulation of the state in relation to society, nor opening a type of bazar where groups would bargain under relatively equal conditions. It does mean approximating groups so that they gradually act less as factions.

Cohen and Rogers's ideas address a point that I mentioned above as being one of those that makes capitalist democracy a system antithetical to full, genuine democracy. I am referring to the lack of popular participation in the decisions of the state. However, although they establish various criteria for composing an order that they consider to be democratic, Cohen and Rogers are silent about another essential aspect. Besides popular sovereignty, civic awareness, good economic performance, state competence, and political equality, distributive equity is also a condition for the democratic ideal on which they base their idea (Cohen and Rogers 1995). Although they treat the economic issue as one of the most important, they do not go farther about the need for economic equality—which they see as a probable consequence of democratic control over the economy—and private property of the means of production is not presented as a threat to their model. For this reason, Cohen and Rogers's model suffers from the same error—although in a reverse direction—which at another moment they accused John Roemer of making for not recognizing democracy as a condition for the realization of his egalitarian economic proposal.

Andrew Levine (1995) was highly wary that Cohen and Rogers's proposal for associative democracy would be possible without socialization of the means of production. Levine doubts that the associative institutions delineated by Cohen and Rogers (1995) could obtain the resources needed for their functioning. It is worth mentioning that years earlier Cohen and Rogers (1983) had proposed a vision closer to an effectively democratic order, whose institutional requirements included: (i) the formal guarantee of individual rights and liberties—thought, expression, collective association, and decision-making—necessary to autonomy for public deliberation based on reason; (ii) the recognition that this first point is necessary but not sufficient, which makes equally necessary the organized expression of political debate, in which the existence of competitive political parties that have access to public financing is crucial to promoting debate between discordant positions, for example, about economic objectives and the means to reach them; (iii) a basic level of material satisfaction—to be defined by a process of public deliberation—because the inexistence of privations of this type is a precondition for a deliberative process free from constraint; (iv) the maintenance of conditions for political equality, which requires that investments be publicly decided and controlled, which can take place under legislative supervision or through a direct democratic route; (v) democracy in the workplace, where all individuals have the opportunity to autonomously exercise their abilities; (vi) equality of opportunities, in the sense of a social commitment in the political and economic arenas to the removal of prior incapacities resulting from material inequalities; and (vii) the extension of all these requirements to international policy in the sense of recognition and promotion so that the democratic order also be respected in relation to foreign peoples.

Although Cohen and Rogers (1983) affirmed in that earlier conception that they were not hostile to movements that were working for reforms of capitalist democracy, they made clear their skepticism about possibilities for reform in two aspects. The first referred to the inter-relationship of the institutional requirements that they identified as part of a system in which the failure of any one of them would seriously compromise the realization of the others. For example, a social order with guarantees of civil liberties, but without public control of investments cannot be considered a democracy.

Cohen and Rogers's second source of skepticism about the democratizing capacity of the reformist movements was the inexistence of any particular motive to envision continuing steps in direction of the complete realization of a genuinely democratic order. Considering that the struggles for reform under the aegis of capitalist democracy also involve consent with capitalism, these struggles can be weakened by aspects that escape their control. For example, if the struggle for control of the political arena is transformed solely into efforts to elect a certain candidate, the original objective would be weakened if that candidate comes to represent little difference in the final distribution of power within the system. Although Cohen and Rogers recognized that reforms could lead to material gains and more political power, they doubted that reformist movements could lead to a future order that is radically democratic. They affirmed that democracy requires the abolition of capitalism precisely because the latter structurally sacrifices freedom. Complementing Poulantzas, 'democracy will be socialist or it will not be at all.'

Conclusion

> Not much? Yes, it's very little, but the direction of the journey is more important than the length of the step.
> AUGUSTO BOAL

∴

The goal of this book was to develop a sociological analysis of economic issues that in times of neoliberal financialization appear to have been barred from debate. In doing so, economic policy in general and the public debt in particular, beyond their so-called technical aspects, appeared to me to be phenomena that can help in the understanding of this sphere of relations in contemporary Brazilian society. The study of the public debt considered other surrounding and broader social phenomena. They were examined considering their connections to the development—not only quantitative, but mainly political—of Brazil's public debt in the approximately two decennia that followed the launching of the Real Plan, in 1994. These phenomena included crisis, financial expansion of the economy, the role of the capitalist state vis-à-vis the financial logic of accumulation, class exploitation, appropriation of economic surpluses, and the lack of democratic social control over key economic decisions.

Without the pretension to explain all of the reasons for certain political decisions, I sought to establish connections between specific choices made and the social structure that conditioned them, but that was simultaneously influenced by those choices. This first point leads to concluding that the state is not—it has actually never been—alien to the capitalist economy. More importantly, nor did the state even distance itself from the economy, as it is said neoliberals would like, or as many critics and opponents of neoliberalism believe. If at one time Brazilian industrialization required a developmentalist state, the financialization of the world economy later imposed its own logic on a new mode of regulation. Thus, it is not possible to speak of a reduction of state intervention in the economy, but of a modified participation—in some respects an even greater one, as can be noticed when examining taxation or public debt—of a state that adapted to the modifications in the historical reality in which it was inserted.

⋯

The expansion of the fictitious economy is one of the moments of articulation between capital and state that belies the supposition of the state's retraction from intervention in market relations. Creating and maintaining the conditions for capitalist accumulation has always been an important role of the modern state. Even social welfare policies—despite the material benefits that they allowed to the ruled classes, mainly in the global North—sought to restore a capitalism in crisis. But another crisis arrived after the so-called glorious thirty years of capitalist development, which had lasted from the mid-1940s through the mid-1970s. The class reaction was to substitute the prevailing dominant ideology with a new thinking that focused economic concerns on savings by identifying them as the key condition for investment and growth. Currency was also placed at the center of these concerns, given that after the crisis of the late 1970s it had to be rescued by the state, which was once again called on to protect capitalism from itself.

One of the most significant effects of this switch of ideologies was to push the former polarization capitalism versus socialism into an even more restricted realm within capitalism itself. This had already taken place during the period of the Keynesian consensus, but reached a more radical form under neoliberalism. Thus, neoliberalism weakened even more the debate about potential *alternatives to* capitalism and strengthened the discussion about how to work *within* capitalism to confront its contradictions. By discussing methods that work within capitalism, any disputes no longer challenged the system itself. In this way, neoliberalism was precisely another conservative revolution.

A few years after the collapse of the Bretton Woods system, which had allowed the United States to inundate world markets with dollars, it was once again the U.S. that changed the conditions of global financial markets. In 1979, the U.S. Federal Reserve raised interest rates to levels much higher than what had been practiced during the previous decades. This had corresponding reflexes on interest rates in the other central economies and in the periphery of the world-system as well. In response to the increase in global liquidity, Brazil, like other peripheral countries undertaking industrialization efforts, took on debt with the international banking system. And in reaction to the rise in interest rates, Brazil 'responded' with economic stagnation, which coincided with the end of its most recent military dictatorship (1964–1985). In the 1970s it had grown at a pace similar to some Asian countries in recent decades, but Brazil then spent the following nearly fifteen years dealing with what various commentators call the crisis of hegemony.

Financial capital was already circulating globally in the 1990s, without as many ties as during the Keynesian consensus, and in amounts much larger than the equivalent material bases of value. It was in this context that the

CONCLUSION 179

hegemonic crisis terminated in Brazil, with finance capital assuming the leading position. Monetary logic, which had been influencing economic policies in the global North in the mid-1970s, reached Brazil nearly two decades later. The Real Plan was the Brazilian response to the crisis of hegemony and, at the same time, it allowed the country's accreditation as a recipient of financial capitals that had been flowing worldwide without sufficient outlets for profitable investments. To do so, besides a series of measures that sought to give it the status of a market economy, Brazil came to attract massive amounts of short-term financial capital through the highest real interest rates among major economies. Upon doing so, it absorbed in practice the ideology that saw savings as the main engine of economic growth.

In this way, the financial realm of the Brazilian economy expanded faster than the material valorization, leading finance to become the hegemonic class fraction. Coherent with its past in which the economy was strongly supported by state action, the financial expansion was also backed by the state. The public debt, which Marx had long ago defined as one of the most important types of fictitious capital, was the great motor of this expansion. Although the Brazilian public debt was notably absent from the Brazilian political debate, its importance to the state budget was highly significant. During the previous nearly twenty years, interest on this debt was the second largest item of federal government spending, exceeded only by expenditures on retirement and other pensions. In this way, the fictitious economy revealed its concrete face—as it does even more clearly in crises—when the effects can assume catastrophic contours for the poorest social segments. If the public debt, like other types of interest-bearing capital, is not concrete in a strict economic sense—because it does not generate value—that debt revealed a concrete capacity to impose material, economic restrictions and forms of behavior over broad segments of Brazilian society.

•••

The expansion of financial logic to various realms of life in society apparently confirmed the realization of the neoliberal aim and the corresponding prescription that the state should not intervene in economic activity. Nevertheless, nation-states have remained active in this sphere, and because of the crisis of Keynesian liberalism, this mode of regulation was substituted by a new type of liberalism. This was perhaps even clearer in Brazil than in economies at the center of the world-system. With greater impetus since the mid-1990s, the Brazilian developmental state began to recoil by privatizing state-owned companies and breaking-up monopolies that it had been holding for some decades.

Nevertheless, this reversal was accompanied by the state's insertion in another realm of capitalist accumulation through the creation of conditions for financial expansion of the economy. In addition to raising real interest rates, the country lifted controls so that in- or outflows of financial capital could take place at virtually any moment and with no substantial restrictions.

High interest rates, the liberalization of capital flows, and growing fiscal deficits—the latter is one of the strongest indications that the state has not removed itself from the economy—led to the expansion of the Brazilian federal public debt, especially the domestic securitized one. On this point, Brazilian neoliberalism confirmed what is said about the contradiction between demanding the withdrawal of the state at the same time as it is called on to create conditions for the development or even the creation of markets. For example, until the mid-1990s, retail investment funds practically did not exist in the country, because they required a secondary market for public bonds that came to develop along with the domestic securitized debt of the federal government. If until the late 1970s the hegemony of industrial capital had been replicated in the state apparatus, since the 1990s finance began to occupy the hegemonic place. In this way, many state actions came to be based on the logic that they would guarantee the profitability of the capital loaned to it by finance.

In this context, the state assumed traits of a class fraction, namely that of finance capital. This was observed in both monetary and fiscal policies. In the first, with inflation control the most important macroeconomic objective and interest policy the sole mechanism envisioned for this control, interest rates were raised to levels high enough to attract substantial amounts of money-capital. Finance capital then found in Brazil a fertile ground from where it could grab economic surpluses, which, we recall, always come from capitalist exploitation, that is, from the labor of others. In terms of fiscal policy, the state was pushed to remove any obstacles to servicing the public debt. This was done, for example, by delinking federal revenues from constitutionally mandated spending for social welfare policies and by limiting primary public expenditures, that is non-financial spending. Thus, since the eve of the Real Plan, the Brazilian state placed finance first on line for the appropriation of the resources that it redistributed.

⋯

An important effect of this macroeconomic configuration was the establishment of a complex of expropriation of surpluses that freed certain capitalists from inconveniences typically encountered in the direct exploitation of others' labor, which takes place in the sphere of material production. More than redistributing surpluses, the fiscal superstructure assembled in Brazil likely raised— I am cautious about making any quantification about this process—ulterior rates of exploitation of labor. The fiscal complex formed by public debt and taxation, allied to a contention of the social wage represented by social welfare policies, placed even more pressure on the working classes. Corporate shareholders were increasingly driven by a logic that pressured their administrators to care more about the market price of company shares than about what it effectively produced came to exercise a new type of pressure on labor. In situations of high interest rates, the expectations for profits in productive activities may have increased to the degree that interest rates had risen.

The Brazilian state became an important competitor for money-capital. Actually, the state always had the advantage of being able to arbitrate rules and thus attract financial resources with greater ease than other institutions. Companies, for example, do not have the same prerogatives of a nation-state to take on debt; states do not disappear and do not go bankrupt with such facility and frequency as do companies. Nevertheless, to take on more debt the Brazilian government had to tax even more, which led to rises in the expected profit rates that in turn increased the pressure on labor. In short, public debt interest signaled rises in the rates of labor exploitation in ulterior production cycles. The state counted on the legitimacy it has to raise taxes to make payments on interest on the public debt and, as we saw, it is the working classes that eventually bear the cost of these taxes. Workers, according to the old Marxian terms, in addition to working one part of the day for themselves, and another part for free for the functioning capital and for the state, may have had to work an additional part of the day for free for finance capital.

Another result of Brazil's public debt, in addition to the impacts on the redistribution of surpluses between labor and capital, was to impose material restrictions on social segments not directly involved with the production process. As I already mentioned in this conclusion, in the past nearly twenty years spending on interest on the public debt was exceeded only by spending on retirement and other pensions. Yet it is important to remember that tens of millions of people depend on those pensions, while interest was appropriated by a very limited population. Other state expenses equally essential to the large mass of society were substantially exceeded by interest paid to rentiers. For example, spending on education, culture, healthcare, and sanitation combined was systematically lower than the spending on interest on the federal public debt.

Thus, the complex comprised by public debt and taxation, protected by institutional guarantees like the delinking of revenues from constitutionally mandated spending on social welfare programs, legal obligations to maintain primary fiscal surpluses, and inflation targets established important mechanisms for the redistribution of surpluses. This specific format caused an encounter of some historical phenomena in contemporary Brazil: a peripheral economy where one of the most important mechanisms of modern capitalism operated and provided important amounts of what Karl Marx once associated to primitive accumulation. This was the public debt, a means of dispossession to which the most advanced capitalist economies turned to at their beginnings and still turn to, and that in Brazil was consolidated even before the country experienced capitalist development similar to that of the countries of the center. Of course, public debt has existed in Brazil since its first days as a nation state, but a debt market sufficiently developed to give a financial character to Brazilian capitalism and its correspondent capitalist state is a relatively recent construction.

⋯

In terms of the implications for democratic politics, though the public debt is a non-capitalist means—it is not even economic sensu stricto, but rather a legal social relation—for extraction of economic surpluses, its importance to the reproduction of inequality makes it an element that expands the antithesis between capitalism and democracy. Concentrated in a few hands, if not in terms of ownership, at least in terms of who controls decisions about it—as are investment funds, which are commonly administered by a few and owned by a multitude of fund shareholders—the Brazilian public debt placed in those few hands a capacity to interfere in economic policies that was higher than anyone else's within society. In this way, a fusion of ideologies and interests between finance and its organic intellectuals installed in the economic apparatus shaped the most important decisions about the allocation of surpluses appropriated by the Brazilian state. Possibly no other social composition or line of thinking had attained such influence in neoliberal Brazil.

One of the mechanisms used for this was what I call ideological insulation. This is different from what in Chapter 4 I called selective bureaucratic insulation. Ideological insulation synthesizes the various mechanisms that we saw in that chapter, by means of which the state and its economic technocracy did not necessarily isolate themselves from society, but did isolate certain issues from democratic debate, that is from popular influence and control. If the class character of the capitalist state was revealed, for example, by not raising anti-capitalist themes for discussion, its character as a class-fraction was revealed when it impeded debate on potentially anti-finance issues. In order to 'depoliticize'—as if this were even possible—the debate about the economy, themes such as fiscal or monetary policy were claimed to be just 'technical' issues, for which politics would only cause instability.

In Brazil, despite some timid initiatives, the legislature did not demonstrate a concrete concern for macroeconomic policy during the period covered by this study. At least not to the point of calling for a sharing of decision-making power with the executive branch. Nearly complete control of Brazil's macroeconomic agenda remained in the hands of the executive and, within it, in the hands of a small number of non-elected bureaucrats not submitted to popular social control. This was first made possible by the process of deliberation over the state budget, which is proposed solely by the executive branch and contains a series of restrictions that prevent the legislature from changing the original proposals. This is the case of the proposed budget allotments for public debt servicing, which wound up impacting the entire state budget. Monetary policy was decided and implemented by an agency—the Central Bank of Brazil—with powers beyond the reach of any substantial type of popular control. Moreover, intellectuals of finance frequently defended the independence of the monetary authority from the popularly elected government.

Despite all these characteristics, and even if they are as significant as the antithesis between democracy and capitalism indicates, one cannot conclude that the situation is unchangeable. In the past nearly forty years, social crises and conflicts have intensified beyond the pace of the nearly thirty years following World War II. This increased the perception that the capitalist system had been entering a process of structural crisis. The growth in the importance of processes of *expropriation*—of which debt interest serves as one of the clearest examples—vis-à-vis the *production* of surpluses is an indication of the structural limits to capital. The system cannot sustain itself by mere redistribution, like that which takes place in the social sphere of finance. This may be sufficient for individual capitalists, but the world-system requires expansion, which in turn depends upon production of surpluses.[1]

Of course, we cannot anticipate how much these limits may expand over time or space. But the very existence of these movements towards the limits of capitalism indicates that it, like the formal democratic system that sustains it, cannot escape its own contradictions. As there are economic limits to the expansion of capital, political limits to it are brought about by the intensification of class conflicts caused by that same expansion. If in the past the primary location of the struggle of progressive movements was the point of capitalist

---

1 I have discussed this hypothesis in "Dispossessions in historical capitalism: expansion or exhaustion of the system?," *International Critical Thought*, April 2019, pp. 194–213.

production, this is now combined with the struggles against expropriation that develop in various other points of social life. This is well synthesized in the reduction or even elimination of social welfare policies to free up resources in the public budget so that finance capitalists can earn the yields expected on money-capital they loaned to the state. To struggle against *exploitation* has always meant to struggle against capital; and in our current times of structural crisis, to struggle against financial *expropriation* is also to struggle against capital. In a genuine democracy, to struggle for expansion of social participation in economic issues is not an end in itself, but a struggle against capital, without which it is not possible to think of a more egalitarian society.

AFTERWORD

The 2016 Coup d'État

> When the house of the great man collapses/ Many small folk will be crushed under the ruins./ Those who never shared the fortune of the mighty/ Will often share their downfall. The/ Swift-plunging wagon/ Drags the sweating draft horses/ Down to the abyss.
>
> BERTOLT BRECHT

∴

At the end of the past decade, while the center of the world economy was experiencing the effects of another capitalist crisis, some in Brazil envisioned that the country could be immune from those effects—though this would be improbable. During the 2003–2010 period, the GDP grew at an annual average of 4.1%; the unemployment rate in the main metropolitan regions, which had begun 2003 at 11%, fell to 5.3% in late 2010; and in the same period, government policies boosted the minimum wage 66% in real terms.[1] In this context, Lula da Silva reached the end of his second term with popular approval ratings that were so high—averaging 77% in the last year of his government—that he was able to name as his party's candidate to succeed him as president a technocrat who had never been a star of the Workers Party and who had never before campaigned for public office. In late 2010, Dilma Rousseff was elected president, leading the Workers Party to its third straight victory over its main contender, the Brazilian Social Democratic Party.

During Rousseff's first two and a half years in office, the Brazilian economy and politics appeared to continue without significant signs of crisis. That situation lasted until mid-2013, when massive street protests erupted throughout Brazil and shook the social scene during the June revolts (Jornadas de Junho in Portuguese). Her government had reached that moment with an average popular approval rating of 57%. By July 2013, the share of the population who considered her government 'excellent' or 'good' fell to 31%. After some stability,

---

[1] Any data presented in this afterword with no source reference are based on the author's calculations from standard databases. Technical aspects or sources not made explicit will be communicated upon request.

which lasted until her re-election, Rousseff's popularity plunged from 40% in December 2014 to 12% in March 2015, remaining at this level until her government was eventually overthrown, in May 2016.[2]

There are many reasons for the coup that unseated the Workers Party from its leadership of the coalition that had been heading the Brazilian government since 2003. For some analysts, it was due to a supposed depletion of popular support for the party, which had become incapable of buffering the class antagonisms. This thesis gained evidence precisely with the revolts of June 2013. Also in the political field, but in the realm of party and electoral issues, other commentators affirmed that the opposition to the Workers Party from the right saw the opportunity to rise to power through a means other than its unsuccessful electoral efforts. These theses are plausible, but I believe that another factor should be added to the list of possible explanations.

Both the thesis of the depletion of popular support for the Workers Party as well as that which emphasized the partisan electoral dispute lack a recognition of the instrumental capitalist rationality that I believe was also subjacent to the movement that culminated with the overthrow of the Rousseff government. In this sense, whoever would come to occupy the presidency would first have to make a commitment to capital. A commitment in relation to that which capital feared it would not attain if there would be a continuation of the political conditions that emerged in 2013, reached their most dramatic point with the re-election of Rousseff, and extended until her removal from office.

In October 2015, the party of the then vice president of Brazil, who would come to seize the presidency—provisorily in May and definitively in August 2016—issued a document entitled A Bridge to the Future (Uma Ponte para o Futuro in Portuguese).[3] It was a type of post-coup government program, in which Vice President Michel Temer was presented for the position to which Rousseff was elected by popular vote. In it, Temer's party indicated the "need" for "a permanent [fiscal] adjustment," which would require "changing laws and even constitutional norms." It also affirmed that it would be "necessary ... to do away with the established constitutional links [of federal tax revenues to mandatory spending], as in the case of outlays for healthcare and education." It proposed "an end to all indexations, whether for wages, social security benefits, and all others" and "that the long-term fiscal equilibrium [should be] one of the constitutional principles." Moreover, it affirmed that it was "necessary to introduce ... a minimum [retirement] age that [should be] no lower than 65 for

---

2   Confederação Nacional da Indústria. "Pesquisa CNI-IBOPE: avaliação do governo." Available at http://www.portaldaindustria.com.br/estatisticas/, accessed October 26, 2016.

3   Fundação Ulysses Guimarães. "Uma ponte para o futuro." Brasília, 29 de outubro de 2015.

men and 60 for women." Also in relation to costs of labor-power, Temer's party maintained that it was essential "to allow that collective bargaining prevail over the legal norms, except in terms of basic rights." What would these proposals be if not part of an effort to revive, and in many aspects make even tighter, the macroeconomic model that I analyzed in previous chapters?

What Temer promised to deliver was precisely a deepening of economic policies that all the governments had implemented since the 1990s, but that in the mid-2010s began to present signs of difficulty of continuation. As we saw earlier, for the first time since 1998, in the last two complete years of the Rousseff administration, the central government ran primary fiscal deficits—that is, not considering financial expenses and revenues (see figure 13). Thus, different from the previous sixteen years, in 2014 and 2015 no fiscal surplus was available to be used for payment of interest on the public debt. And this was one of the trends that the political forces that joined around 'the 2016 coup' committed themselves to reversing, so that macroeconomic policy could resume its original course as required by finance. The program A Bridge to the Future, issued by Temer's party and mentioned above, declared that "the primary objective of a policy for fiscal equilibrium is to first interrupt the growth of the public debt to then initiate the process of its reduction as a percentage of GDP. The normal tool for this is the achievement of a primary surplus capable of covering expenses on interest."

None of this is to say that the Rousseff government had not been making an effort with a similar goal. My argument is rather that the coalition deposed in 2016 reached a point of nearly complete political incapacity to continue with the pro-finance agenda that had marked Rousseff's first term and the governments of her three predecessors—Itamar Franco, Cardoso, and Lula—even if their pro-finance commitments had been clearer and firmer than Rousseff's. Examples of her government's efforts to reconcile with finance could be seen soon after her re-election, in late 2014. It is important to remember that she won by only a small margin—51% compared to 48% for her opponent Aécio Neves—after having appealed to a discourse that revived some issues that had always been dear to the left, for example, the commitment to not weaken labor laws.

Once re-elected, Rousseff's second government abandoned that leftist rhetoric and issued signs favorable to capital in general and finance in particular. First, she appointed as minister of finance an executive from a large private bank who had been a member of the economic team in the first years of the Lula government, a period of deepening of the economic model inaugurated in the second Cardoso government. Another pro-finance measure was the mini-reform in social security enacted in late 2014. By means of two provisional decrees, in late 2014 Rousseff's government changed rules to restrict private-sector worker's access to labor and social security benefits.[4] As we saw in Chapter 3, the measures tightened criteria for access to pensions granted for the death of a spouse, illness assistance, unemployment benefits, and the annual wage bonus paid to workers who received up to two minimum wages. It is important to remember that Cardoso and Lula promoted deep changes in the retirement and other pensions regimes, and Temer, upon seizing the presidency, promised another, and all were larger than those made by Rousseff in terms of reducing the cost of labor-power.

I believe that this pattern can be extrapolated to the general fiscal options of each one of the governments in the past twenty years as well as the government that took political power after 'the 2016 coup.' Cardoso had governed Brazil in a period that coincided with the country's adhesion to the neoliberal mode of regulation, various international financial crises, and low economic growth. During his two governments (1995–2002), annual average GDP growth was 2.3% (0.9% per capita) compared to 4.9% (2.8% per capita) observed in 1970–1994.[5] This did not prevent the government from attaining primary fiscal surpluses in all the years of this period except 1997 (see figure 13). In addition to this class option favorable to finance, the attacks of the Cardoso government on labor were synthesized in the reduction of wages in relation to total national income and in the increase in the portions appropriated by capital, as indicated by the functional distribution of income (see figure 20).

During the Lula governments, the situation was different in some important respects, but all of them allowed the continuity of the monetary and fiscal policies that had been inaugurated in the second Cardoso government (1999–2002). This also contributed to maintaining class confrontations repressed. Economic growth, largely sustained by a more favorable international situation, was significantly higher than Brazil had experienced in the Cardoso period. During the two Lula terms (2003–2010), annual average GDP growth was 4% (2.9% per capita). This also allowed the central government to attain significant primary fiscal surpluses, which reached an annual average of 2.2% of GDP compared to 1.1% on average in the two Cardoso governments (see figure 13). The Lula governments did not need to increase the tax burden, as did the Cardoso governments. The revenues from taxes and social contributions—not including those for retirement and other pensions—during the 2003–2010

---

[4] Brasil. "Medida provisória n. 664, de 30 de dezembro de 2014"; "medida provisória n. 665, de 30 de dezembro de 2014"; "lei n. 13.134, de 16 de junho de 2015"; "lei n. 13.135, de 17 de junho de 2015."

[5] According to the System of National Accounts reference 2000.

period remained on average at the same level reached in the early 2000s, after having grown continuously since the mid-1990s (see figure 14). This context also made viable the increase in wages as a proportion of national income, as we also saw in the functional distribution of income (figure 20).

The proportion of wages in national income continued to rise until 2014. Beginning in 2009—when the first effects of the global financial crisis of 2008 began to be felt in Brazil—federal spending on social welfare policies grew until 2015 (see figure 23). The annual average of total federal spending on housing, urban infrastructure, labor, education, culture, healthcare, and sanitation, which had been 3.7% of GDP in the Cardoso governments and fell to 3.1% in the Lula governments, returned to 3.7% in the five complete years of the Rousseff governments (2011–2015). Spending on retirement and other pensions and social assistance combined—which were significantly impacted by real increases in the minimum wage granted by the Workers Party governments—represented 8% under Cardoso, 9.4% under Lula, and 9.6% of GDP under Rousseff, reaching 9.9% in her last full-year in office, in 2015. At that time, economic growth had already entered a steep decline as did tax revenues, which had actually been falling since the first year of Rousseff's government. One of the consequences, as we saw, was that for the first time since 1998, the central government ran a primary fiscal deficit in 2014, which became much greater in 2015 (see figure 13). That fiscal trend was unacceptable to finance. In fact, the very *goals* set for the primary fiscal results indicated something that finance would not tolerate for long. After averaging 2.9% of GDP in the 2002–2010 period, those goals fell to 1.9% on average in 2011–2015.

The political coalition that seized the government with 'the 2016 coup' was committed precisely to the reversal of those fiscal trends that began under Rousseff. This commitment was expressed, as we saw, in the document A Bridge to the Future issued by Temer's party, which in a certain way was a revised edition—but in a much more radical form—of the Letter to the Brazilian People (Carta ao Povo Brasileiro in Portuguese) that Lula had issued in 2002. Yet, combined with the lesser intensity of the fiscal efforts signaled by Rousseff, her government no longer had the political conditions to implement the so-called austerity agenda imposed by finance. Addressing the alleged fiscal imbalance, the document A Bridge to the Future affirmed that "only an institutional shock [could] reverse it, as well as an integrated vision of the issue and considerable political clarity and authority."

The 'institutional shock' came, executed by the stronger political forces—they had been in the legislature and also within the very deposed government—as well as economic and journalistic forces in addition to those in the judiciary. And the new 'political authority' was used precisely to continue the commitment assumed by the new governing coalition with finance. In late

2016 the Brazilian legislature approved a constitutional amendment proposed by Temer that established a twenty-year budget ceiling on real growth—that is, adjusted for inflation—of all expenditures except interest on public debt. In relation to retirement and other pensions, Congress was then discussing another constitutional amendment, also proposed by Temer, which would establish minimum retirement ages as well as measures aimed at cutting primary expenditures. There were other proposals, but these two summarize well the attempt to return macroeconomic policy to the original pro-finance course of the past nearly twenty years.

I conclude by reaffirming the importance of risking a hypothesis about the fall of the government that, contradictorily, was not able to break with the policies inaugurated in the 1990s, nor able to continue them. It is in the latter that resides my hypothesis that the 2016 coup d'état served to remove from government the political forces that were no longer capable—as they had been until then—of continuing to administer an economic model that remains until our days under the hegemony of finance. It is a bit ironic that in Chapter 1 of this book I discussed what Gérard Duménil and Dominique Lévy called 'the 1979 coup' to identify the sharp monetary shift marked by the hike in real interest rates that initiated in the U.S. and spread throughout the world economy. Later, this study concentrated on analyzing Brazilian macroeconomic policy based on what I called 'the 1994 coup'—recognizing the differences in proportions—which involved the launching of the Real Plan and the sustained high real interest rates in Brazil. I have now concluded the discussion by briefly examining 'the 2016 coup,' which was more explicit than the other two in institutional terms, but all had the same goal: to restore the class power of capital in general and of its financial fraction in particular.

Bibliography

Abu-El-Haj, Jawdat. 2007. "From interdependence to neo-mercantilism: Brazilian capitalism in the age of globalization." *Latin American Perspectives* 34(5): 92–114.

Albo, Greg and Bryan Evans. 2010. "From rescue strategies to exit strategies: the struggle over public sector austerity." Pp. 283–308 in *Socialist register 2011: the crisis this time*, edited by Leo Panitch, Greg Albo, and Vivek Chibber. London: Merlin.

Amin, Samir. 2008. "Economia de mercado ou capitalismo financeiro oligopólico." *Margem Esquerda* 12: 62–73.

Appelbaum, Eileen, Rose Batt, and Ian Clark. 2013. "Implications of financial capitalism for employment relations research: evidence from breach of trust and implicit contracts in private equity buyouts." *British Journal of Industrial Relations* 51(3): 498–518.

Arendt, Hannah. 2006 [1972]. *Crises da república*. São Paulo: Perspectiva.

Arestis, Philip, Luiz F. de Paula, and Fernando Ferrari-Filho. 2009. "A nova política monetária: uma análise do regime de metas de inflação no Brasil." *Economia e Sociedade* 18(1): 1–30.

Aronowitz, Stanley. 2000. *The knowledge factory: dismantling the corporate university and creating true higher learning*. Boston: Beacon.

Arrighi, Giovanni. 1994. *The long twentieth century: money, power, and the origins of our times*. London and New York: Verso.

Asimakopoulus, John. 2009. "Globally segmented labor markets: the coming of the greatest boom and bust, without the boom." *Critical Sociology* 35(2): 175–198.

Babb, Sarah. 2007. "Embeddedness, inflation, and international regimes: the IMF in the early postwar period." *The American Journal of Sociology* 113(1): 128–164.

De la Barra, Ximena. 2006. "Who owes and who pays? the accumulated debt of neoliberalism." *Critical Sociology* 32(1): 125–161.

Barry, Brian. 2002. "Capitalists rule ok? Some puzzles about power." *Politics, Philosophy & Economics* 1(2): 155–184.

Biersteker, Thomas J. 1990. "Reducing the role of the state in the economy: a conceptual exploration of IMF and World Bank prescriptions." *International Studies Quarterly* 34(4): 477–492.

Block, Fred and Peter Evans. 2005. "The state and the economy." Pp. 505–526 in *The handbook of economic sociology*, edited by Neil Joseph Smelser and Richard Swedberg. Princeton: Princeton University Press.

Boito, Armando. 2007. "Class relations in Brazil's new neoliberal phase." *Latin American Perspectives* 34(5): 115–131.

Bonefeld, Werner. 2010. "Free economy and the strong state: some notes on the state." *Capital & Class* 34(1): 15–24.

Bourdieu, Pierre. 1994. "Stratégies de reproduction et modes de domination." *Actes de la Recherche en Science Sociales* 105: 3–12.

Bourdieu, Pierre. 1997. "Le champ économique." *Actes de la Recherche en Sciences Sociales* 119(1): 48–66.

Bourdieu, Pierre. 2001. "Le mystère du ministère: des volontés particulières à la 'volonté générale'." *Actes de la Recherche en Science Sociales* 140(1): 7–11.

Bourdieu, Pierre. 2011 [1996]. *Razões práticas: sobre a teoria da ação*. São Paulo: Papirus.

Bourdieu, Jérôme, Johan Heilbron, and Bénédicte Reynaud. 2003. "Les structures sociales de la finance." *Actes de la Recherche en Sciences Sociales* 146(1): 3–7.

Bowles, Samuel and Herbert Gintis. 1986. *Democracy and capitalism: property, community, and the contradictions of modern social thought*. New York: Basic Books.

Bowles, Samuel and Herbert Gintis. 1990. "Contested exchange: new microfoundations for the political economy of capitalism." *Politics & Society* 18(2): 165–222.

Bowles, Samuel, David M. Gordon, and Thomas E. Weisskopf. 1990. *After the waste land: a democratic economics for the year 2000*. Armonk: M.E. Sharpe.

Boyer, Robert. 1999. "Estado, mercado e desenvolvimento: uma nova síntese para o século XXI?" *Economia e Sociedade* 8(1): 1–20.

Braga, Ruy. 2015. *A pulsão plebeia: trabalho, precariedade e rebeliões sociais*. São Paulo: Alameda.

Bresser-Pereira, Luiz C. 2007. "Burocracia pública e classes dirigentes no Brasil." *Revista de Sociologia e Política* 28: 9–30.

Callon, Michel. 2007. "What does it mean to say that economics is performative?" Pp. 311–357 in *Do economists make markets? on the performativity of economics*, edited by Donald MacKenzie, Fabian Muniesa, and Lucia Siu. Princeton: Princeton University Press.

Camara, Mamadou and Pierre Salama. 2005. "A inserção diferenciada—com efeitos paradoxais—dos países em desenvolvimento na mundialização financeira." Pp. 199–221 in *A finança mundializada: raízes sociais e políticas, configuração, conseqüências*, edited by François Chesnais. São Paulo: Boitempo.

Carcanholo, Reinaldo A. and Paulo Nakatani. 2001. "Capital especulativo parasitario versus capital financiero." *Problemas del Desarrollo* 32(124): 9–31.

Carneiro, Ricardo. 1996. "Liberalização financeira e crescimento econômico." *Economia e Sociedade* 5(1): 193–196.

Carruthers, Bruce G. 1996. *City of capital: politics and markets in the English financial revolution*. Princeton: Princeton University Press.

Carruthers, Bruce G. 2005. "The sociology of money and credit." Pp. 355–378 in *The handbook of economic sociology*, edited by Neil Joseph Smelser and Richard Swedberg. Princeton: Princeton University Press.

Carruthers, Bruce G. and Terence C. Halliday. 2000. "Globalization and institutional convergence: are legal and financial institutions becoming homogeneous?" Working paper n. 2027, American Bar Foundation, Chicago.

Cattani, Antonio D. 2007. "Desigualdades socioeconômicas: conceitos e problemas de pesquisa." *Sociologias* 18: 74–99.

Chesnais, François, ed. 1998. *A mundialização financeira: gênese, custos e riscos*. São Paulo: Xamã.

Chesnais, François. 2002. "A teoria do regime de acumulação financeirizado: conteúdo, alcance e interrogações." *Economia e Sociedade* 11(1): 1–44.

Chesnais, François, ed. 2005a. *A finança mundializada: raízes sociais e políticas, configuração, conseqüências*. São Paulo: Boitempo.

Chesnais, François. 2005b. "Doze teses sobre a mundialização do capital." Pp. 17–31 in *O Brasil frente à ditadura do capital financeiro: reflexões e alternativas*, edited by Carla Ferreira and André Forti Scherer. Lajeado: Univates.

Cohen, Gerald A. 1979. "The labor theory of value and the concept of exploitation." *Philosophy and Public Affairs* 8(4): 338–360.

Cohen, Joshua and Joel Rogers. 1983. *On democracy: toward a transformation of American society*. New York: Penguin.

Cohen, Joshua and Joel Rogers. 1994. "My utopia or yours?" *Politics & Society* 22(4): 507–521.

Cohen, Joshua and Joel Rogers, eds. 1995. *Associations and democracy*. London and New York: Verso.

Corbridge, Stuart. 1993. *Debt and development*. Oxford, UK: Blackwell.

Costilla, Lucio F.O. 2000. "The reconstitution of power and democracy in the age of capital globalization." *Latin American Perspectives* 27(1): 82–104.

Crouch, Colin. 2011. *The strange non-death if neoliberalism*. Cambridge, UK: Polity.

Deflem, Mathieu. 2003. "The sociology of the sociology of money: Simmel and the contemporary battle of the classics." *Journal of Classical Sociology* 3(1): 67–96.

Desai, Radhika. 2013. *Geopolitical economy: after US hegemony, globalization and empire*. London: Pluto.

Deutschmann, Christoph. 1996. "Money as a social construction: on the actuality of Marx and Simmel." *Thesis Eleven* 47(1): 1–19.

Didier, Emmanuel. 2007. "Do statistics "perform" the economy?" Pp. 276–310 in *Do economists make markets? on the performativity of economics*, edited by Donald MacKenzie, Fabian Muniesa, and Lucia Siu. Princeton: Princeton University Press.

Diniz, Eli. 2004. *Globalização, reformas econômicas e elites empresariais: Brasil anos 1990*. Rio de Janeiro: Editora da FGV.

Dufour, Mathieu and Özgür Orhangazi. 2007. "International financial crises: scourge or blessings in disguise?" *Review of Radical Political Economics* 39(3): 342–350.

Duménil, Gérard and Dominique Lévy. 2001. "Costs and benefits of neoliberalism. A class analysis." *Review of International Political Economy* 8(4): 578–607.

Duménil, Gérard and Dominique Lévy. 2004a. *Capital resurgent: roots of the neoliberal revolution*. Cambridge, MA: Harvard University Press.

Duménil, Gérard and Dominique Lévy. 2004b. "The economics of US imperialism at the turn of the 21st century." *Review of International Political Economy* 11(4): 657–676.

Duménil, Gérard and Dominique Lévy. 2011. *The crisis of neoliberalism*. Cambridge, MA: Harvard University Press.

Durkheim, Émile. 2001 [1895]. *As regras do método sociológico*. São Paulo: Companhia Editora Nacional.

Dymski, Gary A. 1992. "Towards a new model of exploitation: the case of racial domination." *International Journal of Social Economics* 19(7/8/9): 292–313.

Elias, Norbert. 1993 [1939]. *O processo civilizador (Vol. 2)*. Rio de Janeiro: Zahar.

Elson, Diane. 1988. "Market socialism or socialization of the market?" *New Left Review* I/172: 3–44.

Elster, Jon. 1982. "The case for methodological individualism." *Theory and Society* 11(4): 453–482.

Elster, Jon, ed. 1998. *Deliberative democracy*. Cambridge, UK: Cambridge University Press.

Engels, Friedrich. 1982 [1895]. "Introdução a Karl Marx, 'As lutas de classes em França de 1848 a 1850'." Pp. 189–208 in *Obras escolhidas (Vol. 1)*. Lisboa: "Avante!."

Evans, Peter. 1996. "Government action, social capital and development: reviewing the evidence on synergy." *World Development* 24(6): 1119–1132.

Evans, Peter. 1997. "The eclipse of the state? reflections on stateness in an era of globalization." *World Politics* 50(1): 62–87.

Evans, Peter. 2008. "Is an alternative globalization possible?" *Politics & Society* 36(2): 271–305.

Eyal, Gil. 2000. "Anti-politics and the spirit of capitalism: dissidents, monetarists, and the Czech transition to capitalism." *Theory and Society* 29(1): 49–92.

Feld, Lars P. and Gebhard Kirchgässner. 2001. "Does direct democracy reduce public debt? evidence from Swiss municipalities." *Public Choice* 109(3–4): 347–370.

Figueiredo, Argelina C. and Fernando Limongi. 2000. "Constitutional change, legislative performance and institutional consolidation." *Brazilian Review of Social Sciences* special issue(1): 73–94.

Filgueiras, Luiz and Reinaldo Gonçalves. 2007. *A economia política do governo Lula*. Rio de Janeiro: Contraponto.

Fine, Ben. 2001. "The continuing imperative of value theory." *Capital & Class* 25(3): 41–52.

Fligstein, Neil. 1996. "Markets as politics: a political-cultural approach to market institutions." *American Sociological Review* 61(4): 656–673.

Fligstein, Neil. 2001a. "Le mythe du marché." *Actes de la Recherche en Sciences Sociales* 139(1): 3–12.

Fligstein, Neil. 2001b. *The architecture of markets: an economic sociology of twenty-first-century capitalist societies.* Princeton: Princeton University Press.

Foster, John B. and Fred Magdoff. 2009. *The great financial crisis: causes and consequences.* New York: Monthly Review.

Foucault, Michel. 1979. *Microfísica do poder.* Rio de Janeiro: Graal.

Foucault, Michel 1981 [1970]. "The order of discourse." In *Untying the text: a poststructuralist reader,* edited by Robert Young. Boston, London, and Henley: Routledge & Kegan Paul.

Frieden, Jeffry A. 1991. "Invested interests: the politics of national economic policies in a world of global finance." *International Organization* 45(4): 425–451.

Frieden, Jeffry A. 2006. *Global capitalism: its fall and rise in the twentieth century.* New York: W.W. Norton.

Fung, Archon and Erik O. Wright, eds. 2003. *Deepening democracy: institutional innovations in empowered participatory governance.* London and New York: Verso.

Furtado, Celso. 2007 [1959]. *Formação econômica do Brasil.* São Paulo: Companhia das Letras.

Garagorry, Jorge A.S. 2007. "Economia e política no processo de financeirização do Brasil (1980–2006)." Tese de doutorado, Programa de Estudos Pós-Graduados em Ciências Sociais, Pontifícia Universidade Católica de São Paulo, São Paulo.

Glaser, Daryl. 1999. "Marxism and democracy." Pp. 239–258 in *Marxism and social science,* edited by Andrew Gamble, David Marsh, and Tony Tant. Urbana: University of Illinois Press.

Gobetti, Sérgio W. and Rodrigo O. Orair. 2010. "Estimativa da carga tributária de 2002 a 2009." Nota Técnica IPEA n. 16, Diretoria de Estudos e Políticas Macroeconômicas, Instituto de Pesquisa Econômica Aplicada, Brasília.

Gorz, André. 2005. *O imaterial: conhecimento, valor e capital.* São Paulo: Annablume.

Grün, Roberto. 2007a. "Decrifra-me ou te devoro! as finanças e a sociedade brasileira." *Mana* 13(2): 381–410.

Grün, Roberto. 2007b. "Entre a plutocracia e a legitimação da dominação financeira." *Revista Brasileira de Ciências Sociais* 22(65): 86–107.

Gramsci, Antonio. 2004 [1932]. *Cadernos do cárcere (Vol. 2).* Rio de Janeiro: Civilização Brasileira.

Greider, William. 1989. *Secrets of the temple: how the Federal Reserve runs the country.* New York: Simon & Schuster.

Hadjimichalis, Costis and Ray Hudson. 2007. "Rethinking local and regional development: implications for radical political practice in Europe." *European Urban and Regional Studies* 14(2): 99–113.

Harrod, Jeffrey. 1992. *Labour and third world debt.* New Delhi: Friedrich-Ebert-Foundation.

Harvey, David. 1990. *The condition of postmodernity: an inquiry into the origins of cultural change*. Malden: Blackwell.
Harvey, David. 2005. *A brief history of neoliberalism*. New York: Oxford University Press.
Harvey, David. 2006a. *A produção capitalista do espaço*. São Paulo: Annablume.
Harvey, David. 2006b. *Spaces of global capitalism: towards a theory of uneven geographical development*. London and New York: Verso.
Harvey, David. 2010. *The enigma of capital: and the crises of capitalism*. New York: Oxford University Press.
Hay, Colin. 1999. "Marxism and the state." Pp. 152–174 in *Marxism and social science*, edited by Andrew Gamble, David Marsh, and Tony Tant. Urbana: University of Illinois Press.
Hermann, Jennifer. 2002. "A macroeconomia da dívida pública: notas sobre o debate teórico e a experiência brasileira recente." *Cadernos Adenauer* 3(4): 41–70.
Hilferding, Rudolf. 2006 [1910]. *Finance capital: a study of the latest phase of capitalist development*. London: Routledge.
Hobsbawm, Eric. 1995. *The age of extremes: a history of the world, 1914–1991*. New York: Vintage.
Ianni, Octavio. 2004 [1989]. *Estado e capitalismo*. São Paulo: Brasiliense.
Ianni, Octavio. 2011. *A sociologia e o mundo moderno*. Rio de Janeiro: Civilização Brasileira.
Ingham, Geoffrey. 1998. "On the underdevelopment of the 'sociology of money'." *Acta Sociologica* 41(1): 3–18.
Jessop, Bob. 1990. *State theory: putting the capitalist state in its place*. University Park: Pennsylvania State University Press.
Jessop, Bob. 2007. *State power: a strategic-relational approach*. Cambridge, UK and Malden: Polity.
Jessop, Bob. 2010. "The 'return' of the national state in the current crisis of the world market." *Capital & Class* 34(1): 38–43.
Jessop, Bob. 2013. "Revisiting the regulation approach: critical reflections on the contradictions, dilemmas, fixes and crisis dynamics of growth regimes." *Capital & Class* 37(1): 5–24.
Johnston, Jim and David P. Dolowitz. 1999. "Marxism and social class." Pp. 129–151 in *Marxism and social science*, edited by Andrew Gamble, David Marsh, and Tony Tant. Urbana: University of Illinois Press.
Kaufman, George G. 2002. "Too big to fail in banking: what remains?" *The Quarterly Review of Economics and Finance* 42(3): 423–436.
Keister, Lisa A. 2002. "Financial markets, money, and banking." *Annual Review of Sociology* 28: 39–61.
Kellner, Douglas. 2002. "Theorizing globalization." *Sociological Theory* 20(3): 285–305.

Krippner, Greta R. 2005. "The financialization of the American economy." *Socio-Economic Review* 3(2): 173–208.

Krippner, Greta R. 2011. *Capitalizing on crisis: the political origins of the rise of finance.* Cambridge, MA: Harvard University Press.

Lapavitsas, Costas. 2011. "Theorizing financialization." *Work, Employment and Society* 25(4): 611–626.

Lapavitsas, Costas. 2013. "Financialised capitalism: crisis and financial expropriation." Pp. 15–50 in *Financialization in crisis*, edited by Costas Lapavitsas. Chicago: Haymarket.

Lebowitz, Michael A. 2005. *Following Marx: method, critique, and crisis.* Chicago: Haymarket.

Lenin, Vladimir I. 1975 [1917]. *Imperialism, the highest satge of capitalism: a popular outline.* Peking: Foreign Languages Press.

Lenin, Vladimir I. 2007 [1917]. *O estado e a revolução: o que ensina o marxismo sobre o estado e o papel do proletariado na revolução.* São Paulo: Expressão Popular.

Levine, Andrew. 1995. "Democratic corporatism and/versus socialism." Pp. 157–166 in *Associations and democracy*, edited by Joshua Cohen and Joel Rogers. London and New York: Verso.

Li, Minqi. 2004. "After neoliberalism: empire, social democracy, or socialism?" *Monthly Review* 55(8): 21–36.

Loureiro, Maria R. 1998. "L'internationalisation des milieux dirigeants au Brésil." *Actes de la Recherche en Sciences Sociales* 121(1): 42–51.

Loureiro, Maria R. and Fernando L. Abrucio. 2004. "Política e reformas fiscais no Brasil recente." *Revista de Economia Política* 24(1): 50–72.

Mészáros, István. 2011. *Para além do capital: rumo a uma teoria da transição.* São Paulo: Boitempo.

MacKenzie, Donald. 2007. "Is economics performative? option theory and the construction of derivatives markets." Pp. 54–86 in *Do economists make markets? on the performativity of economics*, edited by Donald MacKenzie, Fabian Muniesa, and Lucia Siu. Princeton: Princeton University Press.

Mandel, Ernest. 1990. "Introduction." Pp. 11–86 in *Karl Marx. Capital: a critique of political economy (Vol. 1).* London: Penguin.

Mandel, Ernest. 1991. "Introduction." Pp. 9–90 in *Karl Marx. Capital: a critique of political economy (Vol. 3).* London: Penguin.

Marini, Ruy M. 2011 [1991]. "Sobre o estado na América Latina." Pp. 217–226 in *Ruy Mauro Marini: vida e obra*, edited by Roberta Traspadini and João Pedro Stedile. São Paulo: Expressão Popular.

Marx, Karl. 1972 [1850]. *The class struggles in France, 1848 to 1850.* Moscow: Progress Publishers.

Marx, Karl. 1973 [1844]. *Economic and philosophic manuscripts of 1844*. London: Lawrence and Wishart.

Marx, Karl. 1990 [1890]. *Capital: a critique of political economy (Vol. 1)*. London: Penguin.

Marx, Karl. 1991 [1894]. *Capital: a critique of political economy (Vol. 3)*. London: Penguin.

Marx, Karl. 2000 [1863]. *Theories of surplus value (Part I)*. New York: Prometheus.

Marx, Karl. 2010 [1852]. "The eighteenth brumaire of Louis Bonaparte." Pp. 99–197 in *Collected works of Karl Marx and Frederick Engels (Vol. 11)*. London: Lawrence and Wishart.

Marx, Karl. 2010 [1859]. "A contribution to the critique of political economy." Pp. 257–417 in *Collected works of Karl Marx and Frederick Engels (Vol. 29)*. London: Lawrence and Wishart.

Marx, Karl. 2010 [1871]. "The civil war in France." Pp. 307–359 in *Collected works of Karl Marx and Frederick Engels (Vol. 22)*. London: Lawrence and Wishart.

Marx, Karl and Friedrich Engels. 1982 [1846]. "Feuerbach. Oposição das concepções materialista e idealista." Pp. 4–75 in *Obras escolhidas de Karl Marx e Friedrich Engels (Vol. 1)*. Lisboa: "Avante!"

Medeiros, Marcelo. 2003. "O que faz os ricos ricos: um estudo sobre fatores que determinam a riqueza." Tese de doutorado, Departamento de Sociologia, Universidade de Brasília, Brasília.

Miceli, Sergio. 2001. *Intelectuais à brasileira*. São Paulo: Companhia das Letras.

Mills, Charles W. 2000 [1956]. *The power elite*. New York: Oxford.

Mills, Charles W. 2000 [1959]. *The sociological imagination*. New York: Oxford University Press.

Minella, Ary C. 1988. *Banqueiros: organização e poder político no Brasil*. Rio de Janeiro: Espaço e Tempo.

Minella, Ary C. 2007. "Maiores bancos privados no Brasil: um perfil econômico e sociopolítico." *Sociologias* 18: 100–125.

Mollo, Maria de L.R. and Alfredo Saad-Filho. 2006. "Neoliberal economic policies in Brazil (1994–2005): Cardoso, Lula and the need for a democratic alternative." *New Political Economy* 11(1): 99–123.

Moore, Mick. 2004. "Revenues, state formation, and the quality of governance in developing countries." *International Political Science Review* 25(3): 297–319.

Morais, Lecio and Alfredo Saad-Filho. 2003. "Snatching defeat from the jaws of victory?: Lula, the 'Losers' Alliance,' and the prospects for change in Brazil." *Capital & Class* 27(3): 17–23.

Morais, Lecio, Alfredo Saad-Filho, and Walter Coelho. 1999. "Financial liberalisation, currency instability and crisis in Brazil: another plan bites the dust." *Capital & Class* 23(2): 9–14.

Nakatani, Paulo and Rémy Herrera. 2007. "The South has already repaid its external debt to the North: but the North denies its debt to the South." *Monthly Review* 59(2): 31–36.

Neiburg, Federico. 2005. "Inflación y crisis nacional: culturas económicas y espacios públicos en Argentina y Brasil." *Anuario de Estudios Americanos* 62(1): 113–138.

Neiburg, Federico. 2006. "Inflation: economists and economic cultures in Brazil and Argentina." *Comparative Studies in Society and History* 48(3): 604–633.

Nesvetailova, Anastasia. 2006. "Fictitious capital, real debts: systemic illiquidity in the financial crises of the late 1990s." *Review of Radical Political Economics* 38(1): 45–70.

O'Connor, James. 2002. *The fiscal crisis of the state*. New Brunswick: Transaction.

O'Connor, John. 2010. "Marxism and the three movements of neoliberalism." *Critical Sociology* 36(5): 691–715.

Offe, Claus. 1974. "Structural problems of the capitalist state: class rule and the political system. On the selectiveness of political institutions." Pp. 31–57 in *German political studies*, edited by Klaus von Beyme. London: Sage.

Offe, Claus. 1975. "The theory of the capitalist state and the problem of policy formation." Pp. 125–144 in *Stress and contradiction in modern capitalism: public policy and the theory of the state*, edited by Leon N. Lindberg, Robert Alford, Colin Crouch, and Claus Offe. Lexington: Lexington Books.

Offe, Claus. 1984a. *Contradictions of the welfare state*. London: Hutchinson.

Offe, Claus. 1984b. *Problemas estruturais do estado capitalista*. Rio de Janeiro: Tempo Brasileiro.

Offe, Claus. 2001. "Political liberalism, group rights, and the politics of fear and trust." *Studies in East European Thought* 53(3): 167–182.

Offe, Claus. 2004 [1991]. "Capitalism by democratic design? democratic theory facing the triple transition in East Central Europe." *Social Research* 71(3): 501–528.

Offe, Claus and Volker Ronge. 1975. "Theses on the theory of the state." *New German Critique* 6: 137–147.

Offe, Claus and Volker Ronge. 1984. "Teses sobre a fundamentação do conceito de "estado capitalista" e sobre a pesquisa política de orientação materialista." Pp. 121–137 in *Problemas estruturais do estado capitalista*, edited by Claus Offe. Rio de Janeiro: Tempo Brasileiro.

Oliveira, Francisco de. 2006. "Lula in the labyrinth." *New Left Review* 42: 5–22.

Papadatos, Demophanes. 2013. "Central banking in contemporary capitalism: inflation-targeting and financial crises." Pp. 119–141 in *Financialization in crisis*, edited by Costas Lapavitsas. Chicago: Haymarket.

Pastor Jr., Manuel and Gary A. Dymski. 1991. "Debt crisis and class conflict in Latin America." *Capital & Class* 15(1): 203–231.

Paulani, Leda. 2008. *Brasil delivery: servidão financeira e estado de emergência econômico*. São Paulo: Boitempo.

Piketty, Thomas. 2014. *Capital in the twenty-first century*. Cambridge, MA: Belknap.

Pinçon, Michel and Monique Pinçon-Charlot. 2007. "Sociologia da alta burguesia." *Sociologias* 18: 22–37.

Pogrebinschi, Thamy. 2007. "O enigma da democracia em Marx." *Revista Brasileira de Ciências Sociais* 22(63): 55–67.

Polanyi, Karl. 2000 [1944]. *A grande transformação: as origens de nossa época*. Rio de Janeiro: Campus.

Potter, Brian. 2007. "Constricting contestation, coalitions, and purpose: the causes of neoliberal restructuring and its failures." *Latin American Perspectives* 34(3): 3–24.

Poulantzas, Nicos. 1969. "The problem of the capitalist state." *New Left Review* I/58: 67–78.

Poulantzas, Nicos. 1973. "On social classes." *New Left Review* I/78: 27–54.

Poulantzas, Nicos. 1976. "The capitalist state: a reply to Miliband and Laclau." *New Left Review* I/95: 63–83.

Poulantzas, Nicos. 1978a. *Classes in contamporary capitalism*. London: Verso.

Poulantzas, Nicos. 1978b. "Towards a democratic socialism." *New Left Review* I/109: 75–87.

Poulantzas, Nicos. 2000 [1978]. *O Estado, o poder, o socialismo*. São Paulo: Paz e Terra.

Prates, Daniela M. and Leda M. Paulani. 2007. "The financial globalization of Brazil under Lula." *Monthly Review* 58(9): 32–38.

Preda, Alex. 2007. "The sociological approach to financial markets." *Journal of Economic Surveys* 21(3): 506–533.

Przeworski, Adam. 1985. *Capitalism and social democracy*. Cambridge, UK: Cambridge University Press.

Przeworski, Adam. 1992. "The neoliberal fallacy." *Journal of Democracy* 3(3): 45–59.

Przeworski, Adam. 1998. "Deliberation and ideological domination." Pp. 140–160 in *Deliberative democracy*, edited by Jon Elster. Cambridge, UK: Cambridge University Press.

Radice, Hugo. 2010. "Confronting the crisis: a class analysis." Pp. 21–43 in *Socialist register 2011: the crisis this time*, edited by Leo Panitch, Greg Albo, and Vivek Chibber. London: Merlin.

Rocha, Geisa M. 1994. "Redefining the role of the bourgeoisie in dependent capitalist development: privatization and liberalization in Brazil." *Latin American Perspectives* 21(1): 72–98.

Rocha, Geisa M. 2002. "Neo-dependency in Brazil." *New Left Review* 16: 5–33.

Roemer, John E. 1982a. *A general theory of exploitation and class*. Cambridge, MA: Harvard University Press.

Roemer, John E. 1982b. "New directions in the Marxian theory of exploitation and class." *Politics & Society* 11(3): 253–287.

Roemer, John E. 1982c. "Property relations vs. surplus value in Marxian exploitation." *Philosophy and Public Affairs* 11(4): 281–313.

Roemer, John E. 1994. "A future for socialism." *Politics & Society* 22(4): 451–478.
Rousseau, Jean-Jacques. 1968 [1762]. *The social contract*. London: Penguin.
Saes, Décio. 2001. *República do capital: capitalismo e processo político no Brasil*. São Paulo: Boitempo.
Salama, Pierre. 1978. "État et capital. L'état capitaliste comme abstraction réelle." *Critiques de l'Économie Politique. Nouvelle Série* 7–8: 224–261.
Salama, Pierre. 1998. "De la finance à la flexibilité en Amérique latine et en Asie du Nord et du Sud-Est." *Revue Tiers Monde* 39(154): 425–450.
Santos, Paulo L. dos. 2013. "On the content of banking in contemporary capitalism." Pp. 83–118 in *Financialization in crisis*, edited by Costas Lapavitsas. Chicago: Haymarket.
Schmitter, Philippe C. and Terry L. Karl. 1991. "What democracy is... and is not." *Journal of Democracy* 2(3): 75–88.
Schwartz, Herman. 1998. "Social democracy going down or down under: institutions, internationalized capital, and indebted states." *Comparative Politics* 30(3): 253–272.
Sicsú, João. 2006. "Rumos da liberalização financeira brasileira." *Revista de Economia Política* 26(3): 364–380.
Silva, Hélio E.D. 2003. "A reforma do Estado no governo Fernando Henrique Cardoso." Tese de doutorado, Departamento de Sociologia, Universidade de Brasília, Brasília.
Stiglitz, Joseph E. 2002. *Globalization and its discontents*. London: Penguin.
Swanson, Jacinda. 2008. "Economic common sense and the depoliticization of the economic." *Political Research Quarterly* 61(1): 56–67.
Therborn, Göran. 1999. *The ideology of power and the power of ideology*. London and New York: Verso.
Therborn, Göran. 2007. "After dialectics." *New Left Review* 43: 63–113.
Therborn, Göran. 2008 [1978]. *What does the ruling class do when it rules? state apparatuses and state power under feudalism, capitalism and socialism*. London and New York: Verso.
Vernengo, Matias. 2006. "Technology, finance, and dependency: Latin American radical political economy in retrospect." *Review of Radical Political Economics* 38(4): 551–568.
Vernengo, Matías. 2007. "Fiscal squeeze and social policy during the Cardoso administration (1995–2002)." *Latin American Perspectives* 34(5): 81–91.
Wade, Robert. 2008. "Financial regime change?" *New Left Review* 53: 5–21.
Wagner, F. Peter. 1996. *Rudolf Hilferding: theory and politics of democratic socialism*. Atlantic Highlands: Humanities.
Wallerstein, Immanuel. 1979. *The capitalist world-economy*. Cambridge, UK: Cambridge University Press.
Wallerstein, Immanuel. 2013. "Structural crisis, or why capitalists may no longer find capitalism rewarding." Pp. 9–35 in *Does capitalism have a future?*, edited by

Immanuel Wallerstein, Randall Collins, Michael Mann, Georgi Derluguian, and Craig Calhoun. New York: Oxford University Press.

Weber, Max. 1964 [1922]. *Economía y sociedad: esbozo de sociología comprensiva*. México: Fondo de Cultura Económica.

Weber, Max. 1982 [1919]a. "A ciência como vocação." Pp. 97–183 in *Max Weber: ensaios de sociologia*, edited by Hans Heinrich Gerth and Charles Wright Mills. Rio de Janeiro: Livros Técnicos e Científicos.

Weber, Max. 1982 [1919]b. "A política como vocação." Pp. 98–153 in *Max Weber: ensaios de sociologia*, edited by Hans Heinrich Gerth and Charles Wright Mills. Rio de Janeiro: Livros Técnicos e Científicos.

Weber, Max. 2001 [1904–1905]. *The protestant ethic and the spirit of capitalism*. London and New York: Routledge.

Weber, Max. 2003 [1919–1920]. *General economic history*. Mineola: Dover.

Weffort, Francisco C. 1992. "The future of socialism." *Journal of Democracy* 3(3): 90–99.

Williams, Heather. 2001. "Of free trade and debt bondage: fighting banks and the state in Mexico." *Latin American Perspectives* 28(4): 30–51.

Wilson, Hall T. 2002. *Capitalism after postmodernism: neo-conservatism, legitimacy and the theory of public capital*. Leiden: Brill.

Wood, Ellen M. 1981. "The separation of the economic and the political in capitalism." *New Left Review* I/127: 66–95.

Wood, Ellen M. 2003. *Democracia contra capitalismo: a renovação do materialismo histórico*. São Paulo: Boitempo.

Wood, Ellen M. 2005. *Empire of capital*. London and New York: Verso.

Wright, Erik O. 1979. *Class, crisis and the state*. London: Verso.

Wright, Erik O. 1994a. *Interrogating inequality: essays on class analysis, socialism and Marxism*. London and New York: Verso.

Wright, Erik O. 1994b. "Political power, democracy, and coupon socialism." *Politics & Society* 22(4): 535–548.

Wright, Erik O., ed. 1998. *The debate on classes*. London and New York: Verso.

Wright, Erik O. 1999. "Alternative perspectives in Marxist theory of accumulation and crisis." *Critical Sociology* 25(2/3): 111–142.

Wright, Erik O. 2000. *Class counts: student edition*. Cambridge, UK: Cambridge University Press.

Wright, Erik O. 2002. "The shadow of exploitation in Weber's class analysis." *American Sociological Review* 67(6): 832–853.

Wright, Erik O. 2005. "Basic income as a socialist project." *Rutgers Journal of Law & Urban Policy* 2(1): 196–203.

Wright, Erik O. 2006a. "Class." Pp. 62–68 in *International encyclopedia of economic sociology*, edited by Jens Beckert and Milan Zafirovski. London and New York: Routledge.

Wright, Erik O. 2006b. "Compass points: towards a socialist alternative." *New Left Review* 41: 93–124.

Wright, Erik O. 2013. "Transforming capitalism through real utopias." *American Sociological Review* 78(1): 1–25.

Žižek, Slavoj. 2008. "A utopia liberal." *Margem Esquerda* 12: 43–61.

Index

accumulation   37, 85n, 87–89
  cycles of   12, 32
  expansion of   12, 183
  finance and   3, 93, 111
  general formula of capital   32
  regime of   36, 87–88, 95
  state and   35, 41–47, 52, 132
  vs. expropriation   17, 41n, 93, 183–184
agriculture, export-oriented   38, 54
austerity, fiscal and monetary   37, 72–73, 80, 115
authoritarianism   123, 135, 157

balance of payments   21–22, 37–38, 72
banks   107–108, 148
  connections within the state   61, 147–148, 187
  power of   3n, 25, 137
  public debt and   26, 109n, 116–117, 120
Brazilian Social Democratic Party   125, 185
Bretton Woods system   16–17, 178
budget
  ceiling on   189–190
  democracy and   149, 171–172
  discretionary power over   58, 60, 64, 66, 140–142, 154–155
  dispute over   78, 114
  legislation   76–81, 154–155
bureaucracy   56, 59–60, 153
  authoritarian   58, 163–164
  selective insulation of   139, 144, 147

Canada   118
capital
  constant and variable   37
  foreign   28, 140
  interest-bearing   1–2, 32, 99, 179
  international flow of   17, 21–22, 27, 33, 37–38, 72, 178–180
  over-accumulated   37
capital flight   34, 101–102, 126
capitalism
  abolition of   122–123, 167–168, 176, 184
  essential characteristics of   36–37, 93
  historical   32, 36–37, 95, 167
  limits of   131, 183–184
  vs. democracy   120, 122, 128, 131, 167, 175, 182–183
capitalist class
  functioning   90, 93, 113
  hegemonic fraction of   38, 87
Cardoso, Fernando Henrique   54, 70, 110, 163
  government of   37–38, 52, 55, 68, 73, 118n18, 125–126, 187–189
Central Bank of Brazil   20, 73
  class character of   142
  governors of   61, 140, 148, 162–163
  power of   55, 62, 73–75, 144, 157–159, 183
  see also Monetary Policy Committee
central banks   17
  independence of   56–57, 134
circulation of capital   86, 90, 93, 110
civil servants, dismissal of   115
civil society   59, 161
class   86–87
  advantage   101, 154
  appropriating   33, 106, 116
  appropriating vs. productive   106–107
  compromise   125
  location   92, 98, 147, 153
  power   87, 190
  relations, asymmetrical   44, 101
  structure   85–86, 90–91
class struggle   28, 44, 85–86, 92
  buffering of   37, 94–95, 117, 188
  redistributive   57, 63–64, 79, 98, 103–104, 110, 114, 117, 183–184
Collor, Fernando   70, 127
consensus   145, 176
Constitution, the   4, 63–65, 69, 141, 154, 156, 160
contested exchange   92, 94
contract, financial   31, 92
corporate governance   9, 24–25
coup d'état
  1964 military   63, 137
  2016 parliamentary   50, 76, 127, 185–190
credit   50n, 65–66, 91–92
  consumer   125
creditor vs. debtor   15, 85–86, 94
creditworthiness   51–52, 96, 116–118, 165–166

INDEX

crisis   48, 109
  1997 Southeast Asian   21
  1998 Russian   21, 34
  2008 world financial   1–2, 16, 35–36, 47–48, 109
  accumulation   11–13, 19, 33, 47, 183
  class reaction to   10, 12, 18, 46, 178, 190
  fiscal   13, 117
  late 1990s Brazilian   11, 34, 72, 97, 143
  mid-2010s Brazilian   97, 113
  social impacts of   34–35
currency
  as a commodity   88, 92–93
  centrality of   9, 178
  supply of   17

debt interest   84, 88
  class character of   28–29, 91, 93–94
  see also public debt interest
debt-taxation-finance nexus   84, 109
  see also taxation, public debt and
decision-making, economic   130–131, 135–136, 168, 170–171
democracy
  associative   174–175
  capitalist   3–4, 20, 57, 120, 124, 127, 169, 173
  degree of   122, 124, 130, 167
  economic   140, 168, 172, 174
  genuine   122, 128, 170, 175–176
  institutional requirements of   175–176
  participatory   131, 169–170
  representative   58, 124, 173
  socialist   169, 176
  see also socialism, democratic
democratic theory
  Marxist   126–127, 173–174
  Weberian   56, 58, 128
derivative   31–32
dictatorship   58, 75, 124, 126–127
  1964–1985 military   3, 124, 136–137, 157
discourse   153–154
dispossession   182
dollar, U.S.   14, 16–17, 178
Durkheim, Émile   2, 150

earmarked revenue   4, 65
economic growth   75, 102, 111, 124, 185, 188–189

economics, performativity of   150–151
economists   54, 60
  bourgeois   30, 76, 151–152
economy
  debate about   146, 149
  democratic control over   132, 135, 138–139, 158, 164, 168–170, 172, 174–175, 184
  depoliticization of   132–134, 146
  fictitious   10, 178
  fictitious vs. real   1, 31
  political dimension of   2, 11, 57, 168–169, 172
education, public   63–65, 67, 69
elections, presidential   51–52, 126, 133–134, 176, 186–187
Engels, Frederick   121, 173–174
Europe   1n, 17, 172
exchange rate   8n, 16–17, 49, 74
  floating   68, 72–73, 111, 142
  pegged   21, 72, 78
  see also inflation targeting
executive branch, hegemony of   134–135, 154–155, 157, 183
exploitation   28, 59, 87, 90–91, 94, 104
  concealed   90, 94–95, 116
  concept of   85–88
  deepening of   71, 83–84, 86, 90–91, 93, 103–104, 110–112, 117, 181
  secondary vs. original   85, 91–93
  sociological concept of   84, 88, 92
  vs. oppression   88
  see also public debt interest, exploitation through
exploited vs. exploiter   91, 116
expropriation, financial   24, 31, 83–84, 86, 94–95, 104, 117, 183–184
  see also public debt interest, expropriation through

fetishism   134
fictitious capital   24–25, 31–32
  concrete social character of   24, 32, 34, 179
finance as social relation   2–3
finance capital   3n, 31, 55
financial class   40, 116–117, 120
  demands   187, 189
  expectations   144, 147–148

financial class (cont)
    favoring of   30, 65, 69–72, 75, 101–102, 116–117, 165–166, 187–188, 190
    interests   66, 78–79, 107–108, 126–127, 165–166, 189
    power of   9–10, 14, 87, 121, 142, 149, 190
    profits of   28, 35, 111, 152, 180, 184
financial clientelism   144
financial hegemony   14, 22, 38, 54–56, 95, 139, 178–180, 190
financial markets   86, 88, 92
    international, opening of   16–17, 19
financialization
    class character of   11, 36, 93
    concept of   16–17, 40
    consequences of   2, 9–10, 19, 31, 36, 80, 87
    democracy and   120–121, 130, 146, 160
    public debt and   23–24, 26–27, 179
    state and   23–24, 35–36, 41, 43, 46, 64, 88–89, 180
    vs. production   14, 16, 24–25, 31–38, 99, 111–113, 138–139, 179
fiscal adjustment   115, 143–144, 186
fiscal deficit
    nominal   30, 78, 80, 105–106
    primary   78n32, 127, 187, 189
    sustainable   30–31, 98
fiscal equilibrium   77–78, 186–187
fiscal incentive   101–102
fiscal policy   67, 101
    parliamentary coup d'état and 2016   76
    accumulation and   84
    class character of   41, 84
    depoliticization of   82
    vs. monetary policy   73–74, 78, 115–116
fiscal responsibility   60, 76–77, 79–82, 156, 171
fiscal result
    primary   67–68, 79
    primary vs. nominal   74, 77–79
    target for   68, 76–78, 189
fiscal secrecy   166
fiscal structure, regressive   108
fiscal surplus, primary   30, 52, 68–69, 78, 81, 126, 165, 187–188
    target for   77–79, 97, 143–144
Fordist regime of accumulation   89, 93
foreign currency reserves   21, 28–29, 38, 144
Franco, Itamar   54, 70

freedom   170, 176
fungibility
    of money   65–66
    of state revenue   66–67, 69

global markets   33, 38, 47
Gramsci, Antonio   56, 58–59, 95, 125, 134, 152
gross fixed capital formation   24–25, 99, 138–139

healthcare, public   67, 69
hegemony   59, 145–146
    see also financial hegemony
Hilferding, Rudolf   3n, 10–11, 25, 36, 93
Hobsbawm, Eric   18, 123–124
hypothesis of the book   5

ideological insulation   182
ideology   116, 150, 173, 182
    economic   2, 178
income
    capital   96, 100, 111–112, 188
    financial   74, 112
    functional distribution of   112, 188–189
    labor   100, 111–112, 188–189
income transfer programs   125
industrial capital   55, 107
    finance capital's influence on   3n, 25–26
    hegemony of   54, 180
industrialization   45, 59, 146
inequality or equality, economic   128, 130–131, 168–169, 175
inflation   17, 23, 71
    class character of   15, 70–72, 89
    expectations for   153
inflation control   19, 23, 60, 68–71, 73–74, 120, 138, 152, 180
    people's support for   22–23, 70–71, 145
    see also Real Plan
inflation targeting   21, 30, 73–75, 138, 147–148, 151
inflation tax   23, 67
interest rate   15, 22–23, 34, 72–73, 97–99, 113, 138–139, 178
    expectations for   147–148
    in Germany   13
    in Japan   13
    in Korea   20–21
    in Mexico   20–21
    in Russia   35

INDEX

in South Africa   20–21
in the United States   13–15
world's highest   20–21, 50, 73–74, 142, 179–180
see also public debt interest, implicit rate
interest rate, benchmark   34–35, 72–73, 138, 140, 143
   public debt pegged to   34–35, 73, 140–142, 157–159
   target for   73n26–27, 151–152
International Monetary Fund   47, 49, 69, 144, 165
investment   96
   foreign direct   11, 21–22, 37
   foreign portfolio   11, 21–22, 102
   productive   24, 99, 138–139
   see also gross fixed capital formation
investment fund   9, 26–27, 96n
   public debt and   26–27, 116–117, 120, 180
investment grade   62, 68

judiciary   189
June revolts   185–186

Keynesianism   9, 12–13, 36, 46, 69, 89, 114

labor
   autonomy   128, 176
   domination over   28, 46
   industrial   113
   relations   86, 187
   socially necessary   91, 110–111
   see also income, labor
labor laws, weakening of   187
labor-power   91, 104
   costs of   22, 36–37, 113, 187–188
Latin America   47, 70, 114, 126
legislature   172–173, 189–190
   limited power of   134–135, 144, 157
   omission of   141, 144, 155–156, 158, 160–162, 166, 183
legitimacy   63, 149–150, 153
Lenin, Vladimir   31, 174
liberal thinking   1n, 53, 133
liberalization and deregulation   21, 38, 48–49
liberty   123, 127–129
liquidity   22, 33, 65
loan   50n, 66
Lula da Silva, Luiz Inácio   62, 185
   election to the presidency   151
   government of   50, 55, 68, 73, 118n18, 125–126, 187–189
   Letter to the Brazilian People   51–52, 126
   see also Workers Party

macroeconomic policy   61, 63
   democracy and   133–136, 147
   depoliticization of   129, 161–162, 182–183
   makers of   57, 137
Marx, Karl   20, 113, 128, 149–150
   on circulation sphere   90
   on exploitation   91–92
   on fictitious capital   6, 24, 179
   on finance capital   31–32, 88, 93
   on interest   36, 93
   on loans   50n
   on productive agents   85
   on public debt   32, 97–98, 105
   on taxation   97–98
   on the state   28
Marxism   85–86, 174
   on the state   40, 42–43, 49
methodological individualism   92n4
Ministry of Finance   55, 62, 102, 133–134, 157–159, 162–163, 187
monetarism   8n, 9, 20, 69–70
monetary inducement   153
monetary policy   30, 50, 89, 140, 145
   decision-making   73n26–27, 147–148, 151–152, 183
   nominal anchor for   72, 74, 78, 140
Monetary Policy Committee   34, 61n13, 72–73, 139–140, 143–144, 151
monetary stability   60, 75
money-capital   31–33, 89

National Monetary Council   74–75, 136–138
neoliberalism   160, 178
   actually existing   18, 37–38, 134
   arrival in Brazil   4, 19
   consequences of   9–10, 16, 36, 95
   contradictions of   18, 36, 180
   idealized   1n, 18, 47, 57, 76, 89, 146
   idealized vs. actually existing   10, 36–37, 39, 42, 66, 96, 110, 114
   see also state, neoliberal

opportunity cost   113
organic intellectuals   58–60, 149–150
   of finance   58, 60–62, 139, 152, 182

Paris Commune   20, 173
peripheral countries   28, 37–38, 114, 129, 182
Polanyi, Karl   45–46, 53
political domination   59, 88
political power   130–131, 168, 173
poverty   125
press, corporate   76, 189
primary spending
   limit on   180, 189–190
primitive accumulation   97, 182
private property   128, 170, 172–173
privatization   19, 21, 37, 50, 114–115, 179
production cycles, ulterior   98–100, 104, 111, 117, 181
production sphere   50n, 86, 88
productivity   113
professional career   61, 153
profit   37, 86, 95
   expectations for   104, 181
   see also income, capital
provisional decree   101n, 135, 157
public debt   30, 51, 94, 99, 102
   actual debtors of   34, 116
   as class relation   4–5, 28–29, 94, 105
   democracy and   5, 129, 133, 155–156, 171, 182
   domestic vs. external   28–29
   expansion of   16, 23, 30, 80, 97, 120, 180
   institutional apparatus of   6, 85, 157
   labor and   114
   limit on   76, 80, 156–157, 187
   parliamentary investigation on   148, 158–167
   sustainable   30–31, 66, 98, 167
   see also taxation, public debt and
public debt creditors   26, 109n, 116–117
   privileges to   77, 108–110, 120, 166
public debt interest   19
   discretionary power over   74, 140–142, 157–159, 165
   earners of   109n, 116–117, 120
   exploitation through   83–84, 104–105, 110, 114, 181

expropriation through   28–29, 83–84, 98
   implicit rate   28–29
   limit on   81
   spending on   68–69, 74, 78, 102–106, 108–109, 115, 119–120, 125
public debt servicing   77, 80, 120
   budget for   67, 154–155, 183
public services   81, 122

real, currency   62, 67, 72, 78
Real Plan   4, 20–21, 54–55, 62, 64, 70–71, 136–137, 179
reformism   176
regulation, mode of   89, 132, 179
rent   17, 84–85
retirement   115, 186–188, 190
   pensions   118–120, 144, 189
revenue
   expansion of sources of   16, 26–27, 105
   non-financial   79
rights
   democratic vs. property   131
   political   4, 124
   property   118
risk
   credit   26–27
   on public debt   26, 52–53, 68, 102, 143
risk classification agency   62
Rousseau, Jean-Jacques   128
Rousseff, Dilma   68, 118n18, 185–190
ruled class   64, 122
   consent of   59, 69, 95, 120, 124–125, 145
ruling class   59, 125–126
Russia and Soviet Union   46, 123–124
   see also crisis, 1998 Russian

Sarney, José   54, 70
secondary associations   174–175
shareholders   24–25
social formation   87
social movements   160
social security   118n18, 187–188
   see also spending on social security
socialism   58, 134
   actually existing   123
   democratic   168, 170, 176

market 168
  vs. capitalism 123, 174, 178
  see also democracy, socialist
sociology 2–3, 15, 32, 50, 105, 149, 177
social representation 4, 84
Soros, George 48–49
sovereignty 35, 62, 149, 173
spending 41n, 58, 76, 115–116
  delinking of revenues from
    mandatory 64–69, 77, 140–142, 154, 180, 186
  financial 81
  investment 35, 140–142
  mandatory 80, 140–142, 154
  non-financial 23, 68, 79, 81
  on civil servants 80, 115, 117
  on social security 117–120
  on social welfare 63–66, 69, 71, 77, 125, 181, 184, 189
  primary 117
state
  affirmative 175
  autonomy 44, 51, 95, 142
  capitalist character of 40, 42–45, 49, 76, 82, 95, 132, 174
  concept of 40, 42–43, 45n2
  economic role 12, 26, 46–49, 53, 89, 94, 177–178
  finance capital's influence on 26, 35, 54, 57, 62, 144, 147–148
  financial-capitalist character of 49, 55, 63, 65, 74–75, 174, 180, 182
  insulation of 134, 136–137, 175
  legitimacy 44, 95, 104, 181
  mechanisms of selection 132–134, 145
  mediation 44, 53, 58, 94–95
  neoliberal 18, 129, 160
  redistributive function of 50–51, 94
  regulatory 50, 52, 89
state economic apparatus 60–62, 139, 152–153
  hegemony of 56, 129, 141, 160, 163
  legitimacy of 60, 145
state-owned companies 45, 115
stock market 24
superstructure 59, 88, 127, 149
  fiscal 41, 181

surplus
  appropriation of 16, 86, 90–91, 98
  redistribution of 29–32, 50, 58, 90, 106, 131, 167, 181–182
surplus-labor 85n, 98, 110
surplus-value 17, 35, 38, 59, 83–86
Sweden 118
Switzerland 171
symbolic power 132

tax burden 83, 97–98, 100, 105–108, 188–189
tax exemption 102–103
taxation 96–98, 103–104, 189
  capital accumulation and 41n, 84
  direct vs. indirect 100–101, 108
  expansion of 23, 35, 79–81, 83, 97, 104–106, 120
  gross vs. net 108–110
  on financial transactions 107–108
  on profits 96, 106
  public debt and 23, 50, 83–84, 96–97, 104–106, 108–111, 116–117, 181–182
  regressive 100–101
Temer, Michel 50, 186–188, 190

unemployment 71, 185
United Kingdom 17, 45
United States 13–14, 17, 45, 47–48, 61, 96n, 178
unproductive class 85, 90

value 33–34, 38, 86, 113
  labor-theory of 84, 110
Vargas, Getúlio 110n12, 124
vote, popular 124, 173

wage 104
  minimum 125, 185, 189
  social 37, 120, 181
  stagnation 93, 111, 114
Wallerstein, Immanuel 37
Weber, Max 58, 85, 128, 149, 163–164
Workers Party 51–52, 68, 151, 185
  governments led by 38, 125–127, 186, 189
World Bank 47, 49, 61
World War II, years following 12, 69, 183
world-system 2, 28, 39, 70, 114, 179, 183

Wright, Erik Olin   ix
   on budget   79n
   on bureaucrats   60
   on democracy   128, 132, 134–135, 168–169
   on exploitation   84, 88, 104
   on liberty   128
   on socialism   123, 168, 174
   on taxation   103–104
   on the capitalist state   33, 35, 46, 52

CPSIA information can be obtained
at www.ICGtesting.com
Printed in the USA
BVHW042245221021
619690BV00013B/513